Women Workers
and Technological Change
in Europe in the
Nineteenth and Twentieth
Centuries

Women Workers and Technological Change in Europe in the Nineteenth and Twentieth Centuries

Edited by

Gertjan de Groot and Marlou Schrover

Taylor & Francis
Publishers since 1798

UK	Taylor & Francis Ltd, 4 John St., London WC1N 2ET
USA	Taylor & Francis Inc., 1900 Frost Road, Suite 101, Bristol, PA 19007

First published 1995

A Catalogue Record for this book is available from the British Library

ISBN 0 7484 0260 8
ISBN 0 7484 0261 6 (pbk)

Library of Congress Cataloging-in-Publication Data are available on request

Cover design by Kate Hybert.

Typeset in 10/12pt Times
by Solidus (Bristol) Limited

Printed in Great Britain by Burgess Science Press, Basingstoke on paper which has a specified pH value on final paper manufacture of not less than 7.5 and is therefore 'acid free'.

Contents

Acknowledgments

Photograph on p. 4 reproduced from Malcolm Graham (n.d. prob. 1908), Cup & Saucer Land, London.

Imperial War Museum, Woolwich Arsenal, with thanks to the Trustees for permission to reproduce the photographs in figures 6.1, 6.2 and 6.3.

Photographs in figures 7.1, 7.2 and 7.3 reproduced from Malcolm Graham (n.d., prob. 1908), Cup & Saucer Land, London.

Photographs (1939) in figures 9.1, 9.4 and 9.5 reproduced by permission of Aral Dairy Company, Stockholm.

Photograph in figure 10.4 reproduced with permission of the municipal archive Helmond.

Photograph in figure 10.9 reproduced from Public Record Office North Holland; archive Van Houten.

Photograph in figure 10.12 reproduced from Spaarnestad photo archive Haarlem/ NFGC/2311-3 502-7.

List of Tables

List of Figures

Chapter 1

General Introduction

Gertjan de Groot and Marlou Schrover

From the traditional stereotyped viewpoint, femininity and technology clash. Men are traditionally seen as technically competent and creative. Women are seen as incompetent – suited only to work with machines that have been made and are maintained by men. Women use machines, in the home or at work, but are depicted as depending on men as soon as the machinery falters. This negative association between women and technology is one of the features of the sex-typing of jobs. Technological insight has partly replaced strength as a segregative concept, since the advent of the machine era. Men identify themselves with technology, and technology is identified with masculinity.[1] The masculine image of technology is reserved for certain types of technology. Sewing and knitting, requiring knowledge, training and sometimes the use of machines, do not have a technological 'ring'. Moreover, technical competence is part of the male gender identity, but not part of each man's identity. Furthermore, it is class-related. In the lower classes men are expected to be knowledgeable about car mechanics. The higher classes take their cars to the garage.

Technological change is commonly seen as leading to deskilling, opening up possibilities for the replacement of men by women.[2] The relationship between technology, technological change and women's work is complicated. If the concepts 'skill' and 'technology' are regarded critically, this relationship becomes even more complicated. These concepts have been widely used to describe, explain and justify the segregation of work. Studies in this book show that, on the micro level, the interaction between women's work and techno-logical change is much more complex than has hitherto been recognized. The impact of technological change on women's work cannot be generalized. It needs to be examined at the level of individual industries and individual innovations.[3]

This book sheds light on the complicated relationship between work and technology through studies at micro level, examining technological change and its consequences in their social settings. Focusing on specific developments helps to trace the origins of gendering. Technology as such does not determine anything, but its introduction, and the social setting in which it is introduced, do. Technological change can lead to the regendering of existing work, to the disappearance of work, or to the creation of new work. We argue that

1

technological change facilitates the regendering of work. It does not necessarily cause it, but without it regendering seldom occurs. Specific historical and social settings may lead to the gendering of certain techniques, and thus to the creation or abolition of women's work, which may find its repercussions in completely different historical and social settings. Developments in England, with its early industrialization, are contrasted with those in Sweden, Denmark and the Netherlands, where industrialization took off much later.

The textile industry is the traditional field for studying the gendering of work. The idea that the segregation into men's work and women's work was passed on from the cottage system to the factory stems from this field. In this book, Harriet Bradley describes the work of women in the British textile industry; Marianne Rostgård does so for Denmark, and Gertjan de Groot for the Netherlands. Office work is a field now strongly dominated by women. Typing was, however, not women's work from the start. Meta Zimmeck shows that it was first allocated to men and boys, then to boys only and finally to women and girls. In pottery, 'skill' is not the only concept used for segregating work between the genders: 'strength' and 'health risk' may also be used to justify it. Jacqueline Sarsby writes on the pottery industry in England, and Ulla Wikander on that in Sweden. During the First World War, there were rapid changes in the nature of women's employment. Deborah Thom shows that, in England, this did not lead to a permanent modification of ideas about segregation, although it did prove that changes were possible if enforced. Women played an important role in the production of food, both for the family and for the market. The nineteenth century saw radical changes in this field, with the industrialization of food production and the rise of new industries. Women ought to have had a head start as far as 'skills' were concerned. In an attempt to explain women's place in these industries, Lena Sommestad looks at Sweden, and Marlou Schrover at the Netherlands.

Although skill and technology are important concepts in the explanation of the segregation between men's work and women's work, there are many other factors to which the segregation can be attributed.[4] Waged work is sharply differentiated along gender lines. Men's work in one region can be women's work in another, but in virtually all cases there is a clear distinction between 'men's work' and 'women's work'.[5] According to Phillips and Taylor, sexual demarcations were rigidly maintained, even when men and women worked in the same industry.[6] Although this is true, demarcation lines were not inflexible over time, and differences were often minute, as the studies in this book show. Bradley, for instance, describes how in hosiery women worked the smaller specialized machines, and men the larger ones. Rostgård shows that in the Danish textile industry there was hardly any difference between male tacklers and female twisters, except for the name.

Cheap Labour

An important reason for employers to hire women was that they were cheaper than men. Low wages were, however, never the only reason for employing women. Most occupations were gender-segregated, at least for a single time and place. There was little possibility of substituting female for male workers as wage differences changed, unless there were other contiguous changes.[7] When discussing wages, age differences between the male and female workforce have to be taken into account. The average wage of men was higher than the average wage of women, but so was the average age of male employees. In general, however, the low women's wages explain the crowding of women in labour-intensive sectors of production. It is not that women were paid less than men for exactly the same job. Women hardly ever did exactly the same job as men, although differences may have been small. If an employer succeeded in qualifying a certain task as feminine, he could employ women, who were generally paid less. The fact that women were paid less than men is a historical constant, going back before the onset of the industrial era. Even the ratio between women's wages and men's wages hardly varies: women's wages are half to two-thirds of those of men.[8] The explanation for the difference varies. The reason employers gave for paying women lower wages was that women were inferior workers: their production was lower, and they lacked a sense of responsibility. This argument is generally hard to counter, because men and women seldom did exactly the same work. Even when both men and women did do the same work, as Bradley describes for weavers and knitters, women got to work fewer or older machines, thus reducing their output.

The physical strength needed for a job was often used as a justification for higher wages and a preference for men. Women were not considered to be suitable for all jobs, because they allegedly lacked strength, and strength is an ability to be valued, whereas nimbleness is not. The justification is based on two assumptions: that all men are strong and that all men's work requires strength. Most work does not require more strength than women have, and work that requires a lot of strength cannot be done by all men, but only by the stronger ones. Furthermore, the strength required for certain tasks depends on choices that are made. Why should cement or cocoa beans be packed in sacks of fifty kilos? Sarsby shows that in pottery the physical strength argument was only used after men took over tasks requiring strength.

The so-called family wage has been an important factor in sustaining the segregation between men's work and women's work. Employers have assumed that working women lived in families, with working men providing them with support.[9] Both employers and trade union representatives have defended the fact that women were paid less with the argument that women were not the main breadwinners.[10] Women themselves also tended to see their wages in this way, as described by Sarsby, even if they were the main breadwinners during long periods of time while their husbands were unemployed. Pay was related to the social position of the earner, and not to performance.

'Scrap Carriers': young workers carrying clay. In pottery physical strength was only used as a justification for gender segregation after men took over tasks requiring strength.

also seen through education.

Tilly has argued that women were excluded from certain jobs, and from career progression through jobs, because of the expectations that they would marry, have children, and take responsibility for raising them. Employers, according to Tilly, were segregative and inflexible about their designation of the appropriate gender for jobs, because their utilization of fixed capital and organization of work were closely linked to the process of sex-typing of jobs. With a higher concentration of capital, large-scale industrial production, wage labour, and radical spatial separation of home and work, formal or informal gender qualifications for employment affected more and more individuals.[11] Kessler-Harris argues that the sexual division of labour is widely assumed to rest on social conceptions of appropriate male and female work which legitimate the prevailing economic system. Men and women are considered to have different needs of, and requirements in, the workforce. This makes the sources of these conceptions oppositional, and thus self-reinforcing. The economic inefficiency that defined the sexual division of labour was sustained by an ideological conviction that the separate spheres were naturally ordained.[12]

The approaches of Tilly and Kessler-Harris, with their stress on opportunistic choices of both workers and employers, are similar to what Thompson has called the rationalization of wage differences through the concept of the breadwinner in the neo-classical economic theory.[13] Neo-classical economic theory rests on the assumption that economic behaviour is governed by the free choices of individuals attempting to maximize their utility. People marry to increase their utility, and the resulting division of labour between breadwinner and home-maker is based on an assessment of the likely returns from the work of each partner on the market. This circular reasoning is supplemented by the human capital theory. From this perspective, sexual inequalities are not the result of structural discrimination, but of the voluntary smaller investments in their own capital by women, which results from their 'choice' to spend more time in the family. Employers, according to Thompson's summary of this theory, take note of this and place men in the best jobs. It was not only the cheapness that made female labour attractive to employers. A factor of importance was also their high turnover. Women were expected to be ready to accept jobs with little or no career prospects, since marriage, accompanied by withdrawal from paid work, was assumed to be their universal destiny.[14]

We now turn to a key concept in the segregation between women's work and men's work: 'skill'. It is almost impossible to discuss work without referring to this concept.

Skill as a Social Construct

Skill is the ability to perform a certain task. Training, time, and transfer of knowledge can all make somebody better at a certain job. However, whether a job is called 'skilled' or 'unskilled' is mainly determined by the social negotiations that surround the definitions of jobs and skills. Social negotiations are more important than any measurable ability. Women workers have generally been denied access to formal training in traditionally masculine areas of work. Comparing the skill required in women's and men's work is therefore not simply a technical matter. Work is designated as skilled as a result of the workers' collective efforts to protect and secure their conditions of employment, often by excluding outsiders. These efforts have predominantly been made by, and on behalf of, the male working class.

There are hardly any jobs that require no training at all. However, it is not the number of weeks, months or years of training that distinguish a skilled worker from an unskilled one. Jobs that require a training period of a few weeks are sometimes regarded as more skilled than others that require a few months' training. Women's work tends to fall into the unskilled or semi-skilled categories of official classifications.[15] Cooking, for example, which involves complex competencies, is not conventionally defined as skilled unless performed by chefs.[16] The concept 'skill' is saturated with sexual bias, as Phillips and Taylor have shown. Not all unskilled work was women's work, but most work that was considered typically feminine was also considered unskilled. Sommestad shows that there were of course exceptions, such as the dairymaids who were machine operators and not machine assistants. In general, however, most women's work was considered unskilled. Far from being an objective economic fact, Phillips and Taylor claim that skill is an ideological category imposed on certain types of work by virtue of the sex and power of the workers who perform it. Few categories of women's work are designated as skilled, because of the pervasive belief that women's work is by definition unskilled. The male cotton spinners in Lancashire successfully retained their skilled status, and the high earnings which differentiated them from unskilled groups, and they assumed the position of an elite in the cotton industry. Women spinners in the Glasgow cotton industry had no such status, and were generally regarded as socially and morally inferior.[17]

Female skills are considered complementary to male skills. If women lack a certain skill, men are supposed to possess it, and vice versa.[18] All jobs done by men, simply by virtue of that fact, are seen as more skilled than those done by women. Women's skills, such as cooking, caring and sewing, are seen as 'natural'.[19] This also applies to complicated tasks in which the 'natural' aspect is difficult to detect. In hosiery, closing the toes of stockings was the task of women. This was a demanding job, that required expertise and experience if it was to be done effectively and with sufficient speed. The ability to do this work, however, was seen as 'natural'. The 'skill' was seen as hereditary, passed on from mother to daughter, as it seemed impossible to acquire it in the training period that was customary for this work.[20] In the hosiery industry, women's jobs required skills comparable to or even superior than those of men. Although women's qualifications were recognized, they were referred to in different terms from those used with regard to men. Male qualifications were referred to using terms such as skill; female qualifications were specified as speed and accuracy.[21] Even the women themselves, while recognizing that their work was skilled, refrained from using this concept. As Bradley describes, women acknowledged that it took time and effort to become good and quick at certain tasks. Female flatlockers in the hosiery industry considered themselves highly skilled, although their job was one of the lowest paid. Even employers acknowledged the skill of these women, but the women did not use the word skill or craft when they described their work. Zimmeck, however, shows that women typists explicitly stressed the skilled nature of their work. According to the typists, it was not difficult to manipulate the machine, just as it was not difficult to learn to sew, but to produce a finished piece of work was quite another matter.

Language is not simply an innocent instrument through which we express our ideas. It does not express our pre-existing thought, but shapes it. Take the term 'working mother'. Embedded in the phrase are a whole host of shifting, value-laden, gendered and classed characteristics. The term 'working mothers' does not simply stand for working women with children. Rather it stands for women who refuse to give up their jobs to keep house and look after the children. Working men are not split into fathers and non-fathers; their children are not harmed by the fact that they are not around most of the time, and they would be called unemployed if they were 'just' to keep house and look after children.[22]

Skill, as a social construct, must be seen in the light of language. The concept of skill is used to distinguish between men and women. In this book we have attempted to show the ambiguous nature of the concept. We do not, however, advocate replacing it with a different concept, as this would automatically inherit the biased nature of its predecessor.

Denying the existence of an objective meaning of skill has far-reaching consequences for what has for a long time been seen as a major outcome of technological change: deskilling. If skill has no meaning, neither does deskilling.

Deskilling, Reskilling, Upgrading and Feminization

Although the effects of technological change have been studied, these studies are predominantly about men, either because industries were chosen in which men formed the main part of the workforce, or because women were explicitly excluded from the studies.[23]

Two authors have dominated the discussion in how work is influenced by technology and technological change: Marx and Braverman. In Marx's vision, the application of machinery enabled the employer to increase production, and to substitute for men workers with less muscle power: women and children. Thus production costs were reduced, and the workforce became more docile. With the introduction of machinery, the virtuosity with which the worker handled his tools was transferred to the machine. Improvement of machinery led not only to a decrease in the number of adult workers, but also to the substitution of one category of workers by another: skilled by unskilled, adults by children, men by women. Marx's classic example is the introduction of the sewing machine, which caused the originally predominantly male industries involved in the production of wearing apparel to become almost exclusively female. With the introduction of the sewing machine the position of young women, working on the machines, improved. That of male workers, children and old women worsened.

Unlike Marx, Braverman took a gender-blind approach, interpreting the social relations of technology exclusively in class terms.[24] He considered the participation of women to be an extension of the unfinished process of homogenization of labour. Due to changes in production, workers are discarded as well as deskilled. Braverman's ideas about skill and deskilling derive from a conception of the male artisan or mechanic, who is regarded as the 'original' kind of skilled labourer, whose skills have been wrenched away from him. A more complete account could be given if it were recognized that the labour process was gendered. That is, that capitalists created 'men's' and 'women's' jobs when they introduced new techniques and reorganized production. They did so on the basis of characteristics that were socially ascribed to men and women as workers: the 'skill' and 'technological expertise' of men, the 'cheapness' and 'adaptability' of women.[25]

The effects of the combination of deskilling and replacement also differ for those who are replaced and the newcomers. The process has often been described from the position of the replaced person. A sense of wrath may have led to the element of deskilling being overstressed. Women's work in printing is, for example, often far more skilled than is formally recognized, and the jobs women do call for more sustained and exhausting effort than those of the men. However, the pay and the terms and conditions of employment severely deteriorated as women came in. In general, deskilling has received more attention than changes in the job justify, as Zimmeck points out. Women typists may do boring work, often referred to as unskilled, but their work does not differ much from the work of the male copyist who preceded them. Zimmeck shows that the transition from hand copying to typewriting cannot be characterized as 'deskilling'. Hand copying already had the low prestige that was transferred to typewriting and typists. Typing, requiring more training than hand copying, can easily be recognized as more skilled.

The deskilling effects of technological change were stressed and feared, not so much because of their effect on male workers, but because they could lead to feminization. Feminization refers to a process whereby an association develops between the low status, the reward for the job, and the fact that it is performed by women. The orthodox Marxist account suggests that feminization takes place as a result of certain jobs being deskilled, or degraded in a way which facilitates the employment of women as cheap, replacement labour. According to Sullerot's thesis, the image of a job devaluates as women move in.[26] This can be illustrated by the medical profession. Doctors in contemporary Western society usually have quite high prestige. By the mid 1970s in the former USSR, three out of four doctors were women, a figure often cited as proof of women's success in entering male dominated professions. However, following women's entry into this profession its status decreased accordingly.[27]

Feminization can have indirect links with technological change. Hand knitting used to be done by both women and men. Now, with no change in the hand knitting technique, it is mostly done by women, and it has a distinct feminine image. With the introduction of machine knitting, there was a shift from considering knitting in terms of productive labour, to knitting as a leisure activity.

Phillips and Taylor argue that it is rare for women to be introduced directly into male-defined jobs. New jobs are created, the low status of which is evident from the fact that they are performed by women. The work is not feminized because it has been degraded, but is degraded because it has been feminized. Phillips and Taylor argue that the degrading takes place subsequent to jobs being defined as women's work. There is, however, considerable evidence for work having been feminized after it had been deskilled and degraded, and having been feminized during periods in which there was overlap with the employment of men. Rationalization in terms of the feminine virtues of dexterity and patience only came after a job was feminized. Both types of feminization, before and after work has been degraded, may take place, even within a sector.

Skill is a key concept in the discussion on women's work and men's work. Skill, however, is not something that can be measured. It is a social construction; it reflects segregation, but does not explain it. As skill is not a workable concept, the effects of technological change should not be discussed in terms of deskilling, as has widely been done. Regarding technological change, it is important to distinguish between different groups of workers: the replaced and the replacers, the established and the newcomers. The effects of technological change differ for each group.

New Opportunities

The effects of technological change on women's work are often judged with regard to work already in existence. However, technological change also led to the creation of new work, into which women were directly introduced. In the 1920s and 1930s, women were drawn in large numbers into what have been called the new industries. The new industries carried a new range of products, and used new methods of production. They produced consumption goods for the family, rather than heavy capital goods or traditional products. The new industries distinguished themselves by mass-production in plants of unprecedented size. Assembly lines, moving conveyor belts and flow processes assured a fast and continuous output. These industries were characterized by mechanization and rationalization of the production, as well as of the supervision and management. There is a tendency amongst historians to associate women's employment with declining and backward industries. Women's work is associated with less mechanized home-bound work, men's with factories and technical advance. The case of the new industries invalidates such associations. Women held highly mechanized jobs. Rather than regarding these jobs as feminized, they have to be seen as feminine from the start.

Not only in the new industries have women found new opportunities for employment. The administrative sector also saw a massive expansion of work. Opportunities for women in office work have been attributed to new office machinery, primarily typewriters. However, as Zimmeck shows, typewriters were not seen as feminine from the beginning. It was the combination of the rising demand for office workers, and the availability of young women seeking employment, that led to the influx of women.

New opportunities were of course created for women workers during the two world wars. Wartime experience is significant because it reveals the extent to which the sexual division of labour is an artificial construct and not a 'natural' effect of sex differences in physique and personality. It provides an example of how rapidly change can occur if supported by 'national will' and governmental power. The effects that the two world wars had on the nature of women's work have been subject to lengthy discussions. As Thom mentions, much more is known about the work of women in the war periods, than in any other period. Especially in England, many changes in the nature of women's work are attributed to the effect of the wars. Through the years, the effects of the wars have been both over- and underestimated. Although not much might have changed in the short run, wartime experience did alter the ways women and men looked upon women doing certain kinds of work. Assessing the influence of war work is not easy. Memories of war work are ambivalent.

Most women workers during the wars were not new workers at all. The assumption of novelty was an ideological filter through which war work of women was viewed. The First World War was not the breaking point it was often considered to be. The gender segregation hardly changed and most of the work women were doing was women's work anyway. As an example, Thom refers to bullet-making, which was already predominantly women's work. When a task was new, it was labelled male or female work by analogy. Even if women were the first to perform a certain job, it could still be seen as men's work. Thom shows that women's wartime work was the subject of intense ideological negotiation. Not all women readily gave up their work when the war ended. In 1920, the Cardiff tram company took female tram conductors from their jobs when their vehicles had been attacked by ex-servicemen.[28] Women engineers who wanted to continue working after the First World War met widespread opposition.[29] Wartime work did not lead to permanent changes. Women doing work that had formerly been done by men were clearly seen as trespassing into the male realm, and their work was meant to be temporary from the start.

One aspect commonly attributed to changes during the First World War is the subdivision of tasks to facilitate the employment of women. The subdivision was, amongst other things, used to demarcate women's work from the former men's job, thus justifying lower wages with union consent. What the articles in this book show, however, is that the same changes in the production process occurred in the neutral countries Sweden, Denmark and the Netherlands. The subdivision of certain tasks was a necessary phase in the automation of parts of production that reached full bloom in the 1930s. Stress on wartime circumstances may obscure parallels with non-belligerent countries.

Choosing Technologies, Technology Transfer, and Union Strength

New technology was designed with the future operators in mind: men, women or children. This determined the height of the machine, the place of the levers and buttons, and the size and weight of its produce. Machines may, however, not be worked by the kind of person the inventor had in mind. The Laval separator, separating cream from milk, was invented in Sweden for farm use by women. It was used in the Netherlands by men in factories, as described by Schrover, because it was too costly for the smaller scale Dutch farms, and fitted the requirements of the relatively small Dutch creameries.

Although it may take some time, successful technological innovations find their way from one country to the next. However, not only technologies were transferred, but also with the engineers advising on its installation, the division of labour between men and women was transferred. Literature on the transfer of technology is rapidly expanding.[30] Little attention is paid to the influence of foreign technology on the labour process. Most research is directed at the impact of technological transfer on the process of industrialization. However, a few historical studies draw attention to the influence of the transfer of technology on gendering of jobs.

The fact that it was not uncommon for overseers and workers to move from one country to another in order to instruct fellow workers has received little attention. When a Dutch textile industrialist did not manage to produce good jute with Dutch female workers, he recruited a number of female jute spinners from Dundee to teach the local workforce.[31] English potters taught the trade to the Swedish workers at Gustavsberg, and the Dutch potters also had to be instructed by foreigners. The first workers that were imported to teach the trade to the Dutch workers came from Belgium. From the 1850s, English potters from the Staffordshire area came to teach the Dutch workers the Wedgwood style.

With the exchange of workers, not only the employers', designers', machine builders' or instructors' ideas about the division of labour were transferred from one country to another, but also those of the unions. De Groot shows that the division of labour in the Dutch textile industry was not copied in the way it was originally intended to be, but with the alterations the English unions had managed to achieve. The Dutch unions were not strong enough to demand similar alterations, so this was not a precaution taken by the employers. It was just that a system was copied in the way it existed elsewhere, without looking at or discussing its origin.

In most cases, however, the gendering of new technology was not publicly debated; it happened as if it was a natural process. This was so in the case of the Gustavsberg pottery factory. Wikander interprets the instability of the gender division of labour as proof of the fact that the gendering of machinery actually took place. If strong unions existed they could alter or influence the gendering of new technology at the moment of its introduction. A classical example of unions' influence on gendering is the self-acting mule. Although the self-acting mule was invented to be worked by women, men became its operators. In the eighteenth century, spinning was mainly done by women. The early small jennies were used in the homes of the workers. The bigger machines, which were placed in the factories, were still operated by women, but their number decreased and they were in a more dependent position. The spinning mule changed the gender of the operator. According to Berg,[32] male workers were employed because this machine initially required strength. After power had been applied, the machine was claimed to require engineering skills to maintain and repair. Women learned to work the machines and did so until the 1830s. Berg has shown that it was the Mule Spinners' Union, not the machine, which excluded women workers. Printers are another classic example. In England, printers succeeded in blocking management's attempt to change their work or position for an extremely long time before newspaper owners were able to make many men redundant.

Technology is created with the gender of the operator in mind. The ideas of the inventor, and not the technology itself, determine the gendering of the technology. Regional differences in the nature of the industry, as in the case of Swedish and Dutch dairying, or union strength, may cause the gender of the operator to be different than originally intended.

Gertjan de Groot and Marlou Schrover

Technology and Segregation

Because technological change can create a breach in existing work patterns, it offers a unique possibility to study segregative factors on the labour market. The clear demarcation that exists between men's work and women's work has been attributed to many factors. Most of these do not fully, or do not at all, explain the segregation. The characteristics of the job, or the qualifications it is believed to require, cannot explain the segregation, because feminine characteristics were usually attributed to a job after it had got a sex label. Traditional ideas transferred from pre-industrial times had some influence on segregation. Division of work in the pre- or proto-industrial era, however, cannot fully explain segregation in large, expanding or new nineteenth and twentieth century industries. In the nineteenth century, the concept of women's work was developed, and this enforced the segregation. Physical separation on moral grounds led to the strengthening of segregation of work. Legal measures could enhance segregation. All these factors are based on a segregation already in existence. Lower wages and high turnover cannot fully explain segregation. The age of the workers has to be taken into account. Young men and young women do not differ much regarding wages and turnover. A moral obligation, felt by the employer, to provide his young male workers with a career perspective, may have been of influence.

Skill is a highly segregative concept. Women's work was generally seen as unskilled work. Some authors believe that both women themselves, and their employers were less willing to invest in training women, because of the temporary nature of their employment. Skill is however an extremely biased concept. Certain 'skills' are valued and others not. Skills needed in women's work are seen and valued as natural to women.

Contesting the concept of skill also means contesting deskilling as the main consequence of technological change. Deskilling elements have been over stressed out of a sense of wrath amongst those threatened by change. The stress on deskilling has also resulted from a one-sided preoccupation with the stereotypical craftsman. It denies the importance of the numerous workers for whom technological change had upgrading effects, or where it has led to the creation of new work. The Industrial Revolution is often seen as the era in which a whole range of technological developments fundamentally changed the position of women as workers. In this era, the range of jobs women could do was narrowed. Women's participation in the workforce was restricted to low-paid jobs, but in these they dominated. The whole debate on this general level is seriously hindered by a lack of data about women's employment before industrial times, and the nature of their work after it.

Technological change can be crucial for the gendering or regendering of jobs, therefore, it is time to reassess the relationship between technological change and women's work. The traditional picture, in which the introduction of new technology led to deskilling, and thus to the employment of unskilled workers, amongst whom were many women, cannot be maintained. The

12

circumstances in which new technology is introduced determine the effects it will have on the work of women.

If new technology is introduced together with a whole new industry, the gender of the future worker will probably be decided at the moment of the introduction of the technology. This can lead to the creation of work for women. The new technology may be engendered from the beginning, if it was designed explicitly with the gender of the future operative in mind. If new technology is introduced in the new or expanding sector of an established industry, the predominant gender of the existing workforce will determine the gender of the future worker. Thus male workers are very likely to be chosen as the workers for a new technology, when the existing factory workforce is predominantly male. With work that requires little training and offers no career perspective, employers are likely to choose young workers. In an all male industry, these will be boys. As long as no vested interests are threatened, a transitional phase may follow, in which the work is regendered, and girls and women replace the boys (see the chapters by Zimmeck and Schrover). This is one of the rare instances in which the gender of the work remains unclear for a short period, without persisting technological changes. The creation of new work within an existing industry can have an emanation effect on other sectors of the industry not affected by the technological change itself. Once female workers have entered the factory, male workers in other parts of the factory may also be replaced by female workers (see the chapters by Wikander and Schrover). The introduction of female workers in a formerly nearly all-male setting can give rise to more formal demarcations between women's work and men's work, as a greater need is felt to physically separate the sexes. If new technology is introduced in an existing industry, its influence depends on whether the industry is dominated by men or by women.

In a male-dominated industry, men can react in two ways to the new technology: they can object to the new technology and refuse to work with it, or they can, maybe grudgingly, adopt the new technique. In this last case, no regendering takes place. Objections will be raised if the new technology threatens the workers' interests, status or income. The employer's reaction to the objections of his male workers can be twofold. On the one hand, if the men are not well organized in unions, he can introduce the technique despite their protest, and put new workers on the machines. The new workers can be men or boys, but are more likely to be girls and women. The male workers who refused to work with the new technique will, gradually or immediately, become unemployed. On the other hand, if the male workers are well organized in unions, they may be able to stop the introduction of the new technique (see Schrover's chapter), or they may accept to work with the new technique after it has been upgraded so that the threats to interests, status and income are taken away (see the chapter by Sarsby). They may compromise on their demands and revert to this policy after some women have been let into the profession, making the threat of replacement very real (see the chapter by Wikander). The original workers will then probably become the operatives of the new machines, contrary to the initial intentions of the employers and designers, and on higher wages than intended. The older technology, formerly used by men, will gradually become obsolete. While men move to work with the new technology, women may be allowed to work with the technique that is soon to disappear (see the chapters by Wikander and Bradley).

As in male-dominated industry, women in female-dominated industry can react in two ways to the introduction of new techniques: they may object to the new technique and refuse to work with it, or they may adopt it and no regendering occurs. Like the male workers, women will object to the new technique if it threatens their vested position. Unlike the male workers, it is however unlikely, historically speaking, that they will be well enough organized to stop the introduction of the new machinery, or to otherwise influence its introduction. Thus their objections will mean that they will be replaced by different workers, most likely men (see the chapter by Sommestad). The introduction of new technology can help men to move into the industry, claiming the positions of the former female workers (Sarsby).

Once work is gendered, the label becomes rather inflexible, as shown by Bradley. Even periods of considerable social turmoil, such as the two world wars, do not easily lead to regendering, as shown by Thom. Circumstances which are specific for one factory can determine gendering in a much wider setting through the influence of unions, as shown by Rostgård. The union's success in gendering a certain technique in one country may cause the technique to be used in the same way in a different country, although the influence of the union in the adopting country may be negligible (De Groot). Engendered techniques can be transposed to other countries with a very different social setting, without being regendered, as shown by De Groot and Sommestad.

Once a job is gendered, employers will not be able to introduce workers into it whose gender does not match with that of the work. Workers, both male and female, will likewise object to breaches into this pattern. Another technological change is needed to supply the reason or excuse for regendering. In the more dynamic and innovating industries, opportunities for regendering frequently recur. In industries in which technological change is less frequent, feelings about 'tradition' will develop. The opposition to new technology, when introduced, will be stronger, and there is a larger chance that it will not lead to regendering, despite possible intentions of the employer.

Notes

1 Cockburn, C. (1983) *Brothers. Male Dominance and Technological Change*, London. Wajcman, J. (1991) *Feminism confronts technology*, Cambridge, p. 24.
2 Braverman, H. (1974) *Labor and Monopoly Capital: the Degradation of Work in the Twentieth Century*, London.
3 Berg, M. (1987) 'Women's work, mechanisation and the early phases of industrialisation in England', in Joyce, P. (Ed.), *The Historical Meanings of Work*, Cambridge, pp. 64–98.

4 Bradley, H. (1989) *Men's Work, Women's Work: a Sociological History of the Sexual Division of Labour in Employment*, Cambridge, pp. 24–26.

5 Scott, J.W. (1988) 'The problem of invisibility', in Kleinberg, S.J. (Ed.) *Retrieving Women's History. Changing Perceptions of the Role of Women in Politics and Society*, Oxford, pp. 5–29. Roberts, E. (1988) *Women's Work 1840–1940*, Hampshire/London.

6 Phillips, A. and Taylor, B. (1980) 'Sex and skill: notes towards a feminist economics', *Feminist Review* 6, pp. 79–88.

7 Berg, M. (1993) 'What difference did women's work make to the Industrial Revolution?', *History Workshop Journal*, nr. 35 Spring, pp. 24–44, esp. p. 32.

8 Goldin, C. (1990) *Understanding the Gender Gap. An Economic History of American Women*, New York/Oxford.

9 Kessler-Harris, A. (1990) *A Women's Wage. Historical Meanings and Social Consequences*, The University Press of Kentucky.

10 Land, H. (1980) 'The family wage', *Feminist Review*, no. 6, pp. 55–77.

11 Tilly, L.A. (1993) 'Gender and jobs in early twentieth-century French industry', *International Labor and Working-Class History*, no. 43 Spring, pp. 31–47.

12 Kessler-Harris, A. (1989) 'Gender ideology in historical reconstruction: a case study from the 1930s.' *Gender & History* vol. 1 Spring, pp. 31–49.

13 Thompson, P. (1993) *The Nature of Work. An Introduction to Debates on the Labour Process*, London, pp. 180–209.

14 Summerfield, P. (1984) *Women Workers in the Second World War, Production and Patriarchy in Conflict*, London.

15 Wajcman, *Feminism confronts technology*, p. 37.

16 Beechey, V. (1982) 'The sexual division of labour and the labour process: a critical assessment of Braverman', in Wood, S. (Ed.), *The Degradation of Work. Skill, Deskilling and the Labour Process*, London, pp. 63–64.

17 Gordon, E. (1991) *Women and the Labour Movement in Scotland 1850–1914*, Oxford.

18 Phillips and Taylor, 'Sex and Skill', pp. 79–88.

19 Cockburn, C. (1985) *Machinery of Dominance. Women, Men and Technical Know-how*, London, p. 171.

20 Bradley *Men's Work, Women's Work*, p. 142.

21 Parr, J. (1990) *The Gender of the Breadwinner: Women, Men, and Change in Two Industrial Towns 1880–1950*, Toronto.

22 Hamilton, R. (1993) 'Feminist theories', *Left history, an interdisciplinary journal of historical inquiry and debate*, vol. 1, nr 1, Spring, pp. 9–34.

23 Thompson, *The Nature of Work*, p. 185; Cockburn, *Brothers*, p. 4.

24 Braverman, *Labor and Monopoly Capital*.

25 Bradley, H. (1989) *Men's Work, Women's Work, a Sociological History of the Sexual Division of Labour in Employment*, Cambridge.

26 Sullerot, E. (1968) *Histoire et sociologie du travail féminin*, Paris.

27 Stearns, P.N. and Chapman, H. (1992) *European Society in Upheaval, Social History since 1750*. 3rd ed. Ontario, p. 376.

28 Beddoe, D. (1989), *Back to Home and Duty: Women between the Wars 1918–1939*, London, p. 49.

29 Pursell, C. (1993) '"Am I a lady or an engineer?" The origins of the women's engineering society in Britain, 1918–1940', *Technology and Culture*, vol. 34, pp. 78–97.

30 Jeremy, D.J. (Ed.) (1991) *International Technology Transfer: Europe, Japan and the USA, 1700–1914*, Aldershot; Bruland, K. (Ed.) (1991) *Technology Transfer and Scandinavian Industrialism*, New York and Oxford.

31 Gordon, E. (1991) *Women and the Labour Movement in Scotland 1850–1914*, Oxford, pp. 137–211; Bos, J. (1986) *Oude Fabrieks- en bedrijfsgebouwen in Overijssel*, Zwolle, pp. 63–66.

32 Berg, M. (1987) 'Women's work, mechanisation and the early phases of industrialisation in England', in Joyce, P. (Ed.) *The Historical Meanings of Work*, Cambridge. p. 80.

Chapter 2

Frames of Reference: Skill, Gender and New Technology in the Hosiery Industry

Harriet Bradley

Hosiery, like other textile industries, has historically provided women with the chance to acquire craft skills on which to base a lifetime's employment. Yet these 'women's skills' have never received the high social and economic valuation accorded to male craft work such as engineering and printing. This chapter is an exploration of the processes which lie behind this devaluation of women's work. It examines the history of changing technologies and women's work in hosiery in terms of ideas associated with the allocation of tasks and machines to women or to men. In particular, changing ideas and characterizations of female and male attributes have had a strong influence on sex-typing of jobs. In turn, these characterizations have been linked to longstanding debates and conflicts over the definition of skill in the industry. What did 'skill' consist of? How skilled were hosiery workers? How was skill acquired and who could acquire it?

In earlier work I have attempted to trace the history of the sexual division of labour in hosiery from the eighteenth century to the present day.[1] Rather than repeat this story here, I have chosen to concentrate on key moments in the technological evolution of the industry in terms of the debates about gender and skill which were aired in some of the documents relating to the industry. My objects of study, then, are the discourses and ideologies of gender and skill rather than the technologies and tasks themselves, although some details about those are provided where necessary.

My discussion draws upon a series of parliamentary papers dating from 1812 which gives a useful if slanted account of the early period. The papers, relating to a number of petitions from hosiery workers calling for protection for their work and control of the industry, served as an arena where the conflicts within the industry were publicly dramatized. For the early twentieth century I have had to draw more eclectically on union records, company and local histories and civic documents. A limitation of all these sources, however, is the almost total absence of female voices within them. At the end, to try to rectify this, I present some material from the very limited number of female accounts

17

I have been able to locate, notably including taped interviews with women recorded as part of the Leicester Oral History Archive.[2]

The Downplaying of Women's Contribution

Mr Bell: The hosiery and the boot and shoe trade were always largely female labour. . . . In Leicester and Nottingham there was always a very well-paid female population. The hosiery trade, well, they could learn it but it was a fairly skilled job. Women, girls, went to the hosiery trade when they left school and by the time they were in their late teens they were fairly skilled operatives and could earn good money.

Mrs Bell: I mean, let's face it, when we got married I was earning more than you were earning.

Mr Bell: Yes. This was quite common. You got a man and a wife working in the same hosiery factory, and the woman, the wife would be probably earning a little bit more money than her husband. . . . Because women's jobs in the hosiery trade were fairly well paid. . . . The jobs in the hosiery industry for men were rather, counter, packing . . . the lower . . . they weren't skilled jobs in other words.

Mrs Bell: The knitters were.

Mr Bell: Yes.

Mrs Bell: The men who were on the knitting machines earned quite good money.[3]

The dialogue reproduced above is a rare instance of an open if somewhat oblique admission that women in the hosiery industry were performing jobs comparable or even superior in skill to those of male colleagues, although it may be noted that there is a tendency to conflate skill and pay. However, in the formal history of the industry as largely narrated by men (employers and male union officers) women are normally presented as secondary workers in the trade and their skills as inferior to men's. Indeed, documents such as parliamentary reports, union records and industrial histories like that of Wells[4] actually present the industry as a male one, despite the fact that since the 1870s women have been numerically dominant within it. Some of the early parliamentary papers downgraded women's role in the industry to such an extent as to ignore it altogether. Writers who did acknowledge the presence of women and see hosiery as a female industry also upheld the image of women as less skilled and the men in the industry as a skilled elite.[5]

However, as implied above, the question of skill is problematic, a fact which has been recognized by the many writers on women's work who have argued that skill involves a major element of social construction.[6] The premise from which I begin here is that there is some kind of material base to skill in the sense that some jobs are more difficult than others, require more training and more knowledge or are carried out effectively only on the basis of long experience.

However, this material base is overlain, and in some cases quite disguised, by the processes of social negotiation that surround the definitions of jobs and skills. This element of social construction then becomes the dominant part in terms of collective organization, economic rewards and social status.

Thus, in the hosiery industry, there was from the start a great deal of disagreement as to how much skill was involved in the operation of the knitting frame, what exactly that skill consisted of and how long it took to learn. Characteristically male hosiery workers presented the job as highly skilled, seeking thus to enhance their own status and earnings, while at least some of their employers claimed that tasks could be easily learned and carried out by inexperienced workers. These arguments became a great deal more complex and fragmented once issues of gender had entered into the debate in the middle of the nineteenth century.

The Domestic Era

The technological centre of the industry in the first half of the nineteenth century was the knitting frame which had been invented by the Reverend William Lee in 1589. There were different types of frame, producing different types of hosiery, of different gauges (producing finer or coarser garments) but they were all basically adaptations of the same device, essentially a kind of loom in which the operator sat and worked with hands and feet. Frames were housed in the workpeople's homes, occasionally gathered together in small workshops. Although originally knitters had been independent craftsmen, by 1800 the industry was essentially a capitalistic one with entrepreneurial hosiers putting out machinery and work to their operatives. There was still a seven-year apprenticeship system formally in existence which had been established by a royal charter in 1664, but many knitters taught their own children how to work the frame. This was one way in which girls learned the trade, but there were also some cases of girl apprentices, while widows were entitled by the charter to practise the 'art' of framework knitting.[7] However, the majority of knitters up to the 1840s seem to have been men and there were other jobs connected with hosiery production as a family business which women could do and which were more easily combined with childcare and domestic labour: winding yarn, seaming and stitching up the hose and various mending and finishing tasks.

The two first parliamentary reports on the industry, both responses to workers' petitions, were published in 1812 and 1819 and are indicative of this phase in virtually ignoring the issue of gender. The tacit assumption is that this is a male craft; both masters and operatives speak of 'men' or 'workmen' persistently. For example, Thomas Hitchcock, a Leicester hosier, commented that 'there is a great deal of art in qualifying a man to work' and William Jackson, a knitter, spoke of a deputation 'from the workmen of Leicester to the workmen of Nottingham'.[8] Women are subsumed into the male categories.

There was also the assumption of the male as the family breadwinner: 'a man could maintain his family then', said William Watts.[9] It was acknowledged that there were some women in the trade[10] and the appendix listing knitters currently on the poor rate in Leicester gives two women's names. But there is no discussion about women in terms of inferior skill, although there is considerable attention given in both reports to the entry of unskilled *workmen* or 'colts' into the trade.

The operatives were concerned to establish the skill of their trade and were backed by some manufacturers. Gravenor Henson, who wrote the first history of the trade, suggested that it took two years to learn to make stockings 'properly'.[11] Moreover, to be an expert worker, the knitters needed to know more than just how to weave and shape a stocking; they must understand the workings of the frame, get it to run smoothly when they got a newly-made one (this could take up to a week as new frames were rough and could damage stockings), set it up, service it and adapt it to make different products. Henson commented: 'the French are by no means bad workmen but they are extremely bad mechanics; few French stocking makers know how to alter their frames'.[12]

Hosiers confirmed that they themselves lacked the technical knowledge of their operatives, as Braverman[13] has claimed was the case in the early phases of the capitalist labour process: one explained 'I am frequently obliged to leave it to the workman how to make the thing I want and cannot describe it to him perfectly'.[14] John Parker explained that each machine was subtly different: he would not be able to set up a machine, nor did he know how many needles his workmen used.[15]

In sum, during the decades covered by these reports (1800–1820) women were not seen as having an integral part in the industry but neither was there any attempt to suggest that they were incompetent workers on the basis of their sex; indeed, there is no suggestion that they were in any way different as workers. Presumably girls who were apprenticed became skilled operatives, although we do not know if they, like the boys, were also instructed in the mechanics of the frame; this was certainly to become a crucial difference in the future. Inasmuch as the division of labour needed to be legitimated it was on the base of custom and household authority. This may be reading a lot into slender evidence or, more accurately, deducing a lot from significant absences, but such a conclusion would be in line with the body of literature about women's pre-industrial role which suggests a lower social status than that of men but a considerable degree of economic equality.[16]

The Transitional Period 1840–1855

By 1840, the situation had altered dramatically. It was now widely recognized that great numbers of women worked in the industry, both in the seaming and finishing areas and also as knitters. The debate on skill continued but the issue of gender had now become central to it as is demonstrated in the two major reports on the industry from the period from 1840 to 1860, the Royal

Commission on the Condition of the Framework Knitters (1845) and the Select Committee on the Stoppage of Wages (1855). Many (although not all) of the hosiers and operatives who spoke of women categorized them as second-class operatives, ranked with young people and older operatives. For example, hosier William Walker referred to 'women, children and young persons who are incompetent to work the heavier or more skilled machinery'.[17] It is worth pointing out that the 1842 Mines Act and the 1843 Factory Act had already signalled the connection between women and young people and it is likely that opinion in the hosiery industry had been influenced by these broader sweeps in public thinking and debate about the work roles of women.

The prevailing opinion was that women's output was inferior to men's and that they were only competent to carry out the simpler kinds of work, for example in the older style 'narrow frames' which produced 'wrought' hose. Wide frames, becoming widespread in the industry, produced not a fully shaped stocking but flat pieces of cloth which were then cut into stocking shapes, seamed up and shaped on a board. It was argued that greater physical strength was needed to operate these frames, although the evidence for this is inconclusive.

Women were said to produce (and therefore earn) between half and two-thirds of what men did. Three possible reasons for this discrepancy were aired by the witnesses to the reports. First, women were commonly given the inferior machines and types of job to perform. Knitter Thomas Hallard explained that they generally worked on the coarser gauges (24 to 30), specializing in small hose and tops.[18] William Walker alleged that the 'more skilful workmen' had abandoned wrought hose for wide frames and glove frames 'because that work is much better paid than the other'.[19] Given the chance to work these superior frames women's output presumably increased. John Perkins of Kibworth claimed that a 13-year-old girl working on a wide frame could equal the output of three men on wrought work. The important point here, however, is that women were identified with the less productive machinery by the majority of both male knitters and masters; a revealing statement came from Walter Upton of Thurmaston:

> I should apply, of course, for the best work for my own hands, because I am the most expert in the business and if my wife worked she could not work above half her time. . . . They are not so much consequence as we therefore it is in that way that we look out for the best jobs for ourselves. . . . Women and children fall into the bad jobs; men will not work at them if they can get anything that will beat them.[20]

As Upton's words imply, the second reason given for women's lower output was skill deficiency. The debate about how skilled the work was continued. One hosier, Joseph Meadows, described it as 'easy to learn'.[21] Medical Officer Thomas Cotterell opined that 'it requires no vast deal of muscular exertion but it requires attention' and on that basis considered that a young person could do as well as an adult.[22] Dominant opinion, however, seemed to suggest that strength and knowledge were the key attributes. Without the latter a worker could do considerable damage to the frame and the hose. When women worked the frames it was claimed that they needed much more repair and maintenance. According to Isaac Hayes 'they cannot work half as long, perhaps, as a careful man before the frame wants recruiting'.[23] By contrast, experienced knitters claimed that they could make a frame last in good shape for up to fifteen years.[24] Again, this relates to the fact that women lacked mechanics' knowledge: women in the glove branch were described as 'proficient' but 'not to be so that they can keep the machinery in repair'.[25]

Upton had also touched on the third, and possibly paramount, reason for women's lower output, which was simply their responsibility for domestic duties and especially for childcare: 'Of course, those that have a family to attend to, they would not do as much as a person would do that has learnt his trade and has nothing else to do'.[26] Indeed, it was made clear by one manufacturer that the only real difference between men and women resided in this: 'It does not follow that because they are women they are the worst hands; they make as good hands, but their work is uncertain'.[27]

Domestic labour disadvantaged women knitters in two ways: first, they had to keep breaking off their work in the frame to deal with children, cooking and so forth while a man could knit uninterrupted; and second, domestic labour would have interfered with the original process of learning the craft, which was still stated to be a lengthy business. Although it was not clear that the seven-year apprenticeship was really necessary (two years was suggested as a more realistic period), training took time:

> There is a great deal of difference in children, some will take it as quick again as others. I always consider that a boy who has been brought up among it learns it a deal sooner than those who have been utter strangers to it. We do not consider them perfect until they have been five, or six, or seven years in the trade. In the first place, we mostly learn them upon common things, and as soon as they get masters of that we put them into better work and they go on by steps from one sort to another.[28]

As girls were often required to help with household tasks it is likely that their progress through the stages outlined above will have been slower than that of their brothers.

At the end of the domestic phase of the industry, then, a process of gendering of machinery appeared to be under way, although not to the extent that was to prevail under the factory system. Women were generally perceived as less skilled, in terms of strength, experience and knowledge, although some acknowledged this to be due to the constraints placed on them by domestic labour. By now women had come to be seen as inferior men; not different in any radical way but simply lower down the scale, along with children and older men whose strength and dexterity was waning or individually incompetent men of any age. During the next decades, however, ideas about sex-specific skills emerged, linked to a more rigid gendering of particular items of machinery.

The Factory System 1855–1940

As soon as the first automated and steam-powered machines were introduced, employers pointed out that they could easily be worked by women. The first experiments were with what were called 'rotary' machines. Thomas Collins, one of the first to succeed in establishing factory production, explained: 'You have nothing to do but to turn the treadle by the hand, and any boy or girl can turn these frames, if there is anyone to look after them to see that they work'.[29] Thomas Corah, another initiator, used two or three young girls to tend each machine: 'There is no physical force necessary; all they have to do is merely to notice that the thing is going on rightly'.[30] Both Collins and Corah implied a preference for hard-working females (Collins described his workers as 'good hands, active girls and women') in their factories. Earlier experiments to organize male workers on a factory basis had failed because the men refused to accept the accompanying 'time-discipline'.[31]

Factory production involved a deconstruction of the old forms of skill. The knitter's new function was basically that of a caretaker of automated machines. This switch from craftsman to operative was a major threat to male knitters. Data relating to the 1860s and 1870s suggest how vulnerable the men were. Table 2.1 shows women to be numerically dominant on power frames. However, the new machines, like the frames, required to be set up, maintained and repaired. Here men had the potential advantage with their longstanding tradition of mechanical knowledge and the ability to adapt machinery. 'He is clever at expedients and schemes many contrivances to assist in his work' was one observer's comment on the knitter's craft.[32]

The next snapshots we have of affairs within the industry suggest that in the long run the knitters were able to capitalize on these attributes and retain the major role as knitters. Although employers through the decades continually sought to employ women as knitters, knitting retained its image as a male skill. 'Flat' machines, such as Cotton's patents, which produced fully fashioned products rather than an unshaped tube as did the circulars, were considered a male specialism. The unions maintained that only men had the requisite skills to operate these machines. Two factors served to reinforce their campaign. First, some employers acquiesced to the idea that men should be knitters while women specialized in the various jobs linked to the introduction of sewing machines into the trade. Secondly, the number of these finishing jobs (seaming, hemming, mending, embroidering, buttonholing and so on) was dramatically expanding because of the productivity of the new knitting machines. Numerous women were required to fill these jobs.

This significant new phase in the development in the division of labour involved a firmer association between gender and certain types of skills and

Harriet Bradley

Table 2.1 Number of power frames operated by men and women, 1863

	Number of factories	Power frames operated by men	Power frames operated by women
Derby	4	158	340
Nottingham	34	1047	1062
Leicester	27	750	706
Total	65	1955	2108

Source: Factory Inspectors' Reports, 1863, xviii.

machines than in the earlier period. The sewing machine, and its successors, such as the overlocking and linking machines, were seen from the start as female machines. There is no evidence that anyone tried to make men operate sewing machines. These machines were associated with attributes (nimble fingers, close attention) seen as specific to women. With these 'women's jobs' absorbing much of the female labour force, men could stake a claim on the jobs they wanted, declaring these to be 'suitable' only for men. Knitting was the main male job, but a curious and somewhat anomalous 'male' specialism, jealously defended, was countering. This was a process of packing, which involved matching pairs of stockings precisely by colour, shape and size and then folding and boxing them. It is common for this type of job to go to women; however, men succeeded in convincing their employers that some complex skill was involved. In employer Joseph Morley's words, 'part of the work often done by young females, as sorting and folding, is entrusted only to men who have had long training and have acquired a more accurate eye'.[33] A rather more accurate assessment of the work of countering appeared, I would suggest, in the conversation of the Bells which was reproduced earlier. But this example suggests how powerfully processes of social negotiation can generate myths about skill and gender suitability.

One statement embodying these newer ideas about gender and skill came from A.J. Mundella, employer, politician, founder of the Nottingham Arbitration Board and generally an influential man in the industry. He told the 1854 Select Committee:

> I do not think that working in the frame is a healthy occupation for a woman ... I think that the mother of a family ought always to find enough to do without being employed at frame work. There are many things which she might do to assist the family, such, for instance, as seaming, which is quite a woman's work.[34]

Mundella wanted knitting to remain a male monopoly. Himself a knitter in origin, Mundella was in many ways a progressive man, but it is clear that he supported the emergent Victorian ideals of the sexual division of labour: segregation of the sexes at work and the procuring of 'fit' work for women compatible with the maternal role. Sewing had longstanding domestic associations and these were extended to the sewing machine and variations on it; whereas images of 'heaviness' and 'mechanical complexity', however fallacious, could be attached to knitting frames and machines to make them 'unsuitable' for women.

In the Victorian epoch, the idea of 'suitability' seems to have led inexorably to that of 'natural attributes'. These became the leitmotifs of discussions of gender and skill in the subsequent decades. East Midlands women built a reputation as supremely adept and quick: 'what you may call expert hands, who have been at the work for a considerable time, they get from 10/- to 18/- a week' said hosier William Tyler.[35] Although this was linked by Tyler to experience, others associated it with some kind of inbuilt skill, as the following quotations show:

> Can you imagine any women working quicker than your women do in Leicester? The rapidity of the machines, and their natural deftness as they call it is remarkable, is it not?[36]

> Sir Albert Rollit has justly remarked that heredity plays about as important a part in shaping the development of communities as in moulding that of the individual. Only some such hypothesis can account for the skill manufactured and transmitted by successive generations in the great hosiery trade.[37]

> Skilled hosiery workers cannot be trained in a week or two, nor is there any other area of the country where girls and women have that intangible something which makes them not just operatives but good operatives. Employers have argued the pros and cons of heredity for years, but they are faced with the indisputable fact that in the Leicester area hosiery workers, particularly women, have nimble fingers, sure hands and adaptability.[38]

> Either you are a born linker or you are not.[39]

Inherited or otherwise, these female skills were taken to involve quickness, dexterity of fingers, sharp eyesight, quick intelligence and the ability to concentrate closely: 'These quiet jobs are highly skilled, demanding sharp eyes and deft fingers – women's work. They become adept at it and earn good money'.[40]

As we have seen, it was more difficult to define male skills, especially in view of repeated assertions by employers that 'a woman can work the machines by power just as well as a man'.[41] Two reports from the inter-war period indicate how union officers tried to justify male specialisms, the 1919 Report of the War Cabinet on Women and Industry and a follow-up report in 1930. Strength and heaviness remained major issues. The unions declared that women working on Cotton's Patents were not a success and produce less.... In quality and quantity of work the women are not as good as the men. The women do more damage to the machines, they cause more waste and require more supervision.... Manufacturers will realize that on such machines as the Cotton Patent, the Excel Circular Jersey machines ... it is to their advantage to employ men.[42]

Even where women were working the lighter machines such as circulars they were supervising six rather than eight or ten machines. This case might have been undermined by the fact that at Hawick in Scotland women had always operated all types of knitting machine but the union claimed that men were now taking over as 'they are more able to do overtime and repair the machines and are less liable to illness.... A woman does not look after her machine as well as a man and ... requires more overlooking. In some cases an extra mechanic is necessary'.[43] This returns us to the key issue of technical knowledge. The 1930 report made plain that women were still excluded from this, if not formally, then by custom. They did not attend classes at the Technical Colleges. The following comment is interesting, however, in conceding that women *did* acquire practical knowledge of machinery on-the-job: 'women sometimes by practice become very clever at adjusting their machines, but they have not been trained as mechanics and do not undertake repairs'.[44] In the main such 'tacit' skills were conveniently overlooked.

In the factory period, then, special female attributes were proclaimed as the basis for the sexual division of labour. It was acknowledged that in these areas women were superior: 'On their own light machines, the women equalled or surpassed the men in output.... On many machines, owing to their intricacy and delicacy the women are superior'.[45] This was a new note and would seem to reflect the Victorian ideologies of gender which portrayed men and women as each pre-eminent within their separate sphere and suggested that, rather than being an inferior man, woman was a quite different kind of being, superior in many ways because of her domestic and nurturant inclinations. However, sex-specific skills were not equally rewarded. Even the most experienced women were not paid as much as men. For example, in 1880 men on power machines earned 30 to 35 shillings, women 16 to 17 shillings. Rates for the vaunted female jobs of machining, seaming and so forth were lower. This can be linked to the ideology which presented men as breadwinners and therefore deserving of economic supremacy, although in the locality the argument of tradition was more overtly used.

Modernization

Subsequent changes in the industry have been incremental rather than comprehensive. Machines have been modified to improve quality and quantity of output, to handle synthetic materials and so on. Consequently, since 1945 there have been few major changes in the sexual division of labour. A strengthened trade union was able to negotiate with the employers through the Joint Industrial Council after the war and succeeded in re-establishing a kind of apprenticeship system for knitters linked to the 'heavier' machines. Shortage of female labour after the war and the shift system also discouraged employers from trying to use women as knitters except on smaller, more specialized machines. Only a few women have worked as knitters since the war, some remaining in the jobs they took over during wartime. The other jobs (overlocking, linking, machining and making up) have retained their strongly female image. Women workers I interviewed had come across a few cases of men, mainly of Asian origin, working as machinists; but, said one of my informants, 'It's seen as women's work. The young men who started it were inclined to be discouraged.'

A study carried out by a Board of Trade working party in 1946 provides a good account of the division of labour which was consolidated in the post-war period and has basically persisted since. It also presents a somewhat more 'objective' picture of skills than the documents previously discussed. For example, at a number of points it suggests that skills are not fairly rewarded. 'The amount of skill in the various jobs does not seem to be fairly reflected in the relative earning capacity of the job'.[46] There is no further explanation, but it could be a hint of the discrepancy between the rewards for men's and women's skills. For example, the report suggested that linking (generally acknowledged to be the hardest women's job, involving hooking tiny nylon stitches to points on a machine in order to close the toe of the stocking) required eighteen months before an operative could attain a reasonable output. Linking was relatively well-paid, but few girls would gain as much as knitters, where training ranged from six months to a year. Women were found operating some knitting machines (for socks, for example), but would earn less because, although their output was as high per machine, men oversaw more machines, thus marking out their superordinate position.

The report states that some machines, such as hand-operated flat bar machines in outerwear, had been designated women's machines, although 'there are few technical reasons why only women should operate these machines'.[47] Reading the report suggests that the gendering of machines was now largely a matter of tradition and convention although the idea of sex-specific skills lay behind the tradition. Thus, the use of women in making up is ascribed to 'the fineness of so much of the work and the need for nimble fingers'[48] and the fingering of gloves is described as 'a process needing close attention, good eyesight and nimble fingers ... girls of not more than 16 years of age are regarded as the best type of trainees. ... The speed of production is gained by the dexterity of the worker'.[49] It seemed that men either could not or would not master jobs such as glove fingering. Attempts to train them for this job had failed and moreover 'it has been found extremely difficult to replace women by men in those operations which are traditionally female'.[50] Once jobs have become sex-typed as female they are much more impermeable than are male jobs.[51]

Women's Views

All that I have said so far reflects the views of men. Men were primary definers, laying down rules and norms for the industry; it was men who staged among themselves the longstanding debate over skill. However, it may not necessarily be the case that women accept men's views of the world. Although they often lack a voice in the formal sphere in which men make decisions and set standards, women have their own thriving informal culture where their own ideas and meanings may find expression. Unfortunately for the historian, it is hard to uncover a culture which is largely without written documentation. In this final section I draw on a limited amount of material which puts the women's point of view. My main resource is the tapes issued by the Leicester Oral History Archive along with a small amount of interview and questionnaire material.[52] I interviewed two highly experienced female hosiery workers and nine others filled in a small questionnaire for me. What can we learn from these about how women viewed their own achievements?

Back in 1861, Ruth Wills, an employee of Corahs in Leicester, had described 'women's work' as 'dreary and monotonous'.[53] Such a remark suggests that women had fairly low expectations and accepted an industrial ordering that placed them as secondary. While it is clear that many women hosiery workers valued their work and gained enjoyment and satisfaction from many aspects of it,[54] Leicester Oral History Archive materials suggest ambivalence as to how women saw their jobs in terms of skill. Without doubt jobs were hard to learn as one woman from Soar Valley made clear: 'I didn't get on very well, it were on the old machines making army socks, and I didn't get on very well with that, they put me down on the winding and I've always been a winder ever since'.[55] Lily Holmes experienced the common pattern of working up the job hierarchy through 'sitting by Nellie' when she started at Drivers aged 13:

> He says come and sit with me, so I sat at the side of his counter, counting hose.... Then eventually they put me on a machine ... plain hose machines, just one.... And then I went with another woman, she'd got six machines and they put me with her to learn, you see.... Eventually I got machines of my own ... and I worked six machines in the Imperial Room.... Then the woman left her set of machines. There were eight on that set and they were a little bit different, but anyway I learned and that's where I ended up.[56]

Similarly, a Leicester woman described her progress through a number of machines starting at Wolsey aged 14 in 1928 cutting splicings from hose (seen as an unskilled job); at 15 she was promoted to a semi-automatic half-hose (sock) machine; she moved to Byfords where she worked on a more complicated machine, requiring putting two stitches on to a single point, 'which is very hard but you get used to it and it becomes quick and easy to you'. She graduated to fancy half-hose and then during the war worked on automatic sock machines where she took on a man's load (ten machines instead of eight): 'there was no men so we had to work more you see'.[57]

These two women were doing what a man would have called 'learning the trade' and indeed a third woman did describe it in that way: 'I went right through the trade, overlocking, cover seaming, the forelady there learned me the trade'.[58] But this process is described by these women in a matter-of-fact way albeit with some pride ('I could earn my money, I happened to be quick on a machine'[59]). No explicit mention is made of skill or craft. This contrasts with accounts of male workers such as two boot and shoe workers from the Soar Valley, Stanley Trasler and Reuben Widdowson, for whom the idea of skill is crucial:

> It was all hand-clicking in them days. You went round patterns with a knife, you see, and a blade. . . . Then they introduced pressers and a blind man could be a clicker today, there's no skill in it at all. . . . When we were clicking, when it were clicking . . . it took you years didn't it to master your job, but now as they do it you could learn it in a week, no skill at all.[60]

Comparing these accounts suggests that men employed a rhetoric of skill, using it as a yardstick to measure their jobs. By contrast women, though knowledge-able about the machines and processes they operated, taking a pride in their achievements and pleased at mastering a technique, have not in the past developed a discourse of skill with which to counter the marginalization and devaluing of their contributions within the male discourse. Indeed, the very fact of job segregation makes it hard for women to compare their achievements with men. When I asked hosiery worker Norah Gamble if she thought that skills in the industry were fairly rewarded she took me to be asking about the different female jobs when she replied 'the wages don't match up to the amount of skill required'. Jobs like welting (a kind of hemming) were according to her based on speed rather than skill: 'You could earn your money but you had to be like lightning'.

Whereas many accounts of female-specific skills confound speed and skill, Norah, herself in fact a highly skilled operative, implies that skill is something much more technical when describing her own career. Starting at 14 in the inter-war period, she trained as a flatlocker (a type of seaming which she considers more expert than overlocking, as it involves nine strands of cotton to make a stitch rather than three). But she has worked at many other jobs including bar-tacking, seam-covering, cutting, pressing and overlocking. Her skill was acknowledged by her employers who wished to send her to train a new workforce in Portugal (she refused the offer because it would have meant abandoning her work for the trade union). She believes that sitting by Nellie was more effective than going to a training school because of the expertise gained by experienced women: 'With her wealth of experience she would show you an easy way, a quick way'. Although she has spent some thirty-six years working in hosiery factories, she says she is still learning things about flatlocking (she is now working for a company that produces special quality garments for visits to Mecca). Her account makes it clear that technical knowledge is involved. Part of the flatlocker's job was to strip the machine down and clean it every week, and to fit new needles and knives as required: 'You need to know . . . it becomes part of you, the machine'.

Although women may lack a rhetoric of skill, they appreciate their own worth, as Norah does. The nine women who filled in my questionnaire were in their fifties and sixties, and most were flatlockers like Norah. The training they had experienced ranged from none at all to three months. I asked if they considered themselves highly skilled and eight out of the nine replied yes. One described her work as 'one of the highest skilled but normally one of the lowest paid'. Another commented that the job was 'not given the recognition it should'. These responses suggest that women do feel a sense of grievance about the undervaluation of their skills, but such views tend not to surface in the formal spheres of debate which this discussion has reviewed.

Sian Reynolds' study of female compositors in Edinburgh suggests that, although the compositors were in fact highly expert and skilled, they more or less accepted the view that their work was of lower value than that of their male colleagues. They opposed the idea of equal pay which they feared would merely result in loss of jobs for them.[61] Economic pressures can be seen, in this account, to be entangled with acceptance of the existing hierarchy of status and the social privilege accorded the male breadwinner. Something similar may have operated in hosiery. Most women accepted without challenge the idea that they would earn less than men because they had developed no way to contest the lower evaluation of their jobs and of women's worth generally which was offered by men. It is interesting to see whether in the late twentieth century the combined influence of feminist ideas and equal opportunities legislation may lead female hosiery workers to re-evaluate their jobs and affirm their skills more positively. Pat is a woman who has been involved in many activities to do with equal opportunities. She is blunt in her assertion about the relative contributions of men and women: 'Women's skills are far greater'. She believes the attribution of skill to male knitters is based above all on the idea of men as breadwinners, with employers accepting this view. Since the men were a small core employers were prepared to 'appease' them by offering them high pay, which also, she argues, reflects the higher level of investment in the expensive knitting machines. Nonetheless, she sees the knitters in the contemporary context as essentially machine-minders.

Other women have not arrived at such a critical stance. One factor preventing them airing grievances against unequal treatment, especially in the union context, may be feelings of loyalty towards their menfolk and their class. Historically, this extends back to the days when many female hosiery workers were married to knitters. Today, many female union activists reject feminist policies such as positive action, seeing them as divisive and arguing that women are responsible for their own inferior position because of their failure to speak out or become involved in the union. However some women are, in a modest

13 Braverman, H. (1974) *Labor and Monopoly Capital*, New York.
14 Thomas Nelson, Nottingham hosier, in 1812 Report on Framework Knitters' Petition, p. 88.
15 *Ibid.*, p. 69.
16 Clark, A. (1982) *Working Lives of Women in the Seventeenth Century*, London; Snell, K. (1985) *Annals of the Labouring Poor*, Cambridge.
17 Parliamentary Papers, 1845, v, Royal Commission on the Condition of the Framework Knitters, Vol. 1, minute 2831.
18 *Ibid.*, p. 284.
19 *Ibid.*, minute 2831.
20 *Ibid.*, minutes 3447–8.
21 *Ibid.*, minute 2546.
22 *Ibid.*, minute 4514.
23 *Ibid.*, Vol. II, minute 568.
24 *Ibid.*, Vol. I, minute 3866.
25 *Ibid.*, minutes 186–8.
26 *Ibid.*, Vol. II, p. 709.
27 Parliamentary Papers, 1854–5, xiv, Report of the Select Committeee on the Stoppage of Wages (Hosiery), minute 1883.
28 Royal Commission, 1845 (see note 17), Vol. II, p. 123.
29 *A History of the County of Leicester* (The Victoria History of the Counties of England), Vol. III, (Eds) W.G. Hoskins and R.A. McKinley (1955), p. 15.
30 Report of the Select Committee, 1854–5 (see note 27), minute 2245.
31 See Thompson, E.P. (1967) 'Time, Work-Discipline and Industrial Capitalism', *Past and Present* 38, pp. 56–97; and, for the hosiery case, Bradley (1987) (see note 1).
32 Gent, J. (1893) *Robert Finch: A Tale of the Old Leicester Stocking Weavers*, London, p. 5.
33 Parliamentary Papers, 1863, xviii, Factory Inspectors' Reports, p. 269.
34 Report of the Select Committee, 1854–5 (see note 27), minute 2723.
35 Parliamentary Papers, 1892, xxxvi, Pt 2, Royal Commission on Labour, p. 90.
36 *Ibid.*, p. 48.
37 Leicester Corporation Handbook, undated (1920s).
38 Leicester Corporation Handbook, undated (1940s).
39 King, P. (1948) 'Task Perception and Inter-personal Relations in Industrial Training', Pt 1 *Human Relations* Vol. 1, pp. 121–30, 373–412, at p. 379.
40 Johnson and Barnes, hosiery company, publicity material (1951), Leicester Records Office.
41 Royal Commission on Labour, 1892 (see note 35), p. 95.
42 Parliamentary Papers, 1919, xxxi, Report of the War Cabinet on Women in Industry, pp. 90–1.
43 *Ibid.*, p. 90.
44 Parliamentary Papers, 1929–30, xvii, Report on Distribution of Women in Industry, p. 20.
45 Report of the War Cabinet on Women in Industry (see note 42), p. 90.
46 Board of Trade (1946) *Working Reports: Hosiery*, London, p. 17.
47 *Ibid.*, p. 33.
48 *Ibid.*, p. 95.
49 *Ibid.*, p. 50.
50 *Ibid.*

51 See Bradley, H. (1989) *Men's Work, Women's Work*, Cambridge.
52 As I moved away from the Leicester area I was not able to supplement my documentary research with a developed piece of oral history. I did manage to interview two women trade unionists. Norah Gamble of Leicester Outwork Campaign is in her seventies and has a long history of activism in the hosiery workers' union. She also arranged for nine older hosiery workers to fill in a questionnaire for me. Her help and kindness is gratefully acknowledged. For various reasons the other woman I interviewed is simply referred to as Pat.
53 Wills, R. (1861) *Lays of Lowly Life*, London.
54 See Bradley, H. (1990) 'Women in the Factories of Leicester', unpublished paper.
55 This and the following references from the LOHA come from cassette C47, *Soar Valley Working*, compiled by Alice Bilton; cassette C28, *Employment*, compiled by Tim Cobbett, and cassette C29, *Women in Industry*, compiled by M. Carter and T. Simpson.
56 Cassette C47, *Soar Valley Working*.
57 Cassette C28, *Employment*.
58 Cassette C29, *Women in Industry*.
59 Cassette C28, *Employment*.
60 Cassette C47, *Soar Valley Working*.
61 Reynolds, S. (1989) *Britannica's Typesetters*, Edinburgh.
62 National Union of Hosiery and Knitwear Workers (NUHKW) Annual Report 1983.
63 NUHKW Annual Conference Report 1984.

Chapter 3

The Creation of a Gendered Division of Labour in the Danish Textile Industry

Marianne Rostgård

Introduction

Some years ago, I visited a boot and shoe factory. We were guided by one of the foremen – trained as a skilled shoemaker like his father before him. We were there to study ways to widen and expand non-skilled women's field of work, and we looked among other things at the gendered division of labour. At one point I asked the foreman why only women did the stitching (the process where the upper leather is sewn together). He answered, looking a bit bewildered, that stitching had always been done by women, and that was simply the reason why stitching was done by women (and why was I asking such a silly question?). It is true that stitching has been the work of women for a long time. But it has not always been women's work. It became women's work at the end of the nineteenth century, and this tradition has continued ever since. Stitching is an example of a job which at the end of the nineteenth century became labelled as a women's job, and this was what it was for the next century. The question is how and why this happened? Women's work was labelled unskilled at a certain time, too. Skilled and unskilled labour are constructions[1] just as are men's work and women's work. This is the reason why the term 'unskilled' in this chapter is replaced by the term 'non-skilled', to denote that we are talking about work which was not looked upon as skilled, not work which did not require any skills, as the term 'unskilled' suggests.

This chapter presents some of the main conclusions from my thesis.[2] I chose for several reasons to focus on the textile industry, with supplementary studies of the boot and shoe industry. Research based on original sources was limited to the city of Odense. There is, however, reason to believe that many features characterizing the construction of a gendered division of labour in the textile industry are general industrial features, since the main characteristics of the gendering process can be found in the boot and shoe industry as well.

Danish research on the subject has primarily been based on the method of presenting problems in economic history, focusing on industrial growth, the size and composition of the workforce, and so on. The traditional explanation which is given in Danish textbooks on economic history and labour history regarding the number and distribution of women workers in industry is that women became industrial workers as a result of the mechanization process. As machines took over, traditional trade skills became superfluous and non-skilled workers replaced skilled workers. Women workers were preferred by the factory owners simply because women's labour was cheaper than men's.[3] This explanation may account for part of the female labour force in the factories. But it does not explain the gendered division of labour. Indeed, the traditional explanation might lead one to think that factory workers in the textile industry were all female. In fact they were not. If we look at the textile industry, the number of women has of course varied through time, but women have never comprised more than about 60 per cent of the total workforce.

My argument can be outlined as follows. Before industrialization most textiles were made in people's homes in the countryside, either producing for the household itself or producing for sale. The first cloth mills started to operate around the year 1800 in the Copenhagen area, mostly producing for the army and navy. Production of cotton fabrics started out as cottage industry in the 1830s and 1840s, to be replaced by factories in the 1850s and 1860s, which was rather late compared to other European countries. The gendered division of labour varied for a long time from factory to factory and from region to region. A uniformly gendered division of labour was not established until around 1910 as a result of unionization and collective bargaining agreements. In other words, there was no direct connection between mechanization and the gendered division of labour.

In the next section I present a short outline of the industrialization process, focusing on its development in and around Odense, and discuss the composition of the workforce in relation to mechanization. Following this, in the main part of the chapter, I discuss the establishment and institutionalization of a gendered division of labour around the turn of the century. In the final section I describe how the once established division of labour lived on to become an unquestioned tradition.

The Mechanization of the Textile Industry and the Number of Women Workers

As already mentioned, the data collected only represent Odense. Odense, located on the Island of Funen, was in the nineteenth century the second biggest town in Denmark, and a busy industrial town with a substantial textile industry. Before industrialization, the flat lands called Sletten, north and north-west of Odense, had been renowned for their cottage industry. The textiles produced in this area were primarily the work of women – spinning as well as weaving. The men were mostly farming the land, occasionally helping their wives with the weaving in the busy season before the annual markets in July. Because of the substantial cottage industry, Odense seemed to be a good choice, as one of my aims was to study changes in women's work during the process of industrialization. The cottage industry on Funen existed alongside the factories until around 1880. Production for sale seems to have reached a peak in approximately the period 1840–1860, after which it started to decline. It disappeared mainly because the women in the countryside found a new and better way of earning money, namely making butter. This development was part of a new division of labour between the country and the city, which also meant that the new, more affluent peasantry became customers of industrial products.

The cottage industry on Sletten was based on the weaving of linsey-wolsey, a product in which the warp consists of linen, the weft of wool. The textiles woven on Sletten were normally sold at markets in Odense, to townspeople and to merchants for resale. As in every other town around 1830, a number of weavers' workshops and dye works existed as well as the cottage industry. From the 1830s there are examples of workshops which outgrew the normal size of a handicraft-based workshop, marking the beginning of the period of industrialization. These workshops were, however, still based on hand weaving. The spinning was done by hand too, in the towns usually by poor women (widows or unmarried women who had to provide for themselves), or the yarn was imported from England. The first textile factory in Odense began its production in 1841, making woollen cloth. The next factory, a cotton mill, was founded in 1856, mirroring a nationwide development. The first textile mills to be established in Denmark were generally woollen mills, to be followed by a wave of cotton mills in the 1850s and 1860s.

The first census of industrial production was carried out in Denmark in 1855, followed by a second census in 1872. The next public census was delayed until 1897, but we do have material from the local factory inspection that can fill in the gaps between 1872 and 1897. Figure 3.1 shows the number of men and women working in the textile industry in Odense in 1855, 1872, 1890, 1910, 1920 and 1930, as well as the amount of horsepower installed in the form of steam engines. I have also tried to count the number of machines.[4] Until around 1890, it is fair to say that one machine more meant that yet another working process had been mechanized. After around 1890, this correlation becomes less certain, as the new textile machines might replace more working processes or more workers. Replacement of old machines with new ones makes it even more uncertain simply to count the number of machines as a measure of an ongoing mechanization process.

If we take a look at the number of women workers, three periods are discernible. In the period from 1855 to 1872 the number of women workers increased. Between 1872 and 1910 the number of female workers decreased relative to the number of men. After 1910 the rates are reversed again – the number of women employed continued to increase slowly, while the number of men employed decreased after 1910. If we return to the traditional explanation mentioned above, the main point is that the relative number of women decreased in the years from 1870 to 1910 when the textile industry was mechanized. There

number of women,
men, machines and
horsepower

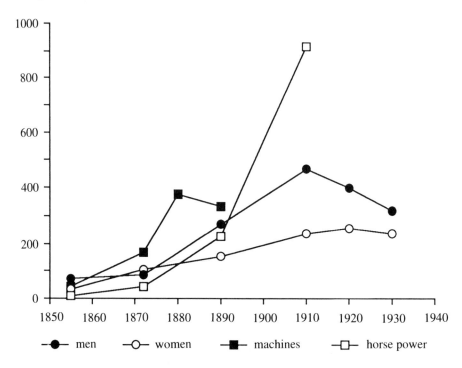

Figure 3.1 *The number of men and women employed in the textile industry in Odense, seen in relation to the degree of mechanization, 1855–1930*

Total number of mills: 3 in 1855, 6 in 1872, 7 in 1890, 8 in 1910.

Sources: Industritællingen 1855, Til oplysning om arbejdernes økonomiske Kaar (Indenrigsministeriet) 1872, Fabriksinspektionsprotokoller 1890 og 1910, Oversigt over det samlede antal beskæftigede i Tekstilindustrien 1918–25, Tekstilfabrikantforeningens arkiv og Brandtaksationsprotokoller, Odense by, 1837–1889.

is a steep increase in the number of machines in the 1870s, which is reflected in the simultaneous rise in the amount of horsepower used. The alteration of the type of mechanization after about 1890 is reflected in a decrease in the number of machines coinciding with a substantial rise in the amount of horsepower.

We can conclude that the mechanization process in the textile industry took place during the rather long period from about 1870 to 1910. And this is exactly the period during which the number of men employed increased. To push it to extremes, one can say that mechanization in the textile industry meant that men got employed instead of women! This explanation is at least as true as the traditional explanation that women were employed in the textile industry due to mechanization of the production process.

But let us leave this discussion aside, and instead take a look at some of the factories one by one. Originally I expected to find a gendered division of labour which might have changed through time – men doing this, and women doing that, in every mill at a certain time. But when I started to look at the factories separately, I found that this was not the case. The picture arising instead showed that the division of labour varied from factory to factory, at least until around 1900. This really puzzled me and annoyed me for some time because the data did not seem to make sense. The reason I looked for a certain pattern in the division of labour was that this was how the literature on the subject described gendered division of labour, and therefore this was what I expected to find in the Danish textile industry.[5]

Woollen Mills and Cotton Mills

There were three woollen mills in Odense both in 1872 and in 1890, although not the same three mills. Beside these mills there were some small spinning mills and dye works, working for peasants, spinning their wool or dyeing home-woven cloth.

One of the mills still running in 1872 was the old mill founded by P.L. Brandt in 1841, though the production was declining. This mill closed down in the second half of the 1880s. P.L. Brandt's brother M.K. Brandt expanded his dye works into becoming a woollen mill in 1869. After the turn of the century, this company, Brandt's Klædefabrik, became the biggest woollen mill in Odense and one of the biggest and best known textile factories in Denmark. Another dyer, Claus Dorch, had started a woollen mill connected to his dye works in the 1850s. This company remained small during its years in business (it burned down in 1878). The second biggest cloth mill in Odense was Munke Mølle Klædefabrik, founded in 1873 by a former merchant, who also owned one of the biggest cotton mills. The last woollen mill, Søndergades Dampvæveri, started out as a spinning mill in 1886 and was turned into a woollen mill in 1889. Comparing the factories one can immediately observe that the relative number of women employed differed from one factory to another in 1872 and 1890, and even more so in 1910 (see table 3.1).

The same pattern can be observed in the cotton industry, as can be seen from table 3.2. The percentage of women employed differs widely in 1890 with respectively 63 per cent (Bierfreund) and 44 per cent (Mogensen) of the adult workers employed being women, whereas the figures from 1910 – 33 per cent (Bierfreund), 36 per cent (Mogensen) and 39 per cent (Hvidevarefabrikken) of the employees being women – are very close to each other. Of the companies existing in 1872 one is a cotton mill (Bierfreund's Dampvæveri), while the two other companies listed were handloom shops; the figures are therefore not immediately comparable. Mogensen's Dampvæveri started operating in 1874 and Hvidevarefabrikken in 1901.

These figures, of course, say nothing about what the women actually did. I

Table 3.1: Number of men and women employed in cloth mills in Odense, 1872-1910

	1872			1890			1910		
	Men	Women	Children	Men	Women	Children	Men	Women	Children
P.L. Brandt	13	7	1	–	–	–	–	–	–
C. Dorch	4	3	0	–	–	–	–	–	–
M.K. Brandt	31	9	13	119	32	31	156	72	37
Munke Mølle	–	–	–	40	15	0	71	31	0
Søndergades	–	–	–	14	10	0	17	9	2

Sources: Industritællingen 1855, Til oplysning om arbejdernes økonomiske Kaar (Indenrigsministeriet) 1872, Fabriksinspektionsprotokoller 1890 og 1910, Oversigt over det samlede antal beskæftigede i Tekstilindustrien 1918–25, Tekstilfabrikantforeningens arkiv og Brandtaksationsprotokoller, Odense by, 1837–1889.

Table 3.2 Number of men and women employed in cotton mills in Odense, 1872-1910

	1872			1890			1910		
	Men	Women	Children	Men	Women	Children	Men	Women	Children
Dehnke	4	3	0	–	–	–	–	–	–
Brodtrüch	10	10	0	–	–	–	–	–	–
Bierfreund	22	71	8	21	36	8	73	36	0
Mogensen	–	–	–	70	55	2	87	50	0
Hvidevare-fabrikken	–	–	–	–	–	–	57	37	0

Sources: Industritællingen 1855, Til oplysning om arbejdernes økonomiske Kaar (Indenrigsministeriet) 1872, Fabriksinspektionsprotokoller 1890 og 1910, Oversigt over det samlede antal beskæftigede i Tekstilindustrien 1918–25, Tekstilfabrikantforeningens arkiv og Brandtaksationsprotokoller, Odense by, 1837–1889.

will return to this question later on. The point is that if we look at the number of women employed, a stabilization of the relative number of women employed in the period from 1890 to 1910 can be observed. In total, the proportion of women employed in the textile industry in Odense (woollen and cotton mills) amounted to 33 per cent in 1855, 55 per cent in 1872, 36 per cent in 1890, and 34 per cent in 1910. We can therefore conclude that it was during the period from 1890 to 1910 that the number of women employed settled at approximately one-third of the textile workers – a proportion which remained stable for many years thereafter.

Another part of the traditional explanation of women's position in industry was that men were replaced by women as the jobs required less skill after the mechanization of the textile industry. It is true, to a certain degree, that women had the most tedious jobs in the factories, but this is not the whole truth. Child labour was restricted for the first time in 1872, further restricted in 1901, and finally abolished in 1913. The jobs previously done by children (boys aged 10 to 14) were taken over by girls aged 14 to 17, girls being the cheapest labour available after 1913. This relates to the types of jobs such as helping hands for the spinners and winders.

If we look at the grown-up women however, such as the weavers, one cannot say that the work of the female weavers required more or less skills than the male weavers' jobs did. If we look at handloom weaving in 'the old days', when the whole process was done by one person, the weaving process would start with designing or otherwise planning the pattern. The yarn had to be wound, the warp had to be cut, the warp transferred to the loom (to mention the main process only), and then the weaver could start weaving. The actual weaving was first and foremost hard work. It took some strength to be able to knock the piece of cloth together on a handloom. The preparation, however, was what required skill and knowledge. Apart from having new machinery, the factories were characterized by an extreme division of labour, meaning that, for instance, the work done by the handicraft weavers was distributed to at least eight people, leaving the weaver by his or her loom as almost a mere machine attendant.

Unionization and the Creation of a Gendered Division of Labour

A weavers' union was founded in Odense in 1885 with fifty-three men and ten women enrolled as members. During the next decade this union was primarily occupied with organizing the weavers in the mills. In 1895, the union in Odense amalgamated with other weavers' unions in Denmark to form the Union of Textile Workers in Denmark. As the name says, it was decided in 1895 to organize all workers in textile mills in the union, not only the weavers. One of the aims of the new union, spelled out in the preamble, was equal pay for men and women. In 1895, 356 textile workers in Odense – about 50 per cent of the total number employed there – had become unionized. At this time the union had finally become strong enough to demand collective bargaining over wages.

The employers started to organize in 1895 as a reaction to the organization of the workers – the initiative was taken by two of the factory owners in Odense. The employers' association was from the outset a nationwide organization, but as was the case with the unions, it took some time before the majority of the employers were organized. These two organizations met for the first time in 1898 to try to make a general agreement about wages. The main claim from both parties – workers and employers – at every national round of collective bargaining from 1898 to 1911 was for 'more uniform wages'. One of the results of the heterogeneous composition of the workforce in the factories was corresponding differences in pay for the same kind of work. The unions, of course, by demanding 'more uniform wages' hoped to raise them to equally high ones, and the employers wanted to lower them to equally low wages. The main objective for the employers was to secure fair competition, as it was phrased, meaning that no employer should benefit from paying lower wages than the other mill owners. It is important to bear in mind that in addition to the general agreements, local unions or clubs were still allowed to bargain local agreements in the period after 1898, but from then on they had to be approved by the central organizations.

One of the reasons why the same tasks were paid differently in each mill was that tasks were done by men in some mills, and by women in other mills. The action for 'more uniform wages' therefore became the start of a long series of conflicts between men and women about who should perform which tasks and how much they should be paid to do them. Wages were in themselves an important issue, but not the only reason struggles between men and women took place in the decades around the turn of the century. At that time the woollen mills in particular still employed a number of craftsmen, who saw the women as a threat both to their employment and to their trade in general. One incident may illustrate the debate and the attitudes towards women workers in the textile industry. It took place at Munke Mølle Klædefabrik in 1898.

The Case of Munke Mølle

In 1898, point 3 on the agenda of a meeting held on 8 February by the union in Odense was 'The conditions at Munke Mølle'.[6] One of the members had complained about 'The bad conditions' (what this meant was not explained in the protocol), and blamed it in sweeping terms on the women workers. The discussion quickly became one about whether or not the union was to try to abolish female labour altogether in the textile factories. Some of the weavers, whose wives worked at the mill too, defended themselves by saying that it was the factory owner who had ordered them to bring their wives to work at the mill. Other men, among them the chairman of the local union, were of the opinion that women should be allowed to work at the factory, but they ought to organize like the men.

The issue of organizing seems to be one example of what was meant by women contributing to the depreciation of conditions at the mill. The question whether the women were to be organized or not turned out to be a discussion about whether the subscription was a family one or not. When the men paid, did they not also pay for their wives? Therefore the wives were members of the union, not unorganized, their husbands stated. Others defied this argument, and stated that only individual membership was obtainable. In the heated debate a woman who had offered to do a certain job for a smaller sum than the man doing it was mentioned – as another proof of how women brought about 'bad conditions' at the mill. The story was contradicted vehemently by her husband. The women said nothing; or, at least, nothing of what they said is recorded in the minutes from the meeting. The accusations raised against the women workers at this meeting are typical. In the 1890s, accusations of this type against women workers can be found in many articles from the journal published by the textile workers' union. The minutes from the meeting in Odense show that the issue of women workers was a very complicated one, and had to do with conflicting views of the situation among the male workers as well as conflicting interests.

The discussion that evening in February ended without any decision being reached. This resulted in the cloth mill workers forming their own organization. The woollen weavers were in general more opposed to female workers than the men in the cotton mills. As mentioned earlier, the first textile factories to be established in Denmark were mainly woollen mills. Apart from Munke Mølle, all the mills in Odense had been founded by craftsmen, and the weavers in the oldest woollen mills were craftsmen too. This meant that craft traditions still lived on in the woollen mills around the turn of the century, whereas cotton, not being a traditional product from the outset, had been worked on by women in the cottage industry, as well as by craftsmen in the cities.

As the local union seemed unable to agree on any action, the woollen mill workers in Odense in June 1898 decided to form their own organization and negotiate their own local agreement. In October 1898, a local agreement was settled which stated that women were only allowed to work 20 per cent of the looms in that particular mill.[7]

The incident gives a glimpse of insight into what was really at stake. One of the reasons why the traditionally apprenticed craft-weavers, especially, wanted to abolish female workers was the threat these non-skilled women formed against the pride the male workers took in their trade. The agreement reached at Munke Mølle in October 1898 amply shows that it was not a question of skills: the women could evidently work the looms as well as the men, and this was precisely the problem! Another incident related by a weaver who had been taught his trade by an old handloom weaver may illustrate this point about the pride the craftsmen took in their trade:

> When I told my master that I would start working at Bloch & Andresen [a cotton mill], he got very angry. I had been working for him nine years and a half, and he had never scolded me before, but now I really got a dressing-down. I cannot remember exactly what he said in his anger, but I can still hear him shouting: 'Do you really think I taught you this trade only to let you get employed afterwards at such a female mill?'[8]

Women's work in factories was never abolished. It could be limited, as the case of Munke Mølle shows, by agreements on how many looms were to be operated by women, but this was not the typical way of limiting female labour in the mills. The typical curtailment of women's work in the textile factories came to be the gendered division of labour.

More Uniform Wages

The difference between men's and women's wages existed from the outset of industrialization – the difference can even be traced back to pre-industrial times – and the fairness of this difference was never really questioned until 1917/18. It is also true that women might work the looms as well as men in the factories, and the women therefore presented a threat to the male workers, as they could do the same job for lower pay. A gendered division of labour came to be the solution to this problem.

Most struggles during the years from 1890 to 1910 arose around the pay for all the different tasks in the mills. Struggles and debates took place under the heading 'more uniform wages', as previously mentioned. Many of these debates and struggles between workers and employers do not mention the words 'female labour' – but this issue was to some extent the hidden agenda. Sources in the archives from the Union of Textile Workers in Denmark are very detailed on these questions of pay, but do not very often relate anything about the setting where these discussions and conflicts took place. Hints in the material, however, suggest that the issues at stake were exactly the same as the ones already mentioned.

The main reason why the male workers never really fought for equal pay for women, although the struggle for equal pay was stressed as one of the aims of the union, was their picture of themselves as breadwinners. The weavers in the factories might not be independent craftsmen any longer, but they still, or instead, took a pride in being breadwinners. Around the turn of the century, it was almost unquestioned that men were breadwinners and women were not. This was never the whole truth, as there were widows and unmarried women who had to feed their children or aged parents. The argument that men were breadwinners was repeated over and over again when men argued that they ought to be better paid than women.

One example illustrates how the demand for more uniform wages contributed to the gendering process. The incident took place in 1895 at Mogensen's Dampvæveri. At a local meeting of the union it was decided to demand 7.50 kroner (crowns) per 100 alen (yards) for the weaving of moleskin (a certain type of cloth). In a letter to the general organization in Copenhagen, the reason for this demand is stated as follows: 'Pay is so low that even the female weavers cannot manage with this pay'. The employer, Chr. Mogensen (who was one of the two factory owners who took the initiative in 1895 to organize the employers), at first refused to negotiate the actual demand. The weavers then went on strike, and Chr. Mogensen countered by a lockout of all workers in the mill. A fortnight later an agreement was reached. Chr. Mogensen agreed to pay the same piece-rate as paid in other mills. There were at that time only two more employers, in Copenhagen, who made this type of cloth. The women working in these two factories were paid 5.50 kroner per 100 alen. This became the piece-rate in Odense too from then on.

According to the correspondence between the local union in Odense and the general union in Copenhagen, the Odense weavers felt really cheated. They had obviously heard rumours of a quite different piece-rate paid in the Copenhagen factories. That was why they had settled for the agreement! But the chairman in Copenhagen retorted that an agreement was an agreement. It was not his fault that the employers seemed to be better informed than the union in Odense; they could have asked before they signed the agreement instead of protesting afterwards.

In this case, the employers won the struggle, and 'more uniform wages' in this case meant female wages. This moleskin cloth was already made by women at Mogensen's mill in 1895. The result of the conflict confirmed that weaving this kind of cloth was women's work, whereas the union in Odense had hoped to alter the situation by demanding higher wages. The main point, though, is that this was the general mechanism at work in the period around 1895–1910. The payment in one factory became the standard pay, and in this way also established a certain gendered division of labour. If we look at statistics and these kind of aggregated data, weaving stayed a non-gender-segregated job. But if we go into detail, there is a gendered division of labour, related to the type of cloth and the type of loom.

Spinning was not done in Danish factories until 1892. Spinning by hand went on until about 1850, but from about 1840 more and more yarn was imported from England. Some entrepreneurs had tried to start spinning mills as early as the 1790s, but had failed. The spinning mill started in 1892 was located in Vejle (a town in Jutland), and the factory owner at first tried to engage men as spinners. This failed, and he then looked to Sweden and engaged some male Swedish spinners. They worked at the spinning mill for rather a short period and were then sent home again. 'The Swedish workers caused trouble as they found it difficult to get used to Danish customs and soon returned to Sweden.'[9] This is all the sources say, so we will never know what kind of trouble the Swedes caused. After having tried to engage Danish men, then Swedish, the owner of the spinning mill gave in and employed some women, and from now on had no more difficulties recruiting workers. The sources do not tell why the employer did not succeed in engaging Danish men for his spinning mill – a guess may be that the wages offered might have been too low.

When Chr. Mogensen started a spinning mill in Odense in 1898 the union in Odense tried to make an agreement fixing the wages at about 15 kr. a week (the normal wages paid to unskilled men in textile factories). The women finally employed in Vejle only got 10 to 12 kr. a week; this therefore became the wage in Odense too, and the workers at the spinning mill in Odense came to be women from the outset. The same was the case at all other spinning mills in Denmark. The first spinning mill in Vejle, by eventually employing women, had set the standard for wages in the spinning mills, and thereby also gendered the job of a spinner in a cotton spinning mill.

'Fair Pay for a Woman'

It appears from union correspondence and other sources that there was an upper limit to a woman's pay. The following case once more comes from Munke Mølle. The issue is the pay for burling. After weaving, the 'raw' cloth is checked and broken threads mended by a burler, before it is fulled and washed to shrink the cloth. Burling was a job normally done by women. I have only come across one example of a male burler. At this time, 1902, the piece-rate for burling was still not written down in any agreement. Four burlers at Munke Mølle had been paid 19.65 kroner for one week's work (nothing was written down in an agreement, but a customary piece-rate existed). As this, according to the employer, 'was too much to pay a woman', he had simply deducted a sum from the wages they had earned according to the customary piece-rates, and now wanted to have piece-rates for burling written down in the agreement. The female burlers went on strike, but the union persuaded them to go back to work again, and started negotiations – the employer proposed a reduction in the pay for burling, and threatened to withdraw a promise of augmenting the pay of some male workers in the mill, if the union did not agree on reducing the pay of the female burlers.[10]

The final letters in this case have disappeared, and I am therefore not able to throw light on what the result of these negotiations was. The point is, however, the existence of what was called 'fair pay for a woman', which meant that women were not allowed to earn as much as men (19.65 kr. was a good wage for one week's work, and there were men who were paid less!).

One more piece of evidence can be offered, clearly stating that the pay of women workers was fixed according to gender, that is 'fair pay for a woman', not according to the actual job done. This case relates to a female weaver in one of the cotton mills in 1899. The mill owner wrote to the chairman of the union in Copenhagen:

> We hereby state that at some of our oldest and most inferior looms, numbers 25 and 26, a woman has in the week starting the 30th of September delivered six pieces of cloth = 17.10 kroner. In the last proposal to an agreement on piece-rates for textile workers, the union demands a weekly pay of 15 kroner for women who operate machines, and for women doing other kinds of casual jobs 12 kroner a week. We must therefore consider the wages in question fair pay, for a female weaver, as long as a weaver who attends to her work can earn the above mentioned sum.[11]

What happened in the years around 1890–1910 was that the gendered division of labour became more uniform. This was first and foremost a result of collective agreements being made, which fixed the wages to be paid at two different levels, one for men, one for women, thereby gendering the jobs. Differences between factories and regions disappeared as a result of the negotiated agreements. At the end of the period women did certain jobs at a certain rate, and the discussions and struggles about who was going to do the job at which level of pay almost disappeared, along with discussions about female labour in the factories.

The breadwinner ideology was the main reason why women were paid less than men. The limitation of women's work to certain fields was the reason women could be paid less than men, without threatening to replace men in the mills. In this period when the gendered division of labour was established and institutionalized through the system of collective agreements, it is important to notice that it was never argued that women could not do certain jobs, nor that they were less skilled than men and therefore did not qualify themselves for equal pay.

To form a full picture of the reason for the differences in pay, however, social factors have to be taken into account as well. Men were not always the breadwinners, but the women were always the ones who took care of the children and the home, even if they worked at a factory. The following incident sheds light on relations in a Copenhagen factory, Rubens, which had a reputation for paying the female weavers badly:

> I was curious to see for myself if the conditions were as bad as the saying went, and I got the job. It was like heaven. Wide rooms with a glass ceiling, light and warm, especially compared to the dark mill where I had been buried for the last eight years. There was nothing wrong with the pay either. The truth is that the factory had an oven, where we could store our bottles with coffee, to keep them warm. But most workers were women with children and married women, and they cooked peas and cabbages and everything in this oven, and they had to look after it, too. And when they came to look after their cooking, they took time for a little chat as well. This, of course, reduced the amount of work done and the pay, as we worked for piece-rates. We also had a system with fines. If we came in too late in the morning or after the break for dinner, the pay was reduced. Many of the women lived in the neighbourhood, and they went home in the morning break and at noon, looking after their children and sending them off to school. Sometimes they came in too late three times a day.[12]

The women's family responsibilities may contribute to an explanation of why women were sometimes paid less than men, as related by this former female weaver.

Women's Work in the Factories

In an account of the total number of employees in the Danish textile industry and their pay from 1907,[13] there are forty-eight entries regarding men and forty-one regarding women. Each entry refers to a certain group of workers with their own designation. Some of the entries, such as 'weaver', are to be found both in the list of women's jobs and in that of men's jobs, others only in one of the lists. Details about who did which jobs would take up too much space and require a thorough explanation of the complicated process of making cloth. It will suffice here to give a short overview.

The group of workers can be divided into three main categories. The ones with the best wages were the foremen and the group of men doing repair and maintenance on machines. The most poorly paid were the young women or old women working as helping hands for other groups of workers and the winders. In between we find a group of semi-skilled workers, such as weavers, spinners, warpers etc., consisting of both men and women.

If we look at the account from 1907, one of the cotton factories in Odense, Mogensen & Dessau, had 160 male weavers and 32 female weavers. The women earned from 20.6 øre to 38.9 øre an hour. The men earned from 24.6 to 50.4 øre an hour. It is characteristic that the pay differences in the group of weavers are in general very wide, and the differences could be as wide between two women as between a woman and a man.

There was a tendency, however, in the 1910s and 1920s for male weavers as a group to become better paid than the similar group of women. It had nothing to do with skills, however, but once again was a result of men seeing themselves, and being seen, as breadwinners.

After 1908 automatic looms were introduced in Denmark, and the first factory to introduce them was Mogensen & Dessau in Odense. These looms differed from mechanical looms in one way only. Their construction allowed an automatic shift of the bobbins in the shuttle, which meant that the weavers no longer had to stop the machine, manually change the bobbin and tie the two ends together with a knot before starting the machine again. The weavers could therefore supervise more looms – in the beginning eight looms, later on twelve and more. This was basically a matter of bargaining the numbers, not of technical possibilities. The price paid per hundred yards of cloth was still the basic unit when prices, and thus the weavers' wages, were bargained for. This price was reduced when the weaver supervised more looms. But the weavers supervising eight or twelve looms still got better pay than weavers supervising three to four looms, which was the custom with mechanical looms. Working at automatic looms seems to have become an exclusively male field.

What was at stake was once more the pay – automatic looms in reality once more deskilled the work of the weavers. What was left for the weavers to do was to inspect the process and stop the loom if a thread broke. In the 1940s and 1950s this problem was solved by adding an automatic stop to the loom, which was released if a thread broke, and then the weavers could supervise even more looms.

Another interesting detail which can illuminate the gendered division of labour is the two categories of tacklers and twisters. The jobs of tacklers and twisters are very similar. When the weaving of a piece of cloth is finished, the loom has to be threaded with a new warp. One must make sure that every thread is in its place – otherwise the whole piece of cloth will be spoiled. Twisters would be allowed to place the new warp in the loom when the same type of cloth was to be woven, tacklers when a new type of cloth with a different pattern was to be woven. I know of no female tacklers, but there were many female twisters. When I once asked an old textile worker about the difference he explained: 'Twisters are women doing the work of tacklers'. There is a slight difference between the two jobs, but it is basically the same job. Constructing differences was yet another strategy to uphold a gendered division of labour. Female twisters perhaps did almost the same job as the male tacklers, but twisters were of course not paid the same as tacklers.

These examples show that women were not in general paid lower wages because they did the most tedious and unskilled jobs. It is true that helping hands in general were low-paid women (after the abolishment of child labour), but even old men can be found in this group. This fact shows that the characteristic feature of this group was just as much 'the ones who could not be used in other jobs' either because they were young and inexperienced or old.

It is true that we find men only at the other end of the scale, among the skilled specialists and foremen. But the biggest group of women working at the textile factories were the semi-skilled weavers, spinners etc. who really did the same tasks and in general were just as qualified or unqualified as their male colleagues – they were just paid less. This was the real problem, and the main reason the men in the textile factories had a good reason to feel threatened. The gendered division of labour in the textile mills was needed first and foremost to secure and justify the differences in pay.

Epilogue

After the conflicts at the turn of the century came some peaceful years. The only time unequal pay was questioned was in 1918/19, when the female textile workers, along with other groups of female workers, raised the question of unequal pay. The women in Denmark won the right to vote in 1917, and influenced by this, and the radicalization of the labour movement in general in 1917/18, the female textile workers for the first time themselves raised the question of equal pay. One result of this movement was that it became illegal to include in writing in agreements that women doing the same jobs as men were paid less, as had been done in the local agreements at Munke Mølle from 1898.

In 1918/19, the men once more argued that men as breadwinners ought to have better pay. Some also argued once more that female labour ought to be abolished, especially that of married women, who ought to stay at home and take care of their husbands and children. An even stronger emphasis was put on the family wage and less on women as scabs.

After the outburst in 1918/19, next to nothing is heard about conflicts between men and women in the textile factories. There are still some incidents resulting from the employers' attempts to make women do work previously done by men. One of the differences from the years before 1911 is that conflicts are now handled as a breach of existing agreements, which turns the incidents into a question about what is legal, not reasons and justifications. The unions in these years seem to have been keen watchers of the established gendered division of labour. At Mogensen & Dessau's factories 44 per cent of the workforce consisted of women in 1920; in 1925 the proportion of women had decreased to 38 per cent, to be raised slightly once more to 41 per cent in 1930. At Brandt's Klædefabrik women comprised 36 per cent of the workforce in 1920; this proportion rose to 41 per cent in 1925, to decrease slightly again to 39 per cent in 1930. I take this as a sign of a very stable gendered division of labour.

In the official union history the story related about the years from 1880 to 1920 can be summed up briefly as follows: 'In the old days we all got lousy pay. But then we organized, and we are now moving towards a better future and better pay, for female workers as well as men.' The conflicts between men and women are rendered as a story of underpaid women who were hard to organize. What is forgotten in this tale is the history I have tried to reconstruct: men in general, whether employers or workers, in reality did not see women as equals and mates. One can say that the employers made use of the existing difference between men and women to try to lower the pay of men by threatening to employ women instead or, as it was said in anniversary speeches and in the official union histories, that the employers sweated the women workers until the unions (the men) came and saved them. In the first case, stressing the basic inequality which had strong cultural and social roots, the gendered division of labour is seen as a way to maintain unequal pay. In the second case, the issue is reduced to women being badly organized and therefore poorly paid. The story which lived on, of course, was the story about the poorly paid and badly organized women, which in the end became the explanation of the inequality. In reality it was the other way round, as I have shown.

The next time the question about female labour arose was in the late 1950s and the early 1960s. Once again unequal pay was tracked down as a problem relating to features characterizing the female workers, not the gendered division of labour and the general societal and cultural inequality. The message had changed, though. If women wanted equal pay, they now had to educate themselves and overcome 'the female handicaps' (more days lost through sickness, for instance). A typical article in *Stof og Saks* (the trade journal) states that women are paid less than men because they do less qualified work. Women are not trained or educated to the same degree as men, which among other things is attributed to a general lack of interest in technical matters among women. In short: women are less qualified workers and therefore of course paid less.[14] The interesting point is that this is the first time lack of skills (especially technical skills) has been introduced as a theme in the debate about unequal pay.

Conclusion

We have come full circle. The reason why women were paid less than men had been forgotten and new explanations of the inequality were offered. But the original reason why women became secondary workers was not the skills. The lower pay did not, therefore, reflect skills. The real reason why women were paid less was the construction of a gendered division of labour which served as an effective borderline, allowing unequal wages to be paid without threatening the male worker's domain. This gendered division of labour grew into a tradition throughout the years, until no one remembered how it came into existence.

Notes

1   Philips, A and Taylor, B, (1980) 'Sex and Skill: Notes towards a Feminist Economics', *Feminist Review* 6.
2   Rostgård, M. (1991) *Teknologiudvikling og kønsarbejdsdeling i tekstilindustrien i Danmark ca. 1830–1915. Hvordan kvinders arbejde blev til kvindearbejde* (Technological Change and the Sexual Division of Labour in the Danish Textile Industry *c.*1830–1915), PhD thesis, Institute of Development and Planning, Aalborg University (in Danish).
3   Johansen, H.C. *et al.* (1983) *Fabrik og bolig. Det industrielle miljø i Odense 1840–1940*, Odense Universitetsforlag, p. 97; Hyldtoft, O. (1984) *Københavns industrialisering 1840–1914*, Systime, pp. 193, 257.
4   Sources: Industritællingen 1855 (Industrial Census), Til oplysning om arbejdernes økonomiske Kaar (Indenrigsministeriet) 1872, Fabriksinspektionsprotokoller 1890 og 1910 (Factory inspectors' reports), Oversigt over det samlede antal beskæftigede i Tekstilindustrien 1918–25 (Overview of the number employed in the textile industry), Tekstilfabrikantforeningens arkiv og Brandtaksationsprotokoller, Odense by, 1837–1889.
5   Ulla Wikander also puts forward the hypothesis that the gendered division of labour in the factories should in no way be seen as a continuation of the pre-industrial division of labour between men and women. On the contrary, industrialization turned the traditional gender roles upside down, and it was some time before a new gendered divison of labour was established. See Wikander, U. (1988), *Kvinnors och mäns arbeten: Gustavsberg 1880–1980. Genusarbetsdelning och arbetets degradering vid en porslinsfabrik*, Lund, Arkiv. Apart from Ulla Wikander there has been a tendency to see the gendered divison of labour as either a continuation of traditions or a sudden change, not a process which went on for several decades. I was working my way through the archives when I first became aware of the work of Ulla Wikander.
6   Minutes from a meeting held on 8 February 1898. Mødeprotokol for Tekstilarbejdernes fagforening i Odense 1885–1900.
7   More examples of this type of local agreement exist from other regions. See Dansk Textilarbejderforbunds arkiv (Danish Textile Workers' Union Archive) pakke 253.
8   Nationalmuseets Industri, Håndværker- og Arbejdererindringer (NIHA), lb. nr. 1535. The incident is related by a former weaver to the Danish National Museum's collection of worker memoirs.
9   Christensen, L.B. (1951) *Aktieselskabet de danske bomuldsspinderier Vejle-København. 1901–1951*, Copenhagen.
10 Dansk Textilarbejderforbund, Korrespondancesager, Odense afd. I, 1893–1911, læg 36.
11 Dansk Textilarbejdreforbund, Korrespondancesager, Odense afd. I, 1893–1911, læg 5.
12 Nationalmuseets Industri- Håndværker og Arbejdererindringer (NIHA), lb. nr. 1507.
13 Oversigt over løn og fortjeneste for mandlige og kvindelige arbejdere på tekstilfabrikkerne i København og provinsen 1. juli 1906 – 1. april 1907. I.H. Rubens' Arkiv, Erhvervsarkivet.
14 *Stof og Saks*, 2.årg. nr. 2 februar 1951, artiklen: Kvinder. Løn. Arbejdsglæde.

Chapter 4

Foreign Technology and the Gender Division of Labour in a Dutch Cotton Spinning Mill

Gertjan de Groot

Since Marx, cotton spinning has been the classical example for studying the relationship between technology and skill. Extensive historical research on cotton spinning has, until very recently, concentrated on the Lancashire situation.[1] By comparing the workforce in British and Dutch cotton spinning, it is possible to evaluate some of the explanations that are often offered for gender segregation. This comparative perspective has the advantage that the application of the same kind of technology can be studied in a different social setting. As the Dutch cotton spinning mill started off employing British technology, the technology itself was identical in both countries. The role of technological change in the process of sex-typing of jobs can thus be demonstrated by comparing the influence of the same technology in two countries. I shall argue in this chapter that the gender division of labour was transferred from one country to another along with the technology.

The English Debate

When a group of Manchester mill owners commissioned Richard Roberts to design a self-acting mule, their principal objective was to break the power of the militant spinners' union. The self-acting mule was to be tended by cheap female or juvenile labour.[2] Contrary to the employers' expectations, however, adult males managed fully to retain their position as spinners in England. Various authors have different explanations for the fact that the employers' expectations were never realized.

Four views can be distinguished on this problem. The first stresses the continuing importance of greater physical strength needed to operate a self-actor. Otherwise unskilled female labour would have replaced skilled male labour at the self-actor.[3] Recently Eleanor Gordon took the edge off this argument: 'the Scottish evidence illustrates the folly of generalizing on the basis of Lancashire experience and the dangers of a posteriori reasoning. Women's work as spinners may have been restricted to the coarser numbers and the smaller mules, but in Glasgow women worked as piecers on all classes of spinning, that is, all sizes and speeds of common mules and self-actors ... with the same number of piecers per self-actor as the Lancashire system, namely, two piecers to one spinner.'[4] The argument that physical strength explains the dominance of men is refuted by the Scottish situation.

A second school of thought has identified the exclusionary rules and practices of male-dominated trade unions as the critical factor which prevented the hiring of unskilled women.[5] This view is shared by Maxine Berg: 'By the 1830s Andrew Ure could represent the factory system and the machine as a method of disciplining labour and dispensing with difficult groups of skilled workers. But the most difficult group of workers, the mulespinners, managed to maintain their position in face of the threat from the self-acting mule, by fighting for control over the new machinery, rather than by trying to stop its progress altogether.'[6]

A third view adopts an eclectic approach and maintains that female exclusion is due to both these factors, linked with the inability of women to exercise authority over piecers.[7] Lazonick insists that the gender division of labour within cotton spinning finds its source in the influence male spinners exercised over their assistants. In his view, men were more able than women to supervise their assistants and thereby increase production. This made spinning a male job.[8]

A fourth perspective is held by Mary Freifeld.[9] Contrary to the prevailing view she maintains that spinning on the self-actor remained skilled work. In her provocative article she argues that the self-actor did not deskill the mule spinners; on the contrary, the new machine provided 'the foundation for the reconstitution of skill on a new basis' so that 'mulespinning on the "self-actor" remained skilled work'.[10] The deskilling interpretation, she insists, is a myth propagated by the machine builders and by Karl Marx, Neil Smelser, Joseph White, Keith Burgess, John Foster, William Lazonick, A.E. Musson, and Isaac Cohen. She undertakes the task of demystifying 'the concept of the deskilled machine tender taken from Marx', noting: 'We are all so much under the influence of Marx ... that evidence to the contrary with respect to the "self-acting" mule is ignored, or explained away'.[11] It is remarkable that she, as the only female author in this debate, defends the 'skilled' work of the male self-actor spinners. The only support for her interpretation that self-actor spinning was skilled work comes from trade unionists. For example in 1919, John Taylor of the Federation of Master Cotton Spinners declared: 'Ninety-nine per cent of the mule spinners are men. The reason why men are employed is that it is a large and complicated machine and requires skilled attention and the rooms in which the work is done are very hot.'[12]

Since the publication of the article 'Sex and Skill' by Anne Phillips and Barbara Taylor,[13] we are warned not to take judgments of men on skill for truth. Phillips and Taylor were the first to show that what generally had been described as skilled work was men's work. The work of most women was automatically labelled as unskilled or semi-skilled. It was not so much the content of labour, but the gender of the performer that defined the ascribed level of skill. Skill was largely a social construct. Seen from this perspective, it is logical that the trade unionist John Taylor defines the spinner's work on the self-actor as skilled in 1919. During the First World War, women took over the work of men who went to the front on a large scale. They showed that they were able to perform the so-called skilled male jobs. During an investigation after the First World War, male trade unionists were very keen on proving that some jobs were really skilled and therefore men's jobs.

Cohen strongly disagrees with Freifeld. He admits that the self-actor did not live up to the claims of its inventor; it did not diminish the skill required of the spinner. Freifeld, according to Cohen, correctly argues that spinning on self-actors required familiarity with different types of raw cotton, knowledge of the influence of humidity and temperature on the yarn fibres, experience in supervision, and the skills that are necessary to maintain the machine and to control yarn quality. But, in addition, she goes on to say that 'while the quality control and mental oversight functions remained unchanged ... all that had been accomplished by the introduction of the "self-actor" was the intensification of the mechanical adjustment tasks of the spinner'.[14] Cohen argues: 'Although the adjustment of the quadrant nut required attentiveness, and although the regulation of the faller demanded a certain degree of dexterity, both these operations could be taught in a relatively brief period of training. By no means did their execution constitute any longer a highly skilled craft, as had been the case with the hand mule and, to a considerable extent, with the power-driven mule as well.'[15]

Freifeld claims that the exclusion of women as spinners was caused by 'the breakdown in the intergenerational transmission of female skills.... It was the lost female craft heritage on short mules that provided the deep structure for the rise of an all-male aristocracy of labour, and the exclusion of women from the skilled work of mulespinning on the "self-actor" during the late nineteenth century.'[16] Gordon argues in her recent study on Scotland:

> Whether or not the loss of the craft of mule spinning to a generation of women explains their exclusion from the Lancashire trade, it has little relevance for the Scottish situation. Admittedly before 1837 there were few women spinners and piecers, but after the strike female piecers were widely recruited, ensuring a plentiful supply of women who had acquired a training in the craft of spinning. Whether or not women were specifically trained as spinners, they seemed to pick up the skill.... From the 1840s in Glasgow there would have been no shortage of trained women with requisite skills, and yet men continued to dominate spinning for twenty years after this.[17]

Dutch Cotton

The Dutch cotton industry started in the region of Twente, in the eastern part of the Netherlands. In this region, the soil was very poor, and peasants used to spin and weave at home in addition to working their land. The Dutch cotton industry was mechanized much later than the British. Even in the 1840s, Ainsworth advised Dutch cotton manufacturers to set up schools to teach homeworkers the technique of weaving, instead of mechanizing weaving. According to him: 'To establish powerlooms, where labour is as low as in this country, would be an undeniable absurdity.' According to Ainsworth, wages in Twente were a quarter of those in Manchester at this time.[18] Cotton spinning was only mechanized on a large scale after the 1860s, and it took another thirty years before weaving was fully mechanized.

The foundation of the Dutch Cotton Spinning Mill in 1865 was one example of the large-scale mechanization that took place in cotton spinning at that time. Veder and Monchy, the two directors of a cotton spinning mill, decided to establish their new factory in Hengelo, a small town near Enschede, the main centre of the Dutch cotton industry, in the east of the Netherlands. Hengelo had just been connected to the railway network. The Dutch Cotton Spinning Mill produced its first cotton in 1867.[19] It was one of the first new large spinning mills. Until then, spinning mills in this region had been very small, employing only thirty or forty workers. The Dutch Cotton Spinning Mill was not only the first spinning mill in Hengelo, but it was also much larger than the older spinning mills in the region. This can be seen when looking at the number of workers employed. At the start, in 1867, there were 275 workers. Between 1875 and 1905, the number of workers remained below 310. After 1905, the growth accelerated to reach 453 in 1916. After the slump of the First World War, there was a sharp increase to 658 workers in 1929. The number of employees declined sharply during the economic crisis of the 1930s, but recovered after a few years.

Technological Changes in the Spinning Process

The major technological changes took place in the final stage of production: the spinning of roving into yarn. I shall concentrate on changes in this process. The technological history of the Dutch Cotton Spinning Mill before 1940 can be divided into four periods. The first, relatively short period started in 1867, and came to an end after a fire in 1872 completely destroyed the factory. The factory was rebuilt in 1873 and entered a very stable period which lasted until 1905. In this second period, there was little technological change or expansion. From 1905 until the Second World War, the firm expanded twice, each time introducing new technology. The third period started with the introduction of ring spinning in 1905. The fourth period started with the building of a complete new spinning department for vigogne-wool spinning in 1916. A bombardment in the Second World War completely destroyed the factory. After the war, the factory was rebuilt and prospered until the crisis in the Dutch cotton industry started in 1967. The Dutch Cotton Spinning Mill merged in 1973 with other textile producers. Even this could not prevent its ultimate disappearance in 1982. My research focuses on the period before the Second World War.

In the first period, before the fire, the Dutch Cotton Spinning Mill bought their preparatory machines and spinning machines from the textile machine manufacturer Parr Curtis & Madeley in Manchester.[20] Veder, as one of the directors, regularly visited Manchester to negotiate the prices and conditions of delivery.[21] In this period in Twente, hand weaving and machine weaving coexisted, each using a different type of yarn. The Dutch Cotton Spinning Mill produced these different types of yarn using two different spinning machines: throstles and self-actors.[22] Throstle spinning was women's work and self-actor spinning was men's work in the Lancashire area.[23] Likewise, the self-actors at the cotton mill in Hengelo were operated by a team of men. Throstles were operated by young women.

In the second period, after the fire (1873–1905), the preparatory machines were delivered by John Mason in Rochdale, who acted as an agent of James Scott & Son in Manchester. The self-acting mules came from Asa Lees & Co. Limited in Oldham.[24] During this period, the Dutch Cotton Spinning Mill specialized in one type of yarn. Handloom weaving was decreasing in Twente. Machine weaving was now dominant. The self-actor had improved so greatly by 1873 that it could be used to produce all the different types of yarn needed in the weaving mills in Twente. Throstle spinning was no longer necessary.[25] Throstles disappeared from the mill, and with them female spinners. In the thirty years following the fire, all spinning was done with self-actors. In 1874, when the firm had fully recovered from the fire, there were thirty-six self-actors. In 1877, this number increased to forty-eight. The number of self-actors continued to rise until the large-scale reorganization of the firm in 1905.

A pair of self-actors was operated by an team headed by an adult male spinner called a minder. He had three assistants: two younger men called the big piecer and the small piecer, and a boy called the doffer. The minder had overall responsibility for his pair of mules in keeping them running at optimum efficiency. He supervised his assistants. As their names suggest, the major job of the assistants was 'piecing': joining together the broken threads. However, they also helped in other tasks. The little piecer was a young man. The big piecer was often a fully experienced operative, waiting his turn for a pair of mules to become vacant. The wage of a big piecer was considerably less than what could be earned by the minder. The doffer replaced the full bobbins with empty ones. Doffers were generally young boys, mostly 12 years old, who in 1890 were obliged to go to school for a few hours a day.[26]

The Dutch Cotton Mill tended to train its own workers. Boys usually started off as doffers, became little piecers after a few years, and big piecers after still another few years. To become a spinner at a self-actor, the big piecers had to be patient. As spinning was the best job in the mill, most men worked as spinners until their retirement. The gradual upward mobility in the team working at the self-actor is a good illustration of an internal job ladder.

Specialization was necessary to enable competition with the Lancashire spinning mills.[27] Employers only noticed that the latest self-actors in Britain were 10 to 20 per cent more productive than the ones used at the Dutch Cotton Spinning Mill ten years after the fire. Still, the employers did not find it necessary to replace the self-actors at the Dutch Cotton Spinning Mill. Experience taught them that they were able to compete with this old stock, because the majority of the spinning mills were doing this. Still, the board was bothered by the idea of being so young, and yet already old-fashioned.[28] The board of directors of the Dutch Cotton Spinning Mill were very persistent in their choice of the self-actor. In 1890, they still claimed that it was the best spinning machine for their production.[29] At that time, however, the demand for coarse-threaded yarn was growing. This could not be spun on the self-actors of the Dutch Cotton Spinning Mill. Thus, at the end of the 1890s, the board of directors was convinced that technological innovations were necessary to keep in pace with the times.[30] Nevertheless, it was more than a decade before these innovations were actually introduced.

The expansion of the firm coincided with the introduction of new spinning technology. Ring spinning was introduced in 1905. This was a more sophisticated form of throstle, which could spin coarse-threaded yarn. Ring spinning had other advantages as well. The Dutch Cotton Spinning Mill bought their ring-spinning frames from Howard & Bullough Limited of Accrington, through the agent James Scott & Son in Manchester. Between July 1904 and March 1916, the Dutch Cotton Spinning Mill bought thirty-four ring frames from Howard & Bullough.[31] In their folders this firm recommended ring spinning as 'great saving in cost of wages as a girl can tend the increased quantity of spindles.'[32] Ring spinning was women's work in the Lancashire area.

> The ring spinner, who is invariably a woman, confines herself to creeling, piecing and clearing. She does not doff the completed packages of yarn. This is done by gangs of doffers and gaiters, again girls or young women, who move around the room dealing with one frame after another as this becomes necessary. Nor is the ring spinner responsible for the general mechanical supervision of her machines. This is carried out by a male worker, known as a ring jobber.[33]

Jewkes and Gray explained the fact that self-actor spinners were men in the Lancashire area, and ring spinners always women, because the work on mules is harder than that on rings. The mule spinner is involved in the arduous task of following the carriage as it moves in and out; the ring has no carriage. Moreover the reparation or piecing of broken threads can be much more strenuous on the mule than on the ring frame. The mule spinner, when piecing, must sometimes reach over the outward moving carriage to join the thread from the spindle to the rollers. This would be a great strain for women, according to Jewkes and Gray. The ring spinner pieces by a simple vertical movement of the arm. Moreover, the mule spinner must frequently manipulate the heavy mule carriage by hand, especially when doffing.[34] Again the argument of physical strength justifies self-actor spinning as men's work. In contrast ring spinning is seen as women's work, because it is easier.

Ring spinning was women's work from the very beginning at the Dutch Cotton Spinning Mill. As the payrolls of the Dutch Cotton Mill show, ring spinners were initially young girls. In 1905 their average age was 14 years. One girl operated two ring frames. These two frames contained 760 bobbins, whereas there were 732 bobbins on a self-actor. The obvious advantage of the change from self-actor spinning to ring spinning was, as the advertising leaflets announced, saving on wages. The girls working on the ring frames earned about 4 guilders in 1905, while the doffer on the self-actor earned 3.27 guilders, the little piecer 6.58 guilders, the big piecer 8.50 guilders and the spinner 11.35 guilders. The total wages earned by a team of men working on a pair of self-actors was nearly 30 guilders. Two girls on four ring frames were able to produce more yarn for only 8 guilders. They were an obvious choice for the employers. In the Dutch cotton industry, unlike the British, there were no strong trade unions obstructing or delaying the introduction of the ring frames.

From 1905 on, the old self-actor was replaced by ring frames. The proportion of spindles on ring frames increased from 12 per cent of all spindles in 1905 to 55 per cent in 1914. The number of self-acting mules declined from forty-eight in 1905 to twenty-four in 1908. In 1914, the board of directors proposed replacing twelve of these old self-actors with forty-eight ring frames.[35] Ten years later, they proposed to buy another forty-six ring frames.[36] During, the crisis of the 1930s the number of self-actors declined even further, and with them the number of self-actor spinners.

At the Dutch Cotton Spinning Mill, as in cotton mills in Twente in general, the introduction of ring frames and abandoning of the self-actor took place faster than in Britain. In 1939, ring spindles still constituted less than 30 per cent of the spindles in Lancashire. The spinners' unions in the Lancashire area were much more powerful than the unions in Twente. In the Lancashire area they were able to prevent the employers from changing from self-actor spinning to ring spinning.[37]

In 1916, the second phase of expansion of the Dutch Cotton Spinning Mill started, when a completely new department, for vigogne-wool spinning, was built. Vigogne-wool spinning used a mixture of cotton waste and wool to make yarn. The introduction of this new way of spinning was another example of major technological change affecting the gender division of labour within the mill. The new technology used was a new type of self-acting mule, which was less complicated to operate. At these new self-actors, the traditional labour hierarchy of doffer, small piecer, big piecer and spinner was replaced by a system of one spinner and one piecer. Again the newly introduced technology was of foreign stock, this time from Germany. To become acquainted with this new technology, the director of the Dutch Cotton Spinning Mill visited three factories building vigogne self-actors in Saxony, the cradle of the vigogne-wool spinning industry. There, he became convinced that the skill of the workforce played a crucial role. The future foreman of the vigogne spinning mill had to have thorough experience of the job. He had to teach the workers at the cards and self-actors the work. The foreman had to come from Saxony and stay for a minimum of a year at the mill. He had to have the freedom to recruit workers, probably from abroad.[38] At this point, the board of directors presumed that the vigogne self-actors would be attended by men. As a result of a second visit to Chemnitz, where they had the opportunity to study a vigogne spinning mill more thoroughly, this opinion was revised. But worries about finding the appropriate workforce for the vigogne spinning mill remained.[39]

The vigogne self-actors were bought from C.E. Schwalbe Werdau, producer of spinning machines in Chemnitz, Saxony. Two German fitters, Max Schierig and Kurt Wild, adjusted the twelve vigogne self-actors. In Saxony, more women than men worked in the vigogne spinning mills. In 1895 there were sixty-nine mills, employing 5,378 women and 2,297 men.[40] The vigogne self-actors were operated by women in this area. As with the introduction of the Lancashire self-actor, the foreign division of labour by gender was copied by the Dutch Cotton Spinning Mill. On the new self-actors at the Dutch Cotton Spinning Mill both jobs, spinning and piecing, were performed by young women.

Again the shift from the old self-actors, with an extended team division of labour of one minder, two piecers and one doffer, to a new system of joiner-minding on the new self-actor was made more swiftly at the Dutch Cotton Spinning Mill than in the Lancashire mills. By 1930, it was estimated that only around 12 per cent of the spinners in Lancashire were joiner-minders.[41] At the Dutch Cotton Spinning Mill, not only had the composition of the team working at the new self-actors changed, but these self-actors were no longer operated by men but by women.

Composition of the Labour Force

The technological changes affected the composition of the labour force. The Dutch Cotton Spinning Mill started off mainly employing men. Figure 4.1 shows that the number of men working there was more stable over time than the number of women. The number of men hardly increased from the opening of the factory in 1867 until 1905. From 1905 onwards there was a gradual increase in the number of men employed. In the period before 1905, except for the period between 1867 and 1872, the number of women lagged behind the number of men. From 1905 to 1929 the number of women rose sharply. After 1914, women outnumbered men. They continued to do so during the 1920s and 1930s. The Dutch Cotton Spinning Mill changed from a men's factory into a women's factory. The number of women fluctuated far more than the number of men. This was partly the result of the introduction of new spinning technology, and partly the result of the introduction of women as piecers and doffers at the old self-actors. Once the economic slump had started in 1929, the directors looked for

Number of
workers

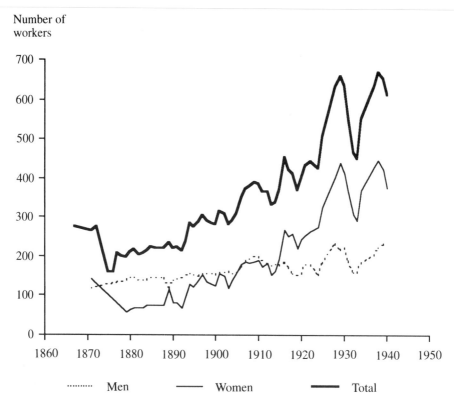

Figure 4.1 Number of men and women employed at the Dutch Cotton Spinning Mill, 1867–1940
Sources: Reports of Chamber of Commerce, Hengelo; Archive of Dutch Cotton Spinning Mill.

ways to cut wage costs. At that point, the big piecer earned 26 guilders a week and the small piecer 17.75 guilders. Young women earned less money, so fifteen men were fired and replaced by young women.[42] From then on only the self-actor spinner was a man. The two piecers and the doffer were women.[43]

Foreign Technology

The Dutch Cotton Spinning Mill bought all their machines abroad. These machines were already engendered. The process of engendering had taken place in the land of their origin. The engendering could have different causes. In Lancashire, self-actor spinning remained men's work, largely due to trade union activity. Newly created work, such as ring spinning, was more likely to become women's work. The result of this engendering process was transferred unaltered to another country, together with the machinery, even when the social context differed. In the Netherlands, there were no trade unions in textiles at the point when the self-actors were introduced. Trade union activity could therefore not be held responsible for self-actor spinning becoming men's work. Neither could any of the other three reasons that have been suggested as responsible for the state of affairs in England account for the Dutch situation.

The first male spinners at the Dutch Cotton Spinning Mill had no experience whatever with modern cotton spinning. As a home industry, hand spinning was mostly done by women. It is not at all surprising that the directors did not for a moment consider the possibility of employing women in self-actor spinning, because hand spinning was not related to machine spinning. The newly recruited male spinners were mainly former peasants, who had to learn the job from scratch. As a result, the directors made numerous complaints about the inexperienced workforce during the first few years.[44] After the Dutch Cotton Spinning Mill burned down in 1872, a great number of workers moved elsewhere, so the process of teaching new labourers the job had to start all over again.[45]

Neither physical strength nor authority were the reason for self-actor spinning becoming a male job in the Netherlands. The system of subcontracting was not employed at the Dutch Cotton Spinning Mill. It was seldom used in Dutch textile factories. Women supervised other women at the drawing, slubbing and roving frames. Thus, although women proved to be capable of supervising, they were not employed as self-actor spinners. None of the four reasons given for the English situation are true for the Dutch situation. The fact that the machines were already engendered is the reason that the gender division of labour in the Dutch Cotton Spinning Mill was identical to the gender division in Lancashire.

The gender division of labour was transferred along with the transfer of technology. How did this occur? The transfer was based on shared ideas. The idea that work on certain machines was men's work, and work on other machines was women's work, generated the notion of men's machines and women's machines. This notion was transferred through regular contact between suppliers and buyers of textile machines. Even before the foundation of the Dutch Cotton Spinning Mill, one of the directors, Veder, established contacts with the future supplier of machines. He became acquainted with the existing gender division of labour in the Lancashire spinning mills by visiting the mills. These visits made him see the existing gender division of labour in Lancashire as a natural division. The Dutch Cotton Spinning Mill is but one example. Most Dutch cotton mills bought their machinery in England, and in the 1870s it was regular practice for employers and their sons to make study trips abroad.[46] For instance, G.J. van Heek, Junior, descendant of one of the most famous Dutch textile families, kept a diary in which he reported all his visits to foreign, mainly English, textile mills. He not only described the machinery of the mills he visited, but also which work was done by men and which was done by women.[47]

Directors and supervisory staff made study trips to the regions in which the textile machinery was purchased during the whole period a mill was in operation.

As one applicant said, the purpose of such trips was 'to acquaint himself with the English method of running a spinning mill'.[48] It became common practice for sons of textile manufacturers to spend time abroad, to acquaint themselves with the newest textile technologies. For example, the son of the proprietor of the Dutch Cotton Spinning Mill, A. de Monchy, spent a fortnight as a volunteer at the factories of Howard & Bullough in Accrington in August 1932.[49] Earlier, in October 1925, Willem Haarding, spinning master at the Dutch Cotton Spinning Mill in Hengelo, visited the Stanhill Ring Spinning factory in Accrington for two weeks. His application was made through James Scott & Son, who delivered the machines to the Dutch Cotton Spinning Mill.[50] Later, Naarding became an expert on cotton spinning in the Netherlands, and even wrote a book on it. In the book he assumed that ring spinning was women's work and self-actor spinning was skilled work, and thus men's work.[51] Women also went abroad to acquaint themselves with the spinners' training. For example, Antje Jongbloed started to work at the Dutch Cotton Spinning Mill in 1901, when she was 12. She was seen as a trustworthy person and was sent to England in 1909, at the age of 20, for further training in spinning. In 1910 she became the first female supervisor in the Dutch Cotton Spinning Mill.[52]

Engendered machinery was not only found in the cotton mills in Twente, such as the Dutch Cotton Spinning Mill; machinery at textile mills in other regions of the Netherlands, using other raw materials, were subject to a similar process. Two examples of such textile mills follow.

The first example is of that of Pieter van Dooren, a wool spinning mill in Tilburg, the wool centre in the south of the Netherlands. In this mill, the spinning machines were operated by men. From 1909, new spinning machines were used, to make vigogne wool. These machines were bought from R. Hartmann in Chemitz, the forerunner of the firm that delivered similar machines to the Dutch Cotton Spinning Mill.[53] Working on these new vigogne self-actors was women's work in the Van Dooren wool spinning mill, as it was in the Dutch Cotton Spinning Mill.[54] In spite of the great differences between the wool industry in Tilburg and the cotton industry in Twente, in both regions women were hired to operate the vigogne self-actors. This practice found its origin in the region where the machinery was built. In Saxony, operating vigogne self-actors was women's work. The vigogne self-acting machines were engendered as women's machines. In Tilburg this changed as a result of local circumstances. As a result of the First World War the production came to a standstill in 1916. This created the possibility of regendering the machines. After the First World War men worked on the vigogne self-actors.[55]

The second example is that of the newly established jute industry in the Netherlands. Before establishing the jute spinning mill in Rijssen in 1863, one of the directors, Bram Ledeboer, tried to get a trainee post in Dundee, to acquaint himself with the methods of making jute. He was unsuccessful. The Dundee spinners were terribly secretive about their production process. It took Bram Ledeboer an enormous effort even to visit a mill. After a lot of trouble, the jute spinning mill was established. The Dutch female jute spinners had great difficulty in producing jute. The directors recruited a number of female jute spinners from Dundee to teach the local workers.[56] The women from Dundee were experienced industrial jute spinners. The Scottish women instructed the Dutch women.[57] This case illustrates that not only was the technology from foreign stock, but it was even necessary to employ foreign workers to give instructions to the Dutch spinners.

The Dutch textile industry is only one example of an industry constructed with foreign technology. The export of English textile technology all over the world can be traced through archives such as the Platt archive. Platt was one of the largest textile machine producers. The massive export of English textile technology, for instance to Asia, can be traced from such archives. The transfer of technology had a similar effect on the gender division of labour in Japanese and Chinese cotton mills as it had in the Dutch Cotton Spinning Mill. This can be illustrated by numerous examples given by Arno Pearse in his 1929 report on the cotton industry in Japan and China.[58]

Conclusion

It was not technology as such that determined whether certain machines were men's machines or women's machines. As I have shown, textile machines were engendered. This was the outcome of a process in their land of origin. Working at certain machines became women's work, while working other machines became men's work. Self-actor spinning was men's work in Lancashire, while throstle and ring spinning was women's work in that area. These sex labels were exported along with the export of the textile technology. As shown through other examples, such as vigogne-wool spinning and jute spinning, the gender division of labour in the region from which the technology came was crucial for the gender division of labour in the textile mills that imported that technology. Regular contacts between importers and exporters of textile technology led to a transmission of the gender division of labour along with the transfer of technology. The contacts made the gender division of labour within the textile mills seem to be natural, so that it was usually not open for debate. The original gender division of labour could only be altered, later on, under the influence of local circumstances. Seen in this way, England was not only the workshop of the world, but also the first exporter of the gender division of labour to the whole world.

Notes

This article is part of my PhD research on men's work and women's work in Dutch industry between 1850 and 1940 at the University of Utrecht in the Netherlands, due to be published in 1995 in Dutch with a summary in English.

1 Other cotton spinning regions, such as Scotland and the United States, are only

recently starting to be extensively studied. See Gordon, E. (1991) *Women and the Labour Movement in Scotland 1850–1914*, Oxford; Cohen, I. (1990) *American Management and British Labor: A Comparative Study of the Cotton Spinning Industry*, New York.

2 Catling, H. (1986) *The Spinning Mule*, The Lancashire Library, p. 147. For a more detailed argument see Bruland, T. (1982) 'Industrial Conflict as a Source of Technical Innovation: Three Cases', *Economy and Society* XI (2), pp. 91–121, esp. pp. 103–4.

3 Lazonick, W. (1979) 'Industrial Relations and Technical Change: The Case of the Self-Acting Mule', *Cambridge Journal of Economics*, vol. CXI, no. 3 p. 239; Chapman, S.J. (1904) *The Lancashire Cotton Industry*, Manchester, p. 68.

4 Gordon (1991) (see note 1), pp. 49–50.

5 Turner, H.A. (1962) *Trade Union Growth, Structure and Policy: A Comparative Study of the Cotton Unions*, Toronto, pp. 114, 128; White, J. (1978) *The Limits of Trade Union Militancy: The Lancashire Textile Workers 1910–1914*, New York, p. 35.

6 Berg, M. (1985) *The Age of Manufactures: Industry, Innovation and Work in Britain 1700–1820*, London, p. 43; see also pp. 194, 257, 262–3.

7 Cohen, I. (1985) 'Workers' Control in the Cotton Industry: A Comparative Study of British and American Mule Spinning', *Labor History* XXVI, 1, p. 72.

8 Lazonick, W. (1979) (see note 3), pp. 231–62. See also Lazonick, W.H. (1976) Historical Origins of the Sex-Based Division of Labour under Capitalism: A Study of the British Textile Industry during the Industrial Revolution, Cambridge, Massachusetts.

9 Freifeld, M. (1986) 'Technological Change and the "Self-Acting" Mule: A Study of Skill and Sexual Division of Labour', *Social History* Vol. 11, pp. 319–34.

10 *Ibid.*, pp. 321–2.

11 *Ibid.*, p. 330.

12 Public Record Office, Parliamentary Papers, 1919, Vol. XXXI, Report of the War Cabinet on Women in Industry, pp. 80–1.

13 Phillips, A. and Taylor, B. (1980) 'Sex and Skill: Notes towards a Feminist Economics', *Feminist Review* 6, pp. 79–88.

14 Freifeld (1986) (see note 9), p. 322.

15 Cohen, I. (1990) *American Management and British Labor*, New York, pp. 76–8, 187–8.

16 Freifeld (1986) (see note 9), p. 343.

17 Gordon (1991) (see note 1), p. 49.

18 Boot, J.A.P.G. (1935) *De Twentsche Katoennijverheid 1830–1873*, Amsterdam, p. 42.

19 The archive of the Dutch Cotton Spinning Mill is held at the Public Record Office of Overijssel (Algemeen Rijksarchief Overijssel) nr. 169.1 Archive Koninklijke Nederlandse Katoenspinnerij, from now on abbreviated as KNKS.

20 KNKS, inv. nr. 4, Minutes of the meeting of the commissioners and board of directors on 3 July 1865, and inv. nr. 28, Report 1889, Retrospective on the period 1865–1889; *Hengelosche Courant*, 20 November 1915. Parr Curtis & Madely constructed machinery for cleaning, preparing and spinning fine and coarse yarn and were established at Phoenix Works, Chapel St Ancouts, Manchester: see *Slater's Directory of Lancashire* (1869), p. 90.

21 KNKS, inv. nr. 0, Letters from Veder to R.A. Monchy concerning the foundation and

management of the Dutch Cotton Spinning Mill.

22 KNKS, inv. nr. 716, Report 1872.

23 See, for instance, Chadwick, D. (1860) *On the Rate of Wages, in 200 Branches of Labour in Manchester and Salford and the Manufacturing District of Lancashire during the 20 Years from 1839 to 1859*, London. Chadwick gives an example of a cotton mill with twenty-four men and ten boys and only one girl working at the self-actors. The throstles in the mill were mostly operated by women and girls. Sixty women and girls were working at the throstles as against only nineteen men and boys.

24 KNKS, inv. nr. 716, Report 1872 and 1873; *Hengelosche Courant*, 20 November 1915.

25 KNKS, inv. nr. 716, Report 29 August 1874.

26 The following is based on a report from a Dutch social democratic engineer, Theo van der Waerden, who visited the factory in 1905. His description is roughly valid for thirty years preceding 1905. Waerden, T. (1911) *Geschooldheid en techniek*, Amsterdam, pp. 143–5.

27 KNKS, inv. nr. 716, Report 29 August 1874.

28 KNKS, inv. nr. 28, Report 1883.

29 KNKS, inv. nr. 723, Report 1890.

30 KNKS, inv. nr. 723, Report 1898, p. 1.

31 Lancashire Record Office (LRO), archive Platt-Saco-Lowell: DDPSL/3/4/1, Overseas order book 71 and DDPSL/3/4/2 overseas order books 85, 100 and 103.

32 KNKS, inv. nr. 175, Technical and sales leaflets on ring-spinning frames.

33 Jewkes, J. and Gray, E.M. (1935) *Wages and Labour in the Lancashire Cotton Spinning Industry*, Manchester, p. 12.

34 *Ibid.*, p. 13.

35 KNKS, inv. nr. 5, Meeting of commissioners and board of directors 26 March 1914.

36 KNKS, inv. nr. 6, Management meeting 12 November 1924.

37 McIvor, A. (1988) 'Cotton Employers' Organisations and Labour Relations, 1890–1939', in Jowitt, J.A. and McIvor, A.J. (Eds) *Employers and Labour in the English Textile Industries, 1850–1939*, London and New York, p. 18.

38 KNKS, inv. nr. 1125, Board of directors to commissioners, 9 January 1916.

39 KNKS, inv. nr. 1125, D.W. de Monchy to the commissioners, 12 February 1916.

40 Queck, J. (1915) *Die Frauenarbeit in der Spinnerei-industrie Sachsens*, Leipzig, especially pp. 31–3.

41 McIvor, A. (1988) (see note 37), p. 18.

42 KNKS, inv. nr. 1074, Report to the commissioners on the Dutch Cotton Spinning Mill in 1930.

43 KNKS, inv. nr. 1155, Retrospective on the 1930s in the report for 1943.

44 KNKS, inv. nr. 28. In the report for 1889 there was a retrospective on the starting problems in 1867: 'new machinery, completely inexperienced workforce, mostly scum from the whole neighbourhood'; inv. nr. 716, Report, 1867: 'bad workforce, bad supervisors . . . on the average only half of the machines working'.

45 KNKS, inv. nr. 27, Report, 1874; inv. nr. 716, Report, 29 August 1874.

46 Quarles van Ufford, J.K.W. (1871) 'Een kijkje in Twenthe', *De Economist*, pp. 247–68.

47 Record Office Enschede, archive Rigtersbleek, inv. nr. 7, Technical notes of G.J. van Heek, Junior, of his visits to other mills between 1904 and 1940.

48 LRO, archive Platt-Saco-Lowell DDPSL/3/34/1, Howard & Bullough, Notes on

work experience volunteers, Nov. 1895 to Nov. 1911, p. 76.

49 LRO, archive Platt-Saco-Lowell DDPSL/3/34/2, Howard & Bullough, Notes on work experience volunteers, Nov. 1911 to Aug. 1933, p. 152.

50 *Ibid.*, p. 62. Willem Johannes Gerrit Naarding of Hengelo arrived on 10 October 1925 and left on 23 October 1925.

51 Naarding, W.J.G. (1954) *De Katoenspinnerij* (The Cotton Spinning Mill) (2 vols), Hengelo, vol. 1, p. 220, 274, 306–7.

52 KNKS, inv. nr. 679–88, wage books; Schelven, A.L. van (1965) *Hengeler wind*, Haarlem, p. 76.

53 Record Office Tilburg, archive Wolspinnerij 'Pieter van Dooren N.V.' inv. nr. 623.

54 *Ibid.*, inv. nr. 706, 707, 708, 686 and 687.

55 *Ibid.*, inv. nr. 710 and 716.

56 Bos, J. (1986) *Oude Fabrieks- en bedrijfsgebouwen in Overijssel*, Zwolle, pp. 57–66.

57 Gordon (1991) (see note 1), pp. 137–211.

58 Pearse, A.S. (1929) *The Cotton Industry of Japan and China*, Manchester.

Chapter 5

'The Mysteries of the Typewriter': Technology and Gender in the British Civil Service, 1870–1914

Meta Zimmeck

Traditional social scientists have been, curiously, little interested in clerical work and even less in the feminization of clerical work. One reason for this is that they impute value and significance primarily to 'men's work' and 'men's technology' and thus doubly damn clerical work and clerical workers. On the one hand, even when done exclusively by men, clerical work is only doubtfully 'men's work', as is indicated by the nineteenth-century aphorism, echoed by later scholars, 'Born a man; died a clerk'. Red-blooded scholars prefer coal-miners, dockers and steeplejacks or inventors and captains of industry to clerical workers, who produce nothing and control nothing. Indeed when they have studied clerical workers, it has only been to compare them with 'real', manual, workers; they show an obsessive interest in 'proletarianization' and in 'degrading' and 'deskilling'. On the other hand, even when operated by men, the tools of office work – variations on pen, ink and paper – do not seem sufficiently like 'real' technology to lure traditionalists away from the superior attractions of industry.[1] They have not been able entirely to ignore feminization, a process common to all industrializing societies, but they deal with women in two ways. Either they treat women as a subset of men, even when women are in the majority, or they treat women as a side-show to the main (men's) event. For example, Giuliano, in his important article on office mechanization, does both. For the most part he files women under 'white-collar workers', 'staff' and 'personnel', but on one occasion he refers directly to 'women' – in a historical context as the passive beneficiaries of technology: 'Large numbers of women were employed in offices as a direct result of the introduction of the typewriter'.[2]

Feminists have challenged this exclusionary view of clerical work as a mere simulacrum of reality. In the first place they reject the determinism, albeit contradictory, of the main traditionalist schools. According to technologists,[3] technology is the independent variable: its existence determines its utilization. However, according to neo-marxists, capitalism is the independent variable: its inexorable appetite for profits determines how, when, by whom, and to what extent technology is utilized.[4] Both groups thus relegate workers to the role of ancillaries, who may resist – irrationally according to technologists and heroically according to neo-marxists – but must ultimately succumb to forces beyond their control. To feminists these approaches demonstrate an alarming 'mismatch of theory and reality'[5] and have blocked rather than stimulated detailed investigation. In accordance with Rothschild's dictum, 'There are no independent variables in history',[6] feminists have postulated a model in which variables interact in complex ways. Thus in response to Giuliano's stark hypothesis that the invention of the typewriter 'caused' women's employment in the office, feminists like Davies provide fuzzier and more complicated causalities:

> Probably the most sensible argument is that the typewriter, like other technological inventions, was one part of complex structural developments ... that changed the face of the office and the sex of the office worker. To pluck the typewriter out of that context and to try to isolate its particular role ... is not only thankless but also an ill-conceived task ... it seems important to remember that technology in no way operates in a vacuum. A successful technological innovation owes its very life to a specific historical situation, and while it in turn may have a great or a small effect on that social context and its development, it is the sociohistorical situation that must be understood first and foremost.[7]

In sum, feminists look not to the grand sweep of inexorable forces but to 'specific historical situations' where unlimited variables of different weights interact in different intensities and to different timetables to produce an outcome which is by no means a foregone conclusion and which, in turn, feeds back into an ongoing process of development.

In the second place, just as feminists have challenged traditional models of causality, they have also challenged those of historical process. From the mid 1970s onwards both technologists and neo-marxists, beguiled by the anticipated widespread adoption of computerization, began to look closely at office work 'almost to the point of constituting as much of a growth industry as the very technology upon which they were commenting'[8] and saw in computerization its ultimate point of development. For technologists the process of change in clerical work is the cumulative accretion of inventions and improvements, which have increased productivity and efficiency and provided for 'the elimination of redundant work and unnecessary tasks' and 'better utilization of human resources'.[9] For neo-marxists, on the contrary, the process of change is the rationalization of work by capitalism – its subdivision, deskilling, and subjection to intensified managerial controls – to the extent that clerical workers are being reduced to the condition of factory workers and immersed in a homogeneous proletarian mass. Both technologists and neo-marxists map a process of development which begins in the 'craft office' of the Dickensian counting house and progresses to the 'industrial' (or perhaps 'post-industrial') office of the 'new information age' via a number of high spots, which include, for example, the introduction of the typewriter, the formulation of 'scientific management', and the introduction of the computer. However, according to feminists this hop, skip and jump approach has two weaknesses. The first is that it is not grounded firmly in empirical evidence. This feminists have attempted to remedy by means of painstaking historical studies.[10] The second is that it rests on a notion of 'skill' which may be flawed. If, as feminists believe, 'the classification of women's jobs as unskilled and men's jobs as skilled or semi-skilled frequently bears little relation to the actual amount of training or ability required for them'[11] and if 'skill' is unpacked and found to consist of little or nothing more objective than the gender (or race or ethnicity or age) of the worker, then to label a historical process which begins with male clerks copying manuscripts by hand and ends with women operators keying in texts on computers as 'deskilling' may miss the point entirely.

Finally, feminists have criticized traditional treatment of the clerical workforce as a uniform group. On the one hand, both technologists and neo-marxists treat clerical workers as a uniform group with the same experiences, interests and expectations. On the other hand, they also substitute parts of the clerical workforce – for example, secretaries or typists and word processor operators – for the whole in a process of meiosis. Dividing their attention between high theory and mechanical minutiae, technologists notice people only when they cannot avoid doing so and then preferably in the aggregate. Their lack of curiosity leads at times to comic non sequiturs, as when Delgado's discovery of feminization in Britain leads him immediately to thoughts of 'equipment':

> In 1851 there were 95,000 office workers out of a working population of 10,207,000, of whom 93,000 were men and 2,000 women. A hundred years later the working population of 20,336,000 accounted for 2,123,500 working in offices and out of the two million odd 845,700 were men and *1,277,800 women*! ... It was a staggering advance, and with the increased numbers of people working in offices there was more and more complex equipment to be housed.[12]

Neo-marxists are better at disaggregating but just as reluctant to impute significance to differences qua differences in the clerical workforce: feminization is not 'about' women but 'about' capital and the working class. Both technologists and neo-marxists also substitute parts of the clerical workforce – for example, secretaries or typists and word processor operators – for the whole. Feminist critics, however, believe that both the failure to differentiate and the propensity to select eponymous groups have resulted in a skewed and partial understanding of clerical workers:

> Our position is that, historically, labor has been divided into many segments, representing separate pools of workers who have access to different types of work and whose interests may be contradictory. These

segments reflect social divisions which are incorporated into the labor market. These divisions are based on ascriptive characteristics such as sex, race, and age; and, within these ascriptive segments, on social characteristics such as class, level of education, and previous job history.[13]

Feminists, therefore, for whom difference is the starting point, approach the workforce from the bottom up rather than the top down.

Drawing on the feminist critique of the literature, this chapter explores the introduction and spread of typewriting in the British Civil Service before the First World War.[14] Typewriting has been seen as *the* critical innovation in office work before computerization. For technologists and neo-marxists it represents the first giant step on the road from the craft to the post-industrial office and for feminists, the occupation most closely identified with and symbolically representative of women office workers. Nevertheless, the reasons for and circumstances of its utilization remain mysterious and 'clouded',[15] and in place of a detailed analysis there is a trite scenario. This trite scenario has three elements. The first is that the adoption of typewriting was automatic – a simple, smooth, linear process. The second is that its adoption led naturally and without resistance to the employment of women, because women had a special aptitude for this type of work and because it was a new occupation to which men had not staked a claim. The third is that its adoption was a significant step in the deskilling of office work – its division into discrete tasks done by specialist workers, the separation of conception from execution, the harnessing of hitherto autonomous 'craft' workers to machines. This paper examines this trite scenario in the light of a specific historical situation and finds it wanting.

The Process of Change: Hand Copying and the Introduction of Typewriting

Contrary to the trite scenario, the introduction of typewriting into the Civil Service was problematic – a protracted, fragmentary and discontinuous process. There were three reasons for this. Firstly, the structure of the Civil Service through which power was diffused and disputed was both horizontally and vertically segmented, so that decision-making was a Byzantine affair – the accumulation of ad hoc decisions negotiated between departments, between departments and groups of civil servants, and between the organization and outside 'political' groups. Each of the parties had different functions, different rationales and different methods of operation. Of these the Treasury (supported by its adjuncts, the Civil Service Commission and the Exchequer and Audit Department) had the clearest and most comprehensive objectives and the greatest might. The Treasury aimed, in the name of 'economy', to exercise a centripetal force over the Civil Service as a whole and thus to counteract departments' drift to individualism and extravagance. This it did by asserting its right to 'control' departments' expenditure and staffing: 'the Treasury is ... responsible for the maintenance of financial order ... I should say that the Treasury has to give its assent to every measure ... of every kind which is proposed, and which has for result the increase, or tendency to increase, the public expenditure'.[16]

Other, less ambitious, departments simply wanted to get on with their own work in their own way. They wanted sufficient resources to do the job and freedom from interference while they were doing it and consequently looked askance at the Treasury's principles of 'economy' and 'control'. Civil servants, who were divided by grade, class, education, and sex, although increasingly inclined to cooperate as time went on, both defended the status quo, their so-called 'vested interests', and opportunistically endeavoured to secure improvements in their position. Finally, forces outside the Civil Service proper – Parliament, in which resided ultimate responsibility for the Civil Service; the women's movement, trade unions, ex-servicemen's associations, etc.; and the press – acted as wild cards whose interest, though episodic, was unpredictable and sometimes decisive. This was particularly true in set-piece confrontations before investigatory committees and commissions. In short, instrumentalities and circumstances made strange bedfellows, and complicated manoeuvres took place and alliances were formed whenever changes, however small, were mooted.

Secondly, before the First World War the incentives to adopt new technology were not strong and departments, satisfied with existing arrangements for copying, were slow to recognize the utility of typewriting. The majority of the work of the Civil Service, its correspondence and internal ruminations, was handwritten and the minority, when the number of copies required was sufficient, was set in type and printed. The division between writing, a general activity engaged in by all civil servants (and one of the basic skills tested by the Civil Service Commission) and copying, a specialist activity, therefore, was blurred, a matter of degree rather than kind. Specialist hand copying was done in most departments not by established (permanent) civil servants but by temporary employees called 'writers' and 'copyists', men and boys who were in principle employed solely on copying but were in practice used as a sort of mobile reserve for overspills of low-grade clerical work. Before 1871 these writers and copyists were hired on a daily basis directly by departments or subcontracted through jobbing law stationers. They were paid by the day (at 5s to 9s 6d), by the hour (1s, with two-thirds or 8d going to the copyists and the remainder to the law stationers as commission) or by the piece (1½d per folio of 100 words). They had none of the benefits enjoyed by established civil servants, which included a rising scale of pay, sick leave, holidays and pensions paid for by their employers. On the whole most departments considered that this system met their needs. It coped with the ebb and flow of work: 'there were [*sic*] a class of law stationers' clerks called Vacher's clerks. Whenever a public office wanted any men to do the drudgery work, all that they had to do was to send to Vacher, and they got as many clerks as they wanted at so much an hour'.[17]

It extracted maximum output: 'You would get less work out of them if they were established clerks. In fact, they would not be so inclined to work as they are now'.[18] And, best of all, it allowed departments to indulge their penchant for 'patronage', hiring and firing in accordance with political chiefs' whims or departmental sentiment.

Although departments were happy with these casual arrangements for copying, the Treasury was not. Firstly, the Treasury came to view the system as structurally anomalous. The whole thrust of reforms in the Civil Service from the Northcote-Trevelyan Report (1854) onwards was to rationalize, standardize, and centralize (processes from which the Treasury benefited mightily). Copyists were, in effect, irrational, because they had no fixed bureaucratic abode, no grade allocated to them, and, moreover, by 'helping out' during times of pressure they were gradually insinuating themselves into the lower reaches of clerical work, which ought to be done only by established civil servants. They were unstandardized, because their skills and character were not 'known' to the same extent as those of established civil servants. And they were uncentralized, because they were hired and managed by departments using their discretion. Secondly, the Treasury felt that the system exposed it to public criticism. Unfettered by the rules limiting established civil servants' political activities, copyists were assiduous in airing their grievances before a string of investigative bodies – the Select Committee on Civil Service Expenditure and their very 'own' committee, the Select Committee on Writers, both in 1873; the Civil Service Inquiry (Playfair) Commission in 1874; the Treasury's Committee of Inquiry to Consider the Memorial of Civil Service Copyists (Welby Committee) and the Royal Commission on Civil Establishments (Ridley Commission), both in 1886. Thirdly, and most tellingly, the Treasury found the system expensive both absolutely, because it was more extensively used by departments than anticipated, and relatively, because cheaper alternatives such as typewriting had appeared on the scene. In applying in 1878 for permission to employ two typists to keep copies of indexes to probate records at Somerset House, the Inland Revenue for the first time (but not the last) performed the felicitous calculus of new technology and cheap labour: cost of three male copyists at 35s to 41s per week – £296 per year; capital cost of two typewriters at £21 each – £42; cost of two women 'Machinists' at 17s to 23s per week – £104 per year; saving – £150 in the first year and increasing thereafter.[19] Thus for organizational, political and financial reasons the Treasury came to the conclusion that the casual system of hand copying ought to be replaced by something more controllable and cost-effective, but it was not immediately obvious what that 'something' was.

Initially the Treasury concentrated on 'control' issues and attempted to shift responsibility for copying from departments' hands into its own. In 1871 the Treasury set up under the Civil Service Commission a General Register of Writers to which recruitment was by open competition and from which allocations were made to departments according to the amount of work available; it also retained a small number of serving writers on a Special Register.[20] It also standardized the rate of pay at 10d per hour (an increase of 2d or 25 per cent) and 1½d per folio. Because it did not anticipate the use of copyists to any large extent, the Treasury was not anxious to enter into vetting the skills and character of copyists, and it established only minimal standards: 'no compulsory qualification beyond handwriting, spelling, and power to copy'.[21] Three years later, though, mindful of copyists' unsavoury reputation as a residuum too old and too unskilled to secure better employment elsewhere (which was explicitly ventilated before the Playfair Commission), it intervened to the extent of fixing a maximum age (30) for registration. In 1878, following the recommendations of the Committee on Copying Machines and Departmental Printing (Winn Committee), the Treasury sought to go beyond the personnel functions of the Registers to fix an organizational framework for copying throughout the Civil Service. It mandated the creation of a central printing press for the Civil Service at the Stationery Office and the concentration of copying work in specialized branches in each department. In addition it gave its blessing to the introduction of the typewriter.[22]

By 1886, when a particularly vehement memorial from disgruntled copyists prompted the appointment of the Welby Committee, the Treasury found that the scale of the problem was such that it needed to make more radical changes. Twelve years previously the Playfair Commission had estimated that, if copyists were employed solely on 'mere copying', 'the number of Copyists [was] not likely to exceed 100 for the whole Service'. However, by 1886 the Welby Committee found that there were 1,564 on the Registers and that of these only 40 per cent were engaged in 'mere copying' and the rest on mixed copying and routine clerical work. Moreover, contrary to the principles of the pool system ('nominally temporary and subject to constant changes'), many copyists had settled into long-term employment in particular departments. Of those on the Registers in 1886, 37 per cent had been employed continuously for more than eight years and 5 per cent for more than fifteen. Finally, a statistical investigation of turnover amongst copyists was interpreted as confirming the image of copyists as 'failures' or, in Treasury-speak:

> These facts go far to show ... that men of ordinary industry and ability taking employment as Copyists have had fair chances of obtaining better and more permanent posts in the Civil Service or elsewhere, and it would follow that those who have been unable to obtain such posts would not command in the open market better terms than they now enjoy.

All this was highly unsatisfactory, and the Treasury knew where to put the blame – on departments' spendthrift ways and lax management. It also thought that it knew what to do. In accordance with the recommendations of the Welby Committee, confirmed by the Ridley Commission in 1890, it closed the Registers, declared men (but not boy) copyists redundant and looked to 'natural wastage' and, exceptionally, retirement based on length of service to make the problem go away.[23]

Finally, in addition to the complexities of decision-making and the lack of push factors for the adoption of new technology, there were difficulties in allocating typewriting to a particular group of cheaper workers. Declaring a problem solved by administrative fiat was not the same as solving it, and the Treasury found that it had in the process unleashed an even bigger problem, gender. As a result the search for a satisfactory alternative to the casual system of hand copying got bogged down when the Treasury and the departments tried to square the circle of economic rationality with patriarchal irrationality. Such were the challenges that many departments – as many as half by 1914 – simply opted out of the changeover to typewriting and stuck with the old methods of hand copying, press copying, and printing. That is, they decided either that they did not have work 'suitable' for conversion to typewriting or, if they did, that the disbenefits outweighed any benefits. Meanwhile these departments continued to provide safe havens for boy copyists and 'redundant' men copyists. For more adventurous departments the gains from converting to typewriting were substantial: one typist could do the work of two or perhaps more hand copyists,[24] and women and girls were cheaper to employ than men and boys. The economics of the choice should have been straightforward, but the emotions were not, and departments found it difficult to deal with the introduction of girls and women into a previously all-male environment.

Contested Suitabilities: The Allocation of Typewriting to Women

Contrary to the trite scenario, women were neither the first choice nor the 'natural' candidates for employment on typewriting duties. Because of conflicting views as to the 'appropriateness' of men, boys, women and girls, based on estimates of their market values and assumptions as to their skills and proclivities, and because of longstanding tensions between the centre and peripheries, both departmental and hierarchical, the Treasury and the departments found it difficult to select just one of these groups. As a result by 1914 they had not, and these groups coexisted, albeit in a state of increasing antagonism. Although there is no comprehensive statistical series for persons engaged in copying by hand and machine in the Civil Service,[25] various snapshots of different groups at different times indicate the general trends. The numbers of men peaked in the mid 1880s at around 900 hand copyists and a few typists and then declined so that by 1897 there were only 100 or so employed on hand copying and/or typing, and the downward trend continued afterwards. There were 368 boy copyists in the mid 1880s, and their numbers thereafter expanded briskly to 878 in 1896 and then, with the introduction of the 'new class' (which combined copying and clerical duties in an undefined way) exponentially to 1,754 in 1897, peaked at 3,837 in 1904 and thereafter declined to 2,752 by 1912. The numbers of women typists grew very slowly from the original two in 1878 to around ten in 1890, 50 in 1892, 75 in 1894, 110 to 120 in 1900, 170 in 1907 and then surged to 600 by 1912. Thus by the First World War, depending on the proportion of boy copyists employed on typing duties, typists comprised one-fifth to one-third of the total copying force and women typists something less than this.[26]

Men were the least-fancied candidates for employment as typists, and, in fact, they were out of the race almost before it began. This was not because typewriting was already feminized but the reverse, because copying was already masculinized. The equation of men copyists with men typists in the official mind, reinforced by some departments' practice of having copyists 'get up' typewriting,[27] was particularly strong in two areas. The Treasury and the departments assumed that men typists, like their predecessors, would be 'failures' for whom typing was a last chance rather than a golden opportunity. Indeed, while departments recorded fulsome praise of women's quickness, neatness and accuracy, their silence about men spoke volumes. They also assumed that men typists, again like their predecessors, would be 'discontented and disappointed [and] difficult to deal with'.[28] To 'prevent the employés from making common cause' the Treasury was careful to inhibit men typists, as it did men copyists, 'from regarding themselves of the Government or State'[29] by making them employees of heads of departments and concealing their existence under lump sum grants.[30] Despite (or perhaps because of) this negative image, the Treasury and the departments treated men typists somewhat indulgently. They were not a threat and, after all, they were *men*, actually or potentially husbands and fathers who had responsibilities and certain financial requirements. Therefore, while not advocating an extension of their employment, the Treasury turned a blind eye when departments, strongly attached to 'their' chaps, wished to promote them, as was the case when the Charity Commission obtained permission to substitute women for men typists:

[This was done] partly for economy, and partly that we desired to promote two of our male typists who were specially meritorious, and we had no opening to put those clerks on as established officers, and the only way in which we could see any likelihood of getting it done was by showing some economy by the change of substituting female for male typists. We did show an economy, and the Treasury allowed us to make the substitution and carry out our promotion.[31]

And it did so, more prosaically, when departments wished to pay them the same wages as men copyists[32] or, in some cases, more.[33]

In contrast to their elders, boys began the race for typing posts as the odds-on favourites but faded before they reached the final stretch. Departments already had considerable experience of employing boys, who comprised around one-third of the copying force in 1886. Some ambitious boys of limited means worked as copyists in order to gain practical experience and support themselves while preparing for the Civil Service's entrance examinations, and a substantial number of established civil servants were, in consequence, ex-boys.[34] The consensus was that boys had one great advantage, cheapness, and one small advantage, their lack of interest in trade unions, but many disadvantages – indiscipline, a short season of employment, and erratic productivity. So long as their advantages outweighed their disadvantages they were considered to be the natural choice to fill the void created by redundant men copyists and to step into newly-created typing posts. The Treasury and the Civil Service Commission were the most forceful advocates of employing boys, and in 1886 they, in effect, defined the advantage of boys by fixing their pay at half the traditional rate for men copyists (5d per hour and ¾d per folio or 17s to 18s per week) and then indicating that future vacancies in copying/typing posts should 'be filled by boys to the utmost extent that may be found practicable'. They showed their determination to secure departments' compliance by putting on a three-line whip: 'If Heads of Departments do not think such substitution of boys ... to be practicable, the point must be considered in concert with their Lordships' Permanent Secretary and the Civil Service Commissioners, and the conclusion must be reported to the Board'.[35] The expectation was, then, that costs would be cut in half and, moreover, the naiveté and rapid turnover of boys would result in a welcome end to the agitations of the copying staff.

Departments' response to the Treasury's plan to allocate typing work to boys was informed by their own less-than-satisfactory experience of employing boys, and their resistance was sufficient to deflect and ultimately to scupper it. First of all boys were boys and engaged in all sorts of merry japes even in the austere halls of government (see, for example, Trollope's *The Three Clerks*), and extra supervision meant extra costs. Secondly, boys had a limited shelf life as workers, and during this time they were not fully efficient, since they had to be trained ('much inconvenience until proficiency attained'[36]) and were somewhat distracted, since, if anxious to get on, they directed their energies to obtaining future employment: 'Directly you have made a boy worth anything, he immediately goes up for examination as a lower division clerk, and off he goes. Then you get another boy to train up, and so it goes.'[37]

Given the widespread concern of social reformers with the dangers of dead-end employment for boys (although not for women and girls), departments had to tread warily 'having regard to [boys'] future advancement in the service', and typing (though not copying) came to be seen as detrimental to boys' prospects. Finally and more seriously, departments came to entertain serious doubts about boys' productivity as typists. In 1889 the Customs and Excise had obligingly furnished the Treasury with 'scientific' costings which not only demonstrated the limited range of options under consideration but also the fact that boy typists were the cheapest (male hand copyists, 1.5d per folio; boy hand copyists, 0.724d; boy typists, 0.627d; women typists, 0.892d).[38] Even when the books were cooked in the boys' favour, their cost advantage was wafer thin, and by 1892, when the Treasury looked again at the data, the figures just did not stack up. The unit costs were calculated to be around 0.75d per folio for boys but 0.33 to 0.5d for women. Even the Treasury had to face facts: 'As My Lords have said these figures tend to throw grave doubts upon the expediency of employing boys on type-writing, not only on piece work at the rates proposed, but at all'.[39]

The Treasury's attempts, increasingly half-hearted, to persuade departments to employ boy typists petered out in the first decade of the twentieth century. The very first application to employ typists, that of the Inland Revenue in 1878, indicated the shape of things to come. The Inland Revenue was keen to have women to explore 'the mysteries of the Type Writer', but the Treasury expressed a preference for boys. Remingtons, which supplied the typewriters, would also have supplied boys, but none were available. Despite a rearguard action ('Can they employ women until the boys are ready?') the Treasury gave in and let the Inland Revenue do as it wished.[40] Most embarrassing was the Treasury's retreat over its own typing arrangements. In 1887, following an office scandal and the enforced retirement of the head of copying, the Treasury combined its registry, copying department and paper room into a single department in belated compliance with the Winn Committee's recommendations. Moreover, it declared, 'Men copyists will in every instance be replaced as vacancies occur by boy copyists'.[41] Yet within two years the Treasury had decided to employ women typists who were 'so much less likely to be troublesome'.[42] Departments which employed women typists wished to retain them. In 1902 when the Treasury circularized departments employing typists, not one went on record as preferring boys. The Foreign Office spoke for all when it 'doubt[ed] the expediency' of substituting boys for women.[43] In addition, departments which employed boys were keen to exchange them for women. In 1903 the Board of Education substituted one 'Supt. lady' and three 'female typists' for seven boy and three men typists: 'The Board of Education have as yet seen no reason to change their opinion that after sufficient experience a woman typist is able to do more and better work than a boy.'[44] More dramatically, between 1911 and 1912 the Post Office converted to typewriting and allocated most of the work to women. However, boys were retained in substantial numbers in copying, largely because these posts were increasingly integrated into the system of recruitment for men's clerical posts and thus provided departments with, in effect, a trainee grade.

Given the deficiencies of the other runners, women should have had an unobstructed gallop past the winning post. On the face of it women had nothing but advantages as candidates for typing jobs. Firstly, because of the peculiar configuration of the labour market for middle-class women – that is, the excess in the supply of educated and fully trained women 'eager to seize the opportunity of earning a livelihood which is neither degrading to their self respect nor trying to their physical powers'[45] over demand for their labour – they outclassed their competition. They were, in effect, the cream to the men and boys' whey. They invariably performed their work diligently, accurately, neatly and expeditiously, and always gave satisfaction:

[In 1878] we [the Inland Revenue] had not much experience of the value of female labour ... and we are bound to say that we did not anticipate that the ladies employed would be capable of doing so much work as has since proved to be the case.

They have however not only shown themselves fully able to do the work originally designed for them, but they have met a gradual and very considerable increase of it, both in quantity and quality.[46]

Secondly, women's expertise could be obtained very cheaply. Their wage scales in the early years of their employment were roughly the same as those of boys (copyists and typists), but their productivity was significantly greater. Finally, as 'voteless females who have to take leave of their office on marriage', women were an ideal counterweight to 'a class of men inflated with the conceit of knowledge but without the reality'.[47] In sum, middle-class ladies could be counted on, their employers thought, to work hard and keep out of trouble (unlike boys) and politics (unlike men).

Although the Treasury did not anticipate that women typists would be 'very numerous' (a piece of futurology consistent with its estimate of the hand copying force in 1874), it was fearful of the consequences of employing women. It took this view not just as a responsible employer pursuing organizational goals but as an organization managed by (and for?) an elite group, perhaps *the* most elite group, of male civil servants whose professional expertise was under threat from a host of reformers including educationalists, women and working-class men, who were demanding equal opportunities.[48] Typists were potentially more threatening than other women civil servants, because they alone would be employed in close proximity to elite men and would have direct knowledge of their work. They would thus be in a position to take a good hard look at the emperor's intellectual and organizational clothes. In order to limit the impact of women typists' employment, the Treasury, in effect, manufactured certain 'disadvantages'. Conditions in the commercial world varied, and in many offices women worked alongside men, but the Treasury took it as axiomatic that women should be kept strictly segregated in self-contained rooms or suites of rooms. This had the effect of rendering women virtually invisible and imparting a special nature to typing as distinct from (rather than as an extension of) copying. The Treasury kept its typists 'at the top of the house' in 'Special Rooms separate from Office. Special stair-case. W.C.' under the basilisk eye of the head of copying. The Foreign Office followed suit with attic rooms and the additional refinement of communication by dumb waiter: 'All papers to be copied pass through [a senior official]. He sends them in Boxes to Lady Type-writer in a hand lift for the purpose. No personal communication with rest of Office'.[49] When typing staff grew more numerous, the size of their accommodation grew, but the basic layout was retained. The 'necessity' of providing segregated accommodation proved costly and troublesome, since it obliged departments to find suitable space and carry out alterations, and ultimately 'structural difficulties' discouraged some departments from making the switch to typewriting.[50] Moreover, the Treasury and departments set certain restrictions on the nature of work allocated to women in the name of chivalry and morality. 'The nature of the cases' dealt with by the Domestic Department of the Home Office was such that they were 'unsuitable' for 'Ladies' to type. So uncivil was the environment that it would be impossible to employ a lone woman 'in a place like the Customs'.[51]

Nevertheless, the Treasury effected a compromise between the incentives, increased productivity and reduced costs, and the disincentives, the threats to homosociability, of employing women and linked it to its somewhat faded plans for boys. According to the Treasury's formula, departments should employ women in large offices where suitable accommodation was available, contact with men was minimal and impersonal, and the subject-matter was of the most inoffensive, and they should employ boys and men in the remainder, small offices where there was face-to-face contact with principals, other civil servants and members of the public, and there were no restrictions about 'appropriate' work:

> The employment of women or girls as type-writing operators may perhaps be more economical in circumstances where their services can be utilized, but the Commissioners apprehend that there must be many small offices where ... the size and arrangements of the building, the nature of the work, and the organisation of staff, afford no facilities for the employment of Female labour.[52]

Thus for the Treasury the typing pool was not so much a form of work organization as of gender organization. But when it suited them, departments ignored these guidelines. As a result, as is shown by a survey of the distribution of women typists presented to the Royal Commission on the Civil Service (Macdonnell Commission) by the Civil Service Typists' Association in 1912, the distribution of women typists was uneven, indeed polarized. Ten departments,[53] 19 per cent of all departments employing women typists, employed only one typist each (1.5 per cent of the total of women typists employed), while the three largest departments[54] (6 per cent), employed a total of 197 women typists (33 per cent). Or, put another way, half of all employing departments employed five or less women typists (10 per cent of the total of women typists), two-thirds, ten or less (21 per cent), and three-quarters fifteen or less (30 per cent). One way, however, for departments to bridge the gap between desire and actuality and hence to reduce anxiety was to employ 'safe' women, the Civil Service equivalent of daughters of the regiment. These women may not have been men, but they, like one of the Treasury's first typists, 'a daughter of an old clerk', and the Board of Education's superintendent of typists, 'the daughter of a late Inspector of Schools',[55] were at least members of the Civil Service's extended family.

Girls appeared relatively late on the scene and in a somewhat ghostly form. So long as women were cheap and docile, there was no incentive to employ girls, who were less likely to lark about than boys but were more likely to cause headaches to managers than women. One official of the Treasury (either a sentimentalist or a cynic) hinted at the vulnerability to scandal of departments which employed young girls: 'Imagine a girl of 17 going backwards and forwards between her office and her home, probably a long way off, every day

– and during winter going home in the dark – and having to work at her office 7 hours and overtime.'[56]

Initially there were no age requirements for women typists, and those selected were highly skilled adults. This was reflected in the age band for recruitment (18 to 30) which was fixed in 1894. In 1889, believing that women's employment was no longer experimental, the Treasury decided to 'take a step in the right direction'.[57] It began a process of tinkering with typists' salary scales which had the effect of turning a portion of women typists into honorary girls. That is, by reducing the starting pay below the market rate and making the scales lengthy and complex, the Treasury gave the impression that the early years of service were an apprenticeship – despite the fact that, unlike all boys and most men, women typists were fully competent at the time of their appointment. Thus in contrast to the Inland Revenue's original weekly scale of 17-3-23s, which had been in effect since 1878, the Treasury scale was fixed at 14-2-24s, increased following considerable 'adverse criticism' from the 'Public Press'[58] to 16-17-2-25s in 1894 and increased again, following a campaign by the women's movement and the CSTA, to 20-2-26s in 1908. Thus, compared to the Inland Revenue's scale, in 1889 typists lost 3s off their minimum and gained 1s on their maximum and five years later gained 2s on their minimum and another 1s on their maximum, so that overall between 1889 and 1894 they lost 1s on their minimum and gained 2s on their maximum, but the configuration of the later scales, with their reduced annual increments, meant that women received the maximum in the sixth rather than the third year of employment (reduced by two years in the 1908 revision).

In the context of campaigns for women's suffrage outside the Civil Service and for equal opportunities within, the Treasury began to think about bringing in real (as opposed to honorary) girls.[59] In 1903 it examined the possibility of hiring girls at 15s per week. However, in anticipation of women's opposition and in the light of adverse findings by the Board of Trade's investigator, Clara Collet, who deprecated the social and economic effects of bringing into typing posts 'young workers of the same class as factory workers, dressmakers and domestic servants',[60] it hesitated. By 1909, humiliated by its retreat the previous year (and already under pressure to make further concessions), the Treasury decided to let the Post Office do its dirty work. Against the whole thrust of its policy of personnel management, which was to decrease departmental (existing in one department only) grades and increase Treasury (common to the Service) grades – i.e., to simplify and centralize – the Treasury permitted the Post Office to establish a departmental grade of typist and shorthand writer which was in every respect inferior to its own to recruit not by patronage but by open competition. Because the Treasury's age band of 18 to 30 was 'too wide' (and had produced worldly-wise, assertive, and socially select women), the Post Office reduced the window for recruitment to 17 to 21 and thereby ensured a supply of (it hoped) innocent, biddable working-class girls and young women. It reduced the scale of pay at the front end, cut the annual increment by 25 per cent (and thus doubled to eight years the length of service required to reach the maximum on the

Treasury's scale), and for the first time explicitly linked low income to age: 16s at 17 years, 17s at 18, 18s at 19 and then by annual increments of 1s 6d to 28s. Moreover, it increased the number of hours from seven to eight per day (from 42 to 48 hours per week), which reduced real wages even further. Finally it added two new features, a minimum height of five feet and an 'undertaking, signed by her parent or guardian, that she will, if successful, reside either with her parents or guardians, or with relatives or friends approved by them',[61] which emphasized the tender years and lack of discretion expected of candidates. Women typists rightly interpreted these actions by the Treasury and the Post Office as an attack on their status and well-being, and they took steps to defend themselves. Not only did they fight their corner on bread-and-butter issues but they also began to demand a revaluing of their skills.

Degrading and Deskilling? Women Typists' Campaign for Recognition and Revaluation

The Treasury's continued efforts to undermine women typists' position and the Post Office's creation of a sub-standard grade and its rapid transfer of typing work from boys to women (which resulted in the department's employment of one-third of all women typists by 1912) had the effect of degrading – 'lowering in honour, estimation, social position, etc.'[62] – but not, contrary to the trite scenario, that of deskilling women typists. In the first place, although the minimum standard of education and training required of women typists was a modest one, the quality of recruits was kept high by patronage, and it was only when departments' desire for quality waned that degrading began in earnest. Prior to 1894, when the Treasury grade was created, women typists were appointed by heads of departments with the Treasury's formal approval. Afterwards they were nominated by heads of departments and then tested as to competence in a 'simple' qualifying examination by the Civil Service Commission. Both the Treasury and the departments agreed that they did not wish to open the floodgates of open competition to 'women in great and increasing numbers', because it might not be possible 'to obtain that full and satisfactory information as to character which should precede admission to examination'.[63] That is, it might not be possible to secure daughters of the department:

> In one department they will not put a name down on the list unless the woman applying has a relative, either past or present, in that department; and in the case of another department there is a leaflet which says that all candidates must state whether they have a relative in the Army or the Navy or the Civil Service, and that preference will be given in the selection in such cases.[64]

This system proved cumbersome and expensive to manage, since 'most Dep[ts] [were] so jealous of their patronage' that they sent sole nominees or one or two candidates for limited competitions to the Civil Service Commission for vetting. In 1908, for example, the Civil Service Commission organized eleven separate examinations for a grand total of eighty-seven candidates (thirty-seven sole nominees and fifty in limited competitions).[65] But high costs and inconvenience were bearable if the system produced what departments wanted, women 'of "gentle breeding"',[66] as indeed it did, but the real problem was that these nice, 'safe' women had, in effect, turned out to be vipers in the bosoms of the departments – career-minded, well-organized, adept, passionate defenders of their 'vested interests'. The Post Office's decision, aided and abetted by the Treasury, to establish its own grade and to go down-market via open competition to the class of persons against whom Collet had so strenuously warned in 1903 implicitly recognized that, particularly if typing were to be done in pools, as it was in the Post Office, the social niceties were not worth the bother and need not be maintained.

In the second place, given the lowering of standards and pay, the Treasury and the departments showed no interest in stemming the resulting haemorrhage of talent to more generous and prestigious employers such as the London County Council. Although they liked to think that the Civil Service was the top employer of women clerical workers, they stoutly refused to do anything to maintain the status of a 'model' employer:

> It is always thought to be fair game to fleece or cheat the Government. In a similar way it is now coming to be regarded as a sort of right that the Government should pay its employees something more than the market rate of wages. This is specially disquieting, coming as it does from persons who don't command votes.[67]

However, by the turn of the century this primacy had been eroded, and departments were having difficulty in recruiting women typists. In 1903 the Civil Service Commission cautioned that even at a low standard of six folios per hour (or ten words per minute) one-quarter of candidates failed to pass and that, if this were raised to eight or nine folios, nearly half would have failed.[68] Departments were also losing women to better employers, a problem which was more acute for typists than other women civil servants, 'because [they were] doing work that is almost comparable with work that has to be done in an outside business'. By 1912, 17 per cent of the typists appointed between 1894 and 1906 had left to take up other work (almost equal to the 21 per cent who had left on marriage), a significant demonstration of independence.[69] A further, even more exhaustive, report by Collet in 1907 showed how far the Civil Service had slipped in the salary league tables, particularly for the more senior posts: 23 per cent of ordinary typists in outside firms earned more than the maximum for Civil Service typists; 50 per cent of shorthand typists earned more than Civil Service shorthand typists; 5 per cent of typists, 9 per cent of shorthand typists and 46 per cent of assistants and superintendents earned more than Civil Service chief super-intendents. And Collet found as well that in other important but less quantifiable respects, the Civil Service was not, as it had been, the employer of the clerical *crème de la crème*. She noted that the Civil Service was an attractive option for 'the younger women who expect to marry and are only aiming at earning enough money to be able to dress and board themselves without their relatives being out of pocket' but an unattractive one for the highly skilled and 'women of mature years'. The Treasury was not alarmed by these findings and, perversely, took the view that, since matters were going according to plan, women typists had 'no claim' to further consideration.[70]

In contrast to their employers' somewhat tortuous manoeuvres women typists aimed, simply, to secure improvements in their position. To begin with they sought secure employment and a decent competence. They wanted to go beyond the temporary and unestablished position which they had, as it were, inherited from men copyists and to 'attain a recognized position with its attendant privileges'.[71] Following a discreet and carefully organized campaign of petitioning heads of departments for establishment, they were successful in 1894 with the creation of the Treasury grade, although their reliance on departmental patronage put them at a disadvantage.[72] Just how important were the actual and emotional benefits of established status can be seen in the plea by the Principal Probate Registry's Miss Andrews, 'probably the senior Typist in the service of the Crown', to be made permanent, despite the fact that since the 1889 reduction she was earning considerably more, on a piece-rate basis and on shorter hours, than the maximum on offer:

> With regard to their Lordships' inference that a pecuniary loss would be sustained should the appointment be acceded to I may remark that I am not unwilling to submit to a small loss as I wish to obtain the benefit of a permanent situation with prospective pension ... it would indeed be an anomaly should I be debarred from obtaining privileges accorded to Typists in all other departments of the Civil Service.[73]

Having regularized their status, women typists then concentrated on improving their conditions of employment and pay, and, as noted above, they secured improved scales in 1894 and 1908 and continued to campaign thereafter, particularly against the Post Office's scale, which, they thought, 'must necessarily tend to attract a less efficient type of worker, and to lower the status of Typists generally'.[74]

As well as quantifiable benefits, women typists wanted the unquantifiable, fulfilling careers. As members of a watertight grade with a short pay scale and few senior appointments, their prospects were poor, limited to sitting at maximum pay until their retirement or until the marriage, resignation or death of a colleague. In their evidence to the Macdonnell Commission the CSTA unveiled an ambitious programme in which they sought an outlet for their abilities:

> I think there should be some prospect before them if they can fit

themselves for it. I do not say that they should have it as a matter of course, but I do not think it is to the advantage of the Service to cause anyone to understand that they will never get a better position, whatever their abilities are, and whatever capabilities they can show.

Firstly they demanded liberation from the straitjacket of their departments. They wished to be considered as an 'interchangeable' or 'fluid' staff able to work in more than one department and thus to benefit from new challenges and new opportunities. The lack of sideways mobility was particularly galling to experienced women stuck in small offices. The CSTA protested vigorously, for example, when the National Health Insurance Commission and other departments took on typists but refused to entertain applications from established women: 'any applicants were told, on presenting themselves, that there was no need for experienced workers, and that they would prefer those with very little service'. They were thus prepared – ironically – to contemplate radical structural change, 'a large general department ... with a proper organization and grading with transfers for members of staff constantly taking place from one branch of the department to another' – in short, something akin to the Registers of hand copyists. Secondly they demanded liberation from the straitjacket of their grade. They wanted the way to be open to them for promotion into both women's and men's grades, as this interchange between the Bishop of Southwark and the CSTA's representative shows:

Q: Then it is at the back of your mind that the whole Civil Service might be open to you?

A: Yes, it is.

Q: Have you considered the possibility of the different grades of the Civil Service being open to women just as they are to men?

A: Yes, they should be open to women in the same way as to men.

Q: You see no reason why that should not work?

A: I see no reason why it should not work.

This bold programme, radical indeed (and in line with the claims of other women civil servants), had a simple purpose, that the woman typist 'need not always be simply a mechanical typist'.[75]

Women typists refused to accept that their work was 'mere' anything and kept up constant pressure on the Treasury and departments to recognize its complexity and value. As early as 1894 the as-yet-unestablished Miss Andrews asserted that she was not engaged in 'mere copying' but in 'working up' letters from rough drafts, and in 1902 Miss Fulcher, superintendent of typists at the Foreign Office, noted that her duties involved organization of work, 'oversight of diverse activities' and 'the many difficulties occasioned by illegible writing or unfamiliar writing'.[76] In the same year women typists opened a 'combined attack' via simultaneous petitions to departments for the improvement of their conditions of service, the centrepiece of which was, in effect, a declaration of skill:

As to the alleged mechanical nature of the work we perform, we would respectfully point out that so far as our actual experience has gone, the work is not more mechanical than other work of the public service which is much more highly paid. But though the operation of typing may appear mechanical to an observer, every person of experience knows that the efficient performance of the duty is impossible without the possession of average judgment and skill.[77]

While not denying the need for 'skill' in the sense of technical facility, they presented this as the beginning, not the end, of their work: 'It is an easy thing to master the manipulation of the machine; a child can do it in just the same way as anyone, almost, can learn to sew; but to produce a garment is quite another matter'. It was 'judgment', however, they asserted, based on a good standard of general education, 'reasoning faculties' and an overview and understanding of the business of the department, which gave value – and a value much greater than hitherto recognized – to their work:

there are many occasions which arise every day in which you could not copy unless there was someone there who had a knowledge of the subject. Contractions are constantly used, and references and allusions by letters only, written ... illegibly, render the operation something more than merely copying words.[78]

Moreover, typists stressed that they (particularly those taking dictation from departmental chiefs) were employed in positions of trust and that departments implicitly relied on their maturity and discretion.[79]

Women typists backed up these assertions with a two-pronged campaign to secure recognition for both their 'skill' and their 'judgment'. For a start they insisted that departments play fair over staffing and proficiency. Supervising posts, which were the only outlet available to typists on promotion, were based on the number of typists employed, but they were frequently left unfilled and special supervising allowances left unpaid by departments. Women typists therefore appealed to departments to honour their commitments: 'We think all those posts should be filled up'.[80] Similarly shorthand, facility in which is quite distinct from typing, was treated by departments as having little independent value:

As girls leaving school nearly always learn shorthand and typewriting I do not see that there is any necessity to pay an additional sum to Female Typists who possess a knowledge of shorthand; and it would no doubt be advantageous to have a number of girls who could take down shorthand notes.[81]

From 1894 the Treasury agreed to the payment of 5d per hour extra for shorthand, but in the 1908 revision it mandated an allowance of 2s per week (regardless of the number of hours worked) but so hedged it with qualifications (payable after the typist had reached the maximum on the scale, passed a qualifying examination and served a year on shorthand duties and payable to not more than 50 per cent of typists) as to render it almost meaningless. Moreover, the Post Office abolished the allowance, conflated the two skills in the grade of typist and shorthand writer, *and* lowered the rate of pay. Women typists demanded an end to this unacceptable situation, either by promoting all typists with a shorthand qualification into a special shorthand grade without regard to any ratio or abolishing the typing grade and replacing it with the grade of shorthand typist – both with proper competitive rates of pay. In the second place they deprecated the 'low test of proficiency'[82] administered by the Civil Service Commission and campaigned for an improved standard. Amongst typists there was a difference of opinion as to how this higher standard – 'equal in value, as a test of general education' to that of women clerks – could be achieved. All believed that there should be one uniform grade (not two) and a uniform method of recruitment. Some were willing to put their trust in open competition 'as a matter of justice'. Others were not, because there was 'a feeling that the Civil Service Commissioners and the Treasury do not take a proper estimate of the value of the work to be done' and would 'be less likely to conduct an examination in the same way as they would conduct, if held for any other branch of the public service' – e.g., the First Division.[83] Showing a very proper sense of their own worth, women typists, then, claimed due recognition of their abilities and parity with women clerks, the highest women's grade recruited by open competition and the 'Amazon Cavalry'[84] of militant women civil servants.

Just how radical was the women typists' stance can be seen not just from their programme but also from their presentation of themselves as 'craft' workers, particularly when compared to the 'industrial' image presented by the few remaining unestablished male typists and shorthand writers employed in the Engineer-in-Chief's Office, who gave evidence to the Select Committee on Post Office Servants (Holt Committee) in 1912. In this most macho of Post Office departments (and one of the last to hold out against the employment of women) unestablished men typists and shorthand writers were paid at the comparatively generous rate of 31s6d-3s6d-52s6d, a maximum nearly twice that of women typists. Their position was, however, threatened by the influx of women typists and shorthand writers acquired by the Post Office via its takeover of the National Telephone Company. Unlike women typists, who claimed parity with women clerks and thus asserted their middle-class status and solidarity with the clerical grades, the men typists of the Engineering Department equated themselves with telegraphists, better paid at a maximum of 63s but manual workers nonetheless. Since their aim was establishment as assistant clerks, preferably without qualifying examination or loss of pay (unlike the egregious Miss Andrews), this claim was a peculiar and somewhat dangerous one to make. Their defence of 'We are just as expert in our work as [telegraphists] are in theirs' was feeble and their desire for even better wages patently obvious: 'I am at my maximum, and I am standing still, and so are ... others'.[85] Whereas women typists emphasized the intellectual demands of their work and the need for constant adaptability to an ever-changing workload, 'a great deal more variety to contend with',[86] men typists emphasized the need for strength and endurance. Although they were not heaving coal or pouring molten iron, they were, in their own eyes, engaged in the clerical equivalent, 'under continual pressure seven hours a day': 'We always have a tray in which work pours incessantly from all the Departments'. Their work was 'specially difficult'; they dealt with 'a great many specifications and special work'. And in the last analysis they were 'men, many of them married, and with families'.[87]

Conclusion

The picture of typewriting which emerges from this examination of the 'specific historical situation' of the Civil Service before the First World War is thus considerably at variance with the trite scenario. In the first place the substitution of typewriting for hand copying was lengthy, begun in 1878 and still not complete after nearly four decades, and bumpy, with longueurs punctuated at increasingly shorter intervals by surges. The Treasury may have been 'anxious to encourage the use of any appliances which can be shown to economize labour',[88] but it also had other, bigger, fish to fry – exercising control over wayward departments, searching for the Holy Grail of cheap *and* docile labour, protecting the power and status of its male mandarins. These different aims were not easy to reconcile, but, because the Treasury also had to contend with an array of volatile and independent-minded departments, groups of civil servants, and outside interested parties, the process of change was even more complex and erratic. In the second place typewriting was not 'from the outset … a female occupation':[89] it was not the case that 'there was no obvious resistance on the part of the existing work-force of the kind we experience today'.[90] Typewriting was first allocated to men and boys, then to boys, and finally to women and girls, but these stages overlapped and the different groups coexisted. Almost every change was contested, but the ultimate triumph of women, which was hinted at but not assured by 1914, was due more to the poor performance and ungovernability of the prime contenders, men and boys, than any sense that typewriting was 'naturally' women's work. In the third place typewriting is hand copying by other means, and, when viewed in the context of its predecessor as well as its successor, it is much harder to characterize the transition from the one to the other as 'deskilling'. The Treasury and the departments imputed low value to hand copying work and to hand copyists and then transferred this low estimation to typewriting and shorthand writing and to typists and shorthand writers. For the women who inherited the somewhat besmirched mantle of hand copyists there was nowhere to go but up.

It is clear that the concept of 'deskilling' should be used with care. Theoretical edifices have been erected on assumptions about the transition from hand copying to typewriting, but this study suggests that the critical factor is not so much technology as the organization of work.[91] That is, the consequences of employing new technology vary according to the size, degree of centralization, extent of division of labour and type of supervision/control of offices. There is, therefore, similarity (and continuity) between the ends of the spectrum of office structures over time – individual work, from men secretaries of the Victorian age to women personal assistants of today, and 'pool' work, from men hand copyists to women typists to ethnic minority keyboarders.[92] But in order to judge whether any significant change has occurred, two conditions must be met. Firstly, like must be compared with like. If it is true that the transition from men secretaries to women word processor operators is 'deskilling', then the opposite is equally true, that the transition from the pool of men copyists to women personal assistants is 'reskilling'. And secondly, aggregate must be compared with aggregate. It is only when (and if) the overall distribution of the many types of office structures has shifted from the personal to the pool that it might be appropriate to describe the transition as 'deskilling' or the converse process as 'reskilling'.

According to the detailed evidence I have examined here, there was little structural difference between hand copying and typewriting as practised by Civil Service departments before the First World War. Departments treated both hand copying and typewriting as specialist tasks in contrast to the day-to-day use of handwriting by most civil servants, although in practice this distinction was not always maintained, since men copyists were utilized as clerks and women typists and shorthand writers as personal secretaries. Departments accorded 'special' status to both men copyists, unestablished but registered and then 'hidden under lump sums', and women typists, initially unestablished and then established but segregated and protected by patronage. From the Northcote-Trevelyan Report onwards departments divided work into 'intellectual' work, which was the province of the small elite, and 'mechanical' work, which was the province of the rest, and in this theoretical separation of conception from execution they put both hand copying and typing into the latter category. There was little difference between the Welby Committee's dismissal of hand copying as 'simple', 'routine', and, damningly, 'mere'[93] and the Treasury's bald assessment of women typists as 'a very limited class of persons engaged on work of a mechanical character'.[94] Finally, depending on the amount and nature of work available, departments' copying arrangements were either 'craft' or 'industrial' or both. Departments employed hand copyists and typists in a similar spectrum of work situations, from small one-person offices to large 'pools', and there does not seem to have been a marked change in their distribution up to the time of the First World War. In small offices with face-to-face contact between principals and copyists, a varied workload, scope for knowledge and discretion, and freedom to organize the working day, copying was 'craft' work, whether done by men hand copyists or women typists. In large offices or pools in which the opposite conditions obtained, copying was 'factory' work, whether done by men hand copyists or women typists, as this discussion between a member of the Macdonnell Commission and a senior civil servant indicates:

Q: What class of work do you propose should be dropped by the boy clerks [employed on typing] and handed over to the women typists?

A: First of all, all mere copying for which the old man-writer, the man-copyist, was introduced (for whom the boy clerk was substituted), should now be transferred to women typists, with a machine that can make six carbon copies at an operation....

Q: Have you considered what effect such a scheme for boys of 15 would have on women of 18 to 30 ...? Have you considered it from the point of view of what the effect would be of transferring this drudgery work of the very commonest description from boys to women?

A: Yes, we have done it; we have transferred it from boys to women typists in our office.... It would make a difference in the number of women typists employed.[95]

The more things changed, the more they stayed the same.

Notes

1   Observing that 'the role of the telephone in social change and social life has never received much attention from the academic community', Lana F. Rakow attributes this primarily to scholars' identification of the telephone with women and women's 'gossip' – a case of trivialization by association. See Rakow, L.F. (1988) 'Women and the Telephone: The Gendering of a Communications Technology', in Kramarae, C. (Ed.) *Technology and Women's Voices: Keeping in Touch*, London and New York, pp. 207–8. Scholars have similarly (and astonishingly) neglected the photocopier.

2   Giuliano, V.E. (1985) 'The Mechanization of Office Work', in Forester, T. (Ed.) *The Information Technology Revolution*, Oxford, p. 299. For other examples of traditional treatments of clerical work with women as honorary men or as tokens see, *inter alia*, Klingender, F.D. (1935) *The Condition of Clerical Labour in Britain*, London: Mills, C. Wright (1951) *White Collar: The American Middle Classes*, New York; Lockwood, D. (1958; second edition 1989) *The Blackcoated Worker: A Study in Class Consciousness*, Oxford (Lockwood attempts to redress the balance in his 'Postscript' to the second edition); Crozier, M. (1963) *The Bureaucratic Phenomenon*, Chicago; Anderson, G. (1976) *Victorian Clerks*, Manchester; Edwards, R. (1979) *Contested Terrain: The Transformation of the Workplace in the Twentieth Century*, London; and from the trade union point of view, Clinton, A. (1984) *Post Office Workers: A Trade Union and Social History*, London, which devotes only ten out of nearly six hundred pages to women.

3   'New technology and more international competition will eventually create more jobs than they destroy, as they have for the past two centuries, if they are only given a chance to work' ('Where are the jobs?', *The Economist*, 22 May 1993, pp. 17–18). For other examples, see Delgado, A. (1979) *The Enormous File: A Social History of the Office*, London; Bevan, S.M. (1987) 'New Office Technology and the Changing Role of Secretaries', in Davidson, M.J. and Cooper, C.L. (Eds) *Women and Information Technology*, Chichester, pp. 179–91; and (more thoughtfully) Beniger, J.R. (1989) 'The Evolution of Control', in Forester, T. (Ed.) *Computers in*

the Human Context: Information Technology, Productivity and People, Oxford, pp. 48–70.

4   A heated debate took place in the wake of the publication of Braverman, H. (1974) *Labor and Monopoly Capital: The Degradation of Work in the Twentieth Century*, New York and London. See also Cooley, M. (1977) 'Taylor in the Office', in Ottaway, R.N. (Ed.) *Humanising the Workplace: New Proposals and Perspectives*, London, pp. 65–77; Cooley, M. 'The Taylorisation of Intellectual Work', in Levidow, L. and Young, B. (Eds) (1981) *Science, Technology and the Labour Process: Marxist Studies, volume I*, London, pp. 46–65; Edwards, R. (1979) *Contested Terrain: The Transformation of the Workplace in the Twentieth Century*, London; Barker, J. and Downing, H. (1980) 'Word Processing and the Transformation of the Patriarchal Relations of Control in the Office', *Capital and Class* 10 (Spring), pp. 64–99; Morgall, J. (1981) 'Typing Our Way to Freedom: Is it True that New Office Technology Can Liberate Women?', *Feminist Review* 9, pp. 87–101; Beechey, V. (1982) 'The Sexual Division of Labour and the Labour Process: A Critical Assessment of Braverman', and Crompton, R. and Reid, S. (1982) 'The Deskilling of Clerical Work', both in Wood, S. (Ed.) *The Degradation of Work? Skill, deskilling and the labour process*, London; pp. 54–73 and 163–78, respectively; and Softley, E. (1985) 'Word Processing: New Opportunities for Women Office Workers?', in Faulkner, W. and Arnold, E. (Eds) *Smothered by Invention: Technology in Women's Lives*, London, pp. 222–37.

5   Carter, V.J. (1987) 'Office Technology and Relations of Control in Clerical Work Organization', in Wright, B.D. *et al.* (Eds) *Women, Work and Technology: Transformations*, Ann Arbor, p. 208.

6   Rothschild, J. (1983) 'Introduction: Why Machina Ex Dea', in Rothschild, J. (Ed.) *Machina Ex Dea: Feminist Perspectives on Technology*, New York, p. xxiv.

7   Davies, M.W. (1988) 'Women Clerical Workers and the Typewriter: The Writing Machine', in Kramarae, C. (Ed.) *Technology and Women's Voices: Keeping in Touch*, London and New York, p. 31. For an extremely useful and flexible pluralistic model of group interaction, which gives scope for class, gender, race, ethnicity, religion, sexuality, physical impairment or disability, and age as potential factors, see Kanter, R.M. (1977) *Men and Women of the Corporation*, New York; Kanter, R.M. and Stein, B. (1980) *A Tale of 'O': On Being Different in an Organisation*, New York.

8   Webster, J. (1990) *Office Automation: The Labour Process and Women's Work in Britain*, Brighton, preface.

9   Giuliano (see note 2), p. 311.

10 See, for example, for clerical work in the United States: Rotella, E.J. (1981) *From Home to Office: US Women at Work, 1870–1930*, Ann Arbor, 1981; Davies, M.W. (1982) *Woman's Place Is At the Typewriter: Office Work and Office Workers, 1870–1930*, Philadelphia; Sondik Aron, C. (1987) *Ladies and Gentlemen of the Civil Service: Middle-Class Workers in Victorian America*, New York and Oxford; and Srole, C. (1987) '"A Blessing to Mankind, and Especially to Womankind": The Typewriter and the Feminization of Clerical Work, Boston, 1860–1920', in Wright, B.D., Marx Ferree, M. and Mellow, G.O. (e.a.) (Eds) (1987) *Women, Work, and Technology. Transformations*, Ann Arbor, pp. 84–100. A closely related area, printing, has been particularly well researched: see Cockburn, C. (1983) *Brothers: Male Dominance and Technological Change*, London; Cockburn, C. (1985) *Machinery of Dominance: Women, Men and Technical Know-How*, London; Baron,

A. (1987) 'Contested Terrain Revisited: Technology and Gender Definition of Work in the Printing Industry, 1850–1920', in Wright, B.D., Marx Ferree, M. and Mellow, G.O. (e.a.) (Eds) *Women, Work, and Technology. Transformations*, Ann Arbor, pp. 58–83; Baron, A. (1989) 'Questions of Gender: Deskilling and Demasculinization in the U.S. Printing Industry, 1830–1915', *Gender and History* I, pp. 178–99; and Reynolds, S. (1989) *Britannica's Typesetters: Women Compositors in Edwardian Edinburgh*, Edinburgh.

11 Phillips, A. and Taylor, B. (1980) 'Sex and Skill: Notes towards a Feminist Economics', *Feminist Review* 6, p. 79.

12 Delgado (1979) (see note 3), p. 93.

13 Feldberg, R.L. and Glenn, E.N. (1983) 'Technology and Work Degradation: Effects of Office Automation on Women Clerical Workers', in Rothschild, J. (Ed.) (1983) *Machina Ex Dea: Feminist Perspectives on Technology*, New York, p. 60.

14 For studies of women civil servants in Britain, see Evans, D. (1934) *Women and the Civil Service: A History of the Employment of Women in the Civil Service, and a Guide to Present Day Opportunities*, London; Martindale, H. (1938) *Women Servants of the State, 1870–1938: A History of Women in the Civil Service*, London; Holcombe, L. (1973) 'Women in the Service of the State: The Civil Service', in Holcombe, L. *Victorian Ladies at Work: Middle-Class Working Women in England and Wales, 1850–1914*, Newton Abbott, pp. 163–93; Brimelow, E. 'Women in the Civil Service', *Public Administration* 59 (Autumn 1981), pp. 313–35; Bagilhole, B. (1984) 'Women and Work: A Study of Underachievement in the Civil Service', PhD, University of Nottingham; Cohn, S. (1985) *The Process of Occupational Sex-Typing: The Feminization of Clerical Labour in Great Britain*, Philadelphia; Davy, T. (1986) '"A Cissy Job for Men; a Nice Job for Girls": Women Shorthand Typists in London, 1900–39', and Sanderson, K. (1986) '"A Pension to Look Forward to . . .?": Women Civil Service Clerks in London, 1925–1939', in Davidoff, L. and Westover, B. (Eds) *Our Work, Our Lives, Our Words: Women's History and Women's Work*, Basingstoke, pp. 124–44 and 145–60 respectively; Grint, K. (1988) 'Women and Equality: The Acquisition of Equal Pay in the Post Office, 1870–1961', *Sociology* 22, pp. 87–108. See also Zimmeck, M. (1984) 'Strategies and Stratagems for the Employment of Women in the British Civil Service, 1919–1939', *Historical Journal* 27, pp. 901–24; Zimmeck, M. (1987) 'We Are All Professionals Now: Professionalisation, Education and Gender in the Civil Service, 1873–1939', *Women, Education and the Professions*, History of Education Society Occasional Publication, no. 8, pp. 66–83; Zimmeck, M. (1988) 'The "New Woman" in the Machinery of Government: A Spanner in the Works?', in MacLeod, R. (Ed.) *Government and Expertise: Specialists, Administrators and Professionals, 1860–1919*, Cambridge, pp. 185–202; Zimmeck, M. (1988) '"Get Out and Get Under": The Impact of Demobilisation on the Civil Service, 1918–32', in Anderson, G. (Ed.) *The White-Blouse Revolution: Female Office Workers since 1870*, Manchester, pp. 88–120; and Zimmeck, M. (1992) 'Marry in Haste, Repent at Leisure: Women, Bureaucracy and the Post Office, 1870–1920', in Savage, M. and Witz, A. (Eds) *Gender and Bureaucracy*, Oxford, pp. 65–93.

15 Srole (see note 10), p. 85.

16 P[arliamentary] P[apers] 1887, c.5226 xix 1, Royal Commission on Civil Establishments, First Report, Minutes of Evidence (hereafter Ridley Commission), evidence of Sir Reginald Welby, permanent secretary, Treasury, 23 November 1886, Q 2.

17 *Ibid.*, evidence of George Dalhousie Ramsay, director of clothing, War Office, 16

February 1887, Q 3009.

18 *Ibid.*, evidence of Sir Gerald Fitzgerald, accountant general of the Navy, 28 March 1887, Q 5839.

19 P[ublic] R[ecord] O[ffice], T1/7670A/8945/78, Algernon West *et al.*, Inland Revenue, to Treasury and E.W. H[amilton] to R.R.W. Lingen, both 18 April 1878.

20 This was, in effect, a concession to departments' wishes. By the Orders in Council of 19 August 1871 and 9 August 1872 the Treasury exceptionally retained without certificate those copyists whom departments found indispensable.

21 PP 1887, c.82 lxvi 331, Return ... dated 16 March 1887 for Copy of Report of the Committee of Inquiry appointed by the Treasury to consider the Memorial of the Civil Service Copyists, 23 December 1886 (hereafter Welby Committee, Report), p. 331.

22 T1/7670A/8945/78, Treasury Minute, 2 March 1878, and Treasury Circular, 25 March 1878.

23 Welby Committee, Report, pp. 332–4, 336, 338 (Appendix II) (calculations by the author).

24 This ratio varied according to circumstances. In 1878 the Inland Revenue brought in two typists to replace three hand copyists. By 1892 the ratio was two for five, and there it remained: 'Their Lordships are assured that the work done by two efficient Type writers is about equal to that of five copyists'. T1/8648B/8571/92, Treasury to Local Government Board, 8 June 1892.

25 In response to a question as to whether boy clerks were employed on typing, one senior civil servant replied: 'It is hard for me to say; we have not got any statistics with regard to that'. PP 1913, cd.6210, Royal Commission on the Civil Service, Appendix to First Report, Minutes of Evidence, 26 March 1912 to 19 April 1912 (hereafter Macdonnell Commission, First Report, Evidence), evidence of Edmund Phipps, principal assistant secretary, Board of Education and honorary secretary, Boy Clerks (Civil Service) Friendly Society, 26 April 1912, Q 2926.

26 The proportions of men and boys were established by applying the ratio supplied by the War Office to the Ridley Commission (82 men and 36 boys or 30 per cent boys), which seems consistent with the Welby Committee's remark that of 1,279 employed copyists 300 men and 368 boys (29 per cent) were employed on 'mere copying', and assuming that boys were not assigned to more complex work. Welby Committee, Report, p. 338 (Appendix II); Ridley Commission, evidence of Sir Ralph Thompson, permanent undersecretary, War Office, 9 December 1886, Q 261; PP 1897, c.288 lvii 863, Return of Persons not Borne on the Permanent Establishment of the Civil Service, and not paid by the Day, whose Salaries are paid out of an Annual Lump-Sum Allowance made to the Head of the Department in which they are respectively serving, and who are Employed by such Head personally without Examination by the Civil Service Commissioners (according to which there were 85 men employed on hand copying and/or typing and/or other duties, 13 on hand copying only and 4 on typewriting only); Macdonnell Commission, First Report, Evidence, Appendix I, pp. 106–7; PRO, HO45/10004/A49679, memo, 27 January 1890, enclosing 'Type-Writers attached to certain Government Offices'; T1/8752C/12759/93, petition of 'female typewriters', 31 December 1892; T1/9545B/11886/00, John Hennell, Civil Service Commission, to [L.J.] H[ewby], Treasury, 22 May 1900, and Hewby, memo, 5 July 1900; T1/10614B/5925/07, GC U[pcott], memo, 5 April 1907; PP 1912, Cd.6535, Royal Commission on Civil Service, Appendix to Second Report, Minutes of Evidence, 25 April 1912 to 2 August 1912 (hereafter Macdonnell Commission,

Second Report, Evidence), Appendix VIII(a) Q 3620, Table Showing the Distribution of Women Typists in Public Departments, pp. 503–4.

27 When the Home Office was seeking permission to employ a typist, it considered hiring a skilled operator from Remingtons or a woman but decided in the end to keep the matter in-house: 'The least difficult plan is to get one of our Copyists to get up Type-writing and one or two of the Boys ...': HO45/10004/A49679, memo, 27 January 1890.

28 'Passing Notes: Women as "Writers"', *Englishwoman's Review* CLXXXIX (15 February 1889), p. 63.

29 T1/8531C/17942/90, GLC(?), memo, 4 July 1890.

30 Or in the words of the Treasury: 'My Lords are obliged to lay down in each such case the rule that the temporary employé is to be considered, and paid as the private employé of the Head of the Branch or Department, the Treasury making a money allowance to such head'. T1/8613C/17690/91, Treasury to Post Office, 17 June 1890.

31 Macdonnell Commission, Second Report, Evidence, evidence of H.W.T. Bowyear, second commissioner, Charity Commission, 28 June 1912, Q 10671.

32 The Civil Service Commission obligingly set out its reasoning on pay: 'so far as this Board is in a position to judge, they think that the ordinary rates of pay for Registered Copyists might reasonably be paid to Male Type-Writing Operators'. And its calculations: six days × seven hours per day × 10d per hour = 35s per week. T1/8613C/17690/91, J.S. Lockhart, Civil Service Commission, to Treasury, 4 February 1891.

33 For example, in 1892 the Exchequer and Audit Department, which ought to have known better, attempted to persuade the Treasury to approve 40s per week for one of its veteran copyists now employed on typewriting on the grounds, it would seem, of male solidarity: 'The poor fellow has a wife and family and finds it very difficult to struggle along'. T1/8642B/6607/92, W. Phillips, Exchequer and Audit Department, to Treasury, 14 April 1892, and J. Harris(?), Exchequer and Audit Department to Blair(?), Treasury, 5 Feburary 1903.

34 A little over 40 per cent of all copyists on the Registers, 1871–1886, secured established posts in the Civil Service, and, given the age limits for appointment, most of these must have been boys. Welby Committee, Report, p. 338 (Appendix II) (calculations by the author).

35 PP 1887, c.66 xlix 161, Return ... dated 1 March 1887 for Copy of the Treasury Minute dated December 1886, with regard to Civil Service Copyists. They were on occasion more oleaginous: 'My Lords think that you may possibly find it convenient to employ a boy yourselves, rather than a woman, upon this work, and would be glad if you would consider this point in concert with the Civil Service Commissioners before They authorise the employment of a woman in your department'. T1/8431A/16487/89, Treasury to Customs and Excise, 21 February 1889.

36 T1/8431A/16487/89, Board of Trade to Treasury, 26 January 1889.

37 Ridley Commission, evidence of Ramsay (see notes 17–18), Q 3111.

38 T1/8431/16487/89, R.T. Trowse, Customs and Excise, to Treasury, 12 February 1889.

39 T1/8752C/12759/93 Hamilton, Treasury, to Civil Service Commission, 24 December 1892.

40 T1/7670A/8945/78, West, Inland Revenue, to Hamilton, Treasury, 13 May 1878.

41 T1/8328B/20227/87, Treasury Minute, 27 August 1887.

42 T1/8371A/18349/88 [J.A. Kempe], memo, 29 October 1888.

43 T1/9988B/14659/03, T.H. Henderson, Foreign Office, to Treasury, 9 April 1903.

44 T1/10026B/19679/03, H.M. Lindsell, Board of Education, to Treasury, 24 February 1903, and Simpkinson, Board of Education, to Treasury, 19 October 1903.

45 'Passing Notes' (see note 29), p. 63.

46 T1/8431A/16487/89, Inland Revenue to Treasury, 6 July 1889.

47 T1/8752C/12759/93, Hervey, Local Government Board, to Welby, Treasury, 6 October 1894.

48 For a discussion of the construction of elite male civil servants' professional expertise, see Zimmeck, 'New Woman' (see note 14).

49 HO45/10004/A49679, 'Type-Writers attached to certain Government Offices', enclosed in memo, 27 January 1890. This was all the more strange since 'the Room is near Office Keeper's Bed Rooms' (!).

50 In 1891 the Board of Trade decided not to employ women: 'Again the accommodation in the Building is far too limited and ill adapted for the employment of female operators'. T1/8613C/17690/9a, Board of Trade to Treasury, 19 January 1891.

51 HO45/10004/A49679, memo, 27 January 1890, and T1/8431A/16487/89, G. G[lendower], memo, 1 March 1889.

52 T1/8752C/12759/93, Lockhart, Civil Service Commission, to Treasury, 17 February 1893.

53 This was an anomalous group – two departments of the Board of Trade (London Traffic and Trade Boards Branches); the Privy Council; three Scottish (Lunacy Commission, Prison Commission and General Record Office) and four Irish (Accounts Office, Valuation and Boundary Commission, Valuation (Finance) Department, Science and Art Department) departments. The strong showing of the Celtic fringe suggests that such unorthodox arrangements were easier to maintain at a distance from the Treasury. Macdonnell Commission, Second Report, Evidence, Appendix VIII(a), Q 3620, Table Showing the Distribution of Women Typists in Public Departments, pp. 503–4.

54 These were the Secretary's Office of the Post Office, the War Office and the Board of Education. *Ibid.*

55 T1/8731A/18349/88, H. Shand, Inland Revenue, to [T.] Durrant, Treasury, 4 May 1889, and PRO, ED23/620, Lindsell, Board of Education, to Treasury, 24 February 1903.

56 T1/8752C/12759/93, RM, 3 October 1894.

57 T1/8431A/16487/89, G[lendower], 5 July 1889.

58 T1/8613C/17690/91, Knox, War Office, to Treasury, 31 March 1891.

59 For similar treatment of women clerks, see Zimmeck, 'Marry in Haste' (see note 14).

60 T1/9988B/14659/03, Clara Collet, Labour Department, Board of Trade, to H. Higgs, Treasury, 19 April 1903.

61 Post Office Archive, POST30/1937/E3991/11, J.C.C., memo, 22 August 1908; A.F. King, Post Office, to Civil Service Commission, 26 November 1908; W.P., memo, 26 August 1908.

62 *Shorter Oxford English Dictionary.*

63 T1/8752C/12759/93, Treasury Minute, 17 March 1894. The required subjects were: writing, spelling, arithmetic (first four rules, simple and compound interest, weights and measures and reduction), and typing. T1/8822B/7837/94, Treasury to G.L. Ryder, Civil Service Commission, 29 May 1894.

64 Macdonnell Commission, Second Report, Evidence, evidence of Miss E.M. Charlesworth, chief superintendent of typists, Local Government Board, and representative, CSTA, 3 May 1912, Q 3898.

65 T1/11172/25824/09, J.L. Hammond, Civil Service Commission, to Treasury, 5 January 1909, and B.B.B., memo, 11 January 1909.

66 POST30/1937/E3991/11, W.P., memo, 26 August 1908.

67 T1/10117/11113/04, H[amilton], memo, 5 October 1904.

68 T1/9988B/14659/03, S.C.P., memo, 19 June 1903, referring to a total of fifty-nine candidates tested in the preceding eighteen months.

69 Macdonnell Commission, Second Report, Evidence, evidence of Charlesworth, Qs 3905, 3907, Appendix VIII(b), Q 3839, Statistics showing the Number of Women Typists in Government Departments who resigned for various causes, 1894 to 1906.

70 T1/10614B/5925/07, Collet, 'Salaries and Conditions of Employment of Women 18 Years and Upwards Employed as Typists in April 1907' (calculations by the author); U[pcott], 21 June 1907. Collet's sample included fifty-seven insurance companies, twenty-seven finance and steam navigation companies, eighty-three typewriting offices and agencies collectively employing 480 typists as well as the Board of Education, the Metropolitan Water Board, the Metropolitan Asylums Board and the London County Council.

71 T1/8752C/12759/93, petition of 'female typewriters', 31 December 1892; A.B., memo, 5 January 1893; Durrant, memo, 5 January 1893.

72 It also left them vulnerable to criticism. For example, Charles Bradlaugh MP demanded to know 'whether, in introducing female typists into the Service, the Government proposed to recognise a return to the system of appointment by private patronage without examination by the Civil Service Commissioners, notwithstanding that such a system had long been practically abolished as regarded the appointment of men'. *The Times*, 26 July 1890, cutting in HO45/10004/A49679.

73 T1/8840/10974/94, L.M. Andrews to Sir Francis Jeune, president, Probate, Divorce and Admiralty Division, Supreme Court, 18 June 1894. Miss Andrews gave up 2s per week (7 per cent) and her colleague 5s (18 per cent). Francis Mowatt, Treasury, to Principal Probate Registry, 6 July 1894.

74 T1/11074/17400/09, memorial, 'To the Postmaster General', enclosed in H. Babington Smith, Post Office, to Treasury, 19 August 1909.

75 Macdonnell Commission, Second Report, Evidence, evidence of Charlesworth, Qs 3991, 3794, 3791 (this phrase, to which the witness agreed, was in a question asked by Mrs Deane Streatfield). The witness hedged her bets by adding the proviso: 'There is only one objection that I see to it, and that is that the work of each department takes a certain time to learn, and it would only be a certain number who could be drafted like that'). *Ibid.*, 3885–7, 3973.

76 T1/8840A/10974/94, Andrews to Jeune, 18 June 1894; T1/9796B/4628/02, S.I. Fulcher to W.C. Cartwright, Foreign Office, 12 March 1902.

77 T1/9988B/14659/03, petition of Agnes Healey *et al.* to Treasury, 2 April 1902, and S.E. Spring-Rice, memo, 19 April 1902.

78 Macdonnell Commission, Second Report, Evidence, evidence of Charlesworth, Qs 3830, 3695, 3698.

79 Women typists attempted to turn the tables and assert that it was men who were natural gossips: 'A great deal of [typists and shorthand writers'] work is very confidential work, and I think that should be recognised. Many employers of outside labour, clerks to municipal authorities, and so on, have told me that they prefer

women clerks because they are loyal to their employers, and do not communicate the contents of documents to other people interested; they consider women are less likely to do so than men.' *Ibid.*, Q 3707.

80 The method of calculating senior posts was as follows: if there were more than three but less than six typists, then there should be one superintendent; more than six but less than ten, two superintendents; more than ten, one superintendent and one chief superintendent; more than twenty, special allowances for superintendents and chief superintendents. The failure to appoint chief superintendents was particularly acute at the Post Office and the War Office. In answer to a question as to whether women suffered more than men from this form of neglect Charlesworth answered: 'It might occur, but I think the men's associations would have something to say about it and would get it altered'. *Ibid.*, Qs 4009, 4011.

81 POST30/1937/E3991/11, WP(?), memo, 26 August 1908.

82 T1/9988B/14659/03, petition of Healey *et al.*

83 Macdonnell Commission, Second Report, Evidence, evidence of Charlesworth, Qs 3690, 3676, 3676, 3683, 3788.

84 PRO, T162/47/E3506/1, W.R. Fraser, memo, 20 August 1920.

85 PP 1913 cd.268 x, Select Committee on Post Office Servants (Wages and Conditions of Employment), Minutes of Evidence, 3 December 1912 to 1 May 1913 (hereafter Holt Committee, Evidence), evidence of S. Levey, 18 December 1912, Q 21,532.

86 Macdonnell Commission, Second Report, Evidence, evidence of Charlesworth, Q 3958.

87 Holt Committee, Evidence, evidence of Levey, Qs 21,532, 21,536, 21,552, 21,522, 21,531.

88 T1/8313A/17893/87, Treasury to War Office, 25 June 1887.

89 Softley (see note 4), p. 225.

90 Barker and Downing (see note 4), p. 70.

91 A point adumbrated, *inter alia*, by Carter (see note 5), pp. 208 *passim*.

92 For a discussion of the further refinement of ethnicity, see Glenn, E.N. and Tolbert, C.M. (1987) 'Technology and the Emerging Patterns of Stratification for Women of Colour: Race and Gender Segregation in Computer Occupations', in Wright *et al.*, pp. 318–31; and Machung, A. (1988) '"Who Needs a Personality to Talk to a Machine?": Communication in the Automated Office', in Kramarae, C. (Ed.) *Technology and Women's Voices*, London and New York, pp. 62–81.

93 Welby Committee, Report, pp. 331–3 *passim*.

94 T1/8752C/12759/93, Treasury Minute, 17 March 1894.

95 Macdonnell Commission, First Report, Evidence, evidence of Phipps, Qs 2929, 2936, 2937 (questions asked by Mrs Deane Streatfield).

Chapter 6

'A Revolution in the Workplace'? Women's Work in Munitions Factories and Technological Change 1914–1918

Deborah Thom

The history of wartime employment is often seen as typical of the process of the social inscription of work in the lives of women. It is certainly influentially mythical in creating a story of women's work which has emphasized women's secondary wage earning, vulnerability to male hostility and reliance upon government rather than their own organizations for improvement. Work is a cultural formation in the lives of women as much as for men despite the history of overgendering characteristic of most accounts of wartime innovation.[1]

The account of the turning of young women into women war-workers, then, is one that looks at the experience of learning to be a factory worker. It also raises the question of the contribution of the women workers of the day to social change. Paul Thompson, in *The Edwardians*,[2] argues for the profound effect of the experience of war on people's understanding of their world, and the experience of war-work for the woman worker should also demonstrate such change. Motherhood has famously been described in this period as 'women's highest service to the state', which women had, it was argued, set aside to perform war-service.[3] One of the problems of histories of work is the layer of understanding imposed on the worker's experience by her subsequent labour history. In this instance, this presents a substantial methodological problem precisely because war-work was so unlike much of the industrial employment, not of all women, but of the women who were war-workers. The rhythms of work, the nature of the training on the job, the social relations of the workplace were all altered by the fact that the work was undertaken by women who were addressed, in a threefold description, as women war-workers. The evidence is also more than usually opaque, even though it is voluminous and thorough, and so looks so much better than most evidence about women, which is so often sparse and subject to the random accidents of survival. However, the abundance of evidence reflects the political needs served by record-keeping at the time. The best collections about working women are those of the Imperial War Museum in London, which were explicitly gathered to demonstrate the novelty and success of war-work for women; and, in a more restricted way, the Gertrude Tuckwell collection at the Trades Union Congress which focused around the Women's Trade Union League, and its daughter organization, the National Federation of Women Workers, which became in wartime, as its leader Mary Macarthur said, 'virtually a union of women war-workers, especially munitions workers'.[4] The government demonstrated an unusually keen interest in these women and produced a massive survey of their activities, the Report of the War Cabinet Committee on Women in Industry, in 1919.[5] This committee was set up to exonerate the government from the claim made by striking transport workers and munitions factory workers that they had not honoured their promises to award equal pay to the women doing men's work. At the time it was not clear to women themselves whether they were doing a man's or a woman's job, whether it was skilled or not, even, or perhaps especially, whether they were paid on the basis agreed by their trade union. Hence, in order to understand how much innovation there was, it is necessary to investigate the perceptions of the government, employers and the workers themselves while remaining aware that the history of women's work itself was a political counter in debates about the responsibility of the government, and thus makes any final conclusions difficult.

The state was the innovator in the field of women's employment and this too makes this a history which is both better recorded and more polemical than most accounts of women's contribution to technological change. Winston Churchill was briefly the minister of munitions and he called it, ironically enthusiastic, a 'great argument for state socialism'.[6] The process by which women were turned into new sorts of workers was one that was overlaid with a specific and contingent kind of paternalism. This paternalism had limits, as when many workers began to show signs of the toxic effects of TNT (trinitrotoluene). The solution was to ensure that processes of management would be used to guarantee that no single worker would be exposed for very long to the poison.[7] However, this paternalism shaped and defined the debates about women's labour and therefore the historical record. The theory of dilution and substitution was based on a discourse about the woman worker which presumed that she was weaker, undisciplined, and uninterested in technical knowledge because women were not usually factory workers in engineering. The government orchestrated this view and produced propaganda based on this assumption, much of it pictorially vivid. Women's own industrial organization tended to work on some of the same sets of assumptions, exploiting them in the interests of their members but thus reproducing an argument which has been attributed only to their male peers. When this theory is examined, it will be found that the placing of technological change in a discourse of innovation peculiar to wartime creates a misleading impression of innovation and novelty. The change is not in the area of technology, nor in the capacities or skills of women; it is in the management of large groups of women, occurring as a result of dilution and substitution. The machinery on which they worked and the organization of production was either imported from the United States, or borrowed from factories where it was already in use, copied and reproduced in much greater volume.[8] The organization of production was different only in that larger numbers of semi-skilled workers were engaged in workshops where previously skilled workers had been producing the same goods more slowly.

Substitutes and Dilutees

The labour theorist and historian G.D.H. Cole was one of the most interested theoreticians to write about the wartime processes of dilution and substitution. In his book on workers' control in the workplace he defined dilution thus:

> the introduction of less skilled workers to undertake the whole, or a part of the work previously done by workers of greater skill or experience, often, but not always, accompanied by simplification of machinery, or the breaking up of a job into a number of simpler operations.[9]

This book was written in 1923, and the clarity of the definition was in part the result of the debates over what had been dilution in wartime, when, as Ministry of Munitions officials pointed out in 1917, dilution became 'synonymous with the introduction of women'.[10] The record has remained muddled as to who was a substitute and who a dilutee. For government and employers, as well as men's trade union officials, the problem of dilution was the spreading of scarce skills; for workers it was the relationship between labour and conscription. Labour management was integrally related to the management of soldier supply. When dilution could be achieved in the context of mass conscription, male workers, mostly, became replaceable. Paradoxically, those men whose skill was essential to maintain semi-skilled or unskilled workers' machines became more in demand than ever before. Engineers, in particular, resisted the introduction of dilution as they had done since American practices of innovation in engineering had been mooted in Britain in the years before the war. They were to remain central in the process of job definition because they were essential to the smooth expansion of production of wartime, as they both made and set machine tools which made the armaments used so prodigally in France and the Dardanelles.[11] Agreements about dilution then were primarily about skill, not gender, and they do not mention women as such at all. Much dilution did involve men without completed apprenticeships, so the question of dilution cannot be reduced to the question of the introduction of women, any more than all women should be assumed to have been replacing skilled men on diluted tasks.

In 1915, after a major scandal about the production of shells, a new government investigated the possibility of reorganizing production and conscription. The two were integrally related. The cabinet rejected all alternatives in favour of women, whom they were already being urged to employ by women's organizations of the left, worried about unemployment, and of the right, worried about prostitution. In March the Women's War Register was set up to enrol women, whatever their labour history, for war-work.[12] The Ministry of Munitions was set up in May as soon as the trade unions, led by the Amalgamated Society of Engineers, had signed the Treasury Agreement that, in exchange for an industrial truce and accepting dilution, they would have a guarantee of equal pay for dilutees doing men's work. Government did not thereby get the kind of direct control over the labour market which some had advocated, since enlisting women was not the same as training them, and agreeing equal pay for some women was not the same as ensuring that they got equal earnings. Trade unions and employers were essential for the smooth acceptance of the scheme and for running it in practice. Women's organizations participated in the celebrations of the new war register, the equal pay agreement and the labour exchanges with mixed feelings. Many women were opposed to the war, which they regarded as man-made, and the biggest suffrage organization split on the subject. The Women's Social and Political Union on the other hand, which was the leading non-constitutional suffrage organization, had been largely responsible for organizing the march of women demanding the 'Right to Serve'. Emmeline Pankhurst had negotiated a substantial sum from Lloyd George to pay for costumes and publicity. They had originally called the march a 'Right to Work' march, but that presumably had too many connotations of male demands of 1908 marches against unemployment.[13]

The existing skills of industrial women were hidden by this process. Willingness to work had really never been in doubt, but the capacity to replace skilled engineers in munitions factories was, and incapacity was emphasized by the description of all women as in the same position. In war all their other characteristics became submerged in a general, and generalized, relationship to the labour market of wartime. Mary Macarthur had described women workers as 'meantime' workers, in the labour force between school and marriage; they now became 'meantime' for the period of war. Differences of labour history, social class or racial or regional origin were submerged in descriptions of them as gendered labour power. The discourse of the day, and the shaping of experience that four years of war gave to their lives, meant their temporary status was always included in the description which linked their gender to their role as workers in wartime. All working women tended to be referred to as women war-workers, and many used the compound phrase themselves.

Organizing Women

Trade unions anticipated exploitation as a consequence of the mass enrolment of inexperienced women factory workers. The anonymous official historian of the Ministry of Munitions described it thus:

> women were badly organised, prone to manipulation by employers, ignorant of workshop practices, in particular defensive, restrictive practices; and content to work in lowly position for low pay. Women did

not enjoy the protection of custom, they were not organised in strong Trade Unions nor could such organisations be built up in an emergency.[14]

This account represents the view of male trade unionists as represented in the War Emergency Workers' National Committee, as well as government and employers. Most importantly for the impact of change on women themselves, it represented the views to some extent of trade unions organizing women. For them it was an opportunity to improve organization among women, and thus demonstrate that these were not innate characteristics of the woman worker, but contingent upon a history when women had had much less opportunity to exploit labour shortage in their own interests. The education and propaganda of women trade union leaders similarly emphasized inexperience in women, their lack of training and need for organization. High unemployment in the first years of war gave support to this position, which meant that women were seen as recipients of change, rather than innovators in their own right.[15] When the process of dilution was being discussed by employers and trade unions in engineering and shipbuilding, 'No representative of the women was consulted: and this was not unreasonable in itself as the women at the time had no *locus standi* in the matter', as Mary Macarthur wrote in 1918.[16]

Yet the introduction of dilution in 1915 through the Defence of the Realm Act (DORA) and the Munitions of War Act of March 1915 had removed several important rights for organized labour. No employee could leave a job on munitions without an employer's certificate, strike action was outlawed, and pay was detached from the workplace and subject to government scrutiny in tribunals.[17] Dilution was introduced after agreement in May 1915, and the discussion about what it meant in practice continued throughout the war, but most closely affected women's experience of the wartime workplace in the year after the Treasury agreement.[18] Once conscription was introduced in 1916, the issue shifted from skilled men's work being done by women to substitution, a woman replacing an unskilled or semi-skilled man for the war effort. The views of women's organizations at this time have to be interpreted as recognizing that war-work was not the same in legal status or public discourse throughout the war. Much of the discussion of work and work process is actually about more general issues than whether women are or are not engaged in technological change.

The first agreement on dilution was signed in November 1914 between Vickers, a major armaments firm, and the Amalgamated Society of Engineers, at Crayford. Dilution was to be limited to women working on automatic machines,[19] which therefore meant more shells could be produced, but any expansion would increase or maintain the need for skilled engineers who set and mended the machines these women used. Women in engineering already worked on mass production tasks making fuses, cartridges and bullets, so their representatives would have been seen as irrelevant to the discussion. Women were lined up in this way with unskilled men, and both groups of the unskilled seen as having no identity of interest with skilled men. The Treasury agreement of 1915 formalized this by giving the TUC formal control over its own members 'that the existing supply of labour be more economically used',[20] and ensuring that dilutees should be the first to leave their jobs. Dilutees were used only for the duration of war, subject to arbitration to make up for the loss of collective bargaining by strike and superintended by a National Labour Advisory Committee.

In March 1916, government moved into manufacture in its own right as well as exercising more extensive control over existing armaments manufactures. The hated leaving certificate system was to be replaced by conscription with a system of reserved occupations for men and voluntary registration for war-work. Government had moved into control of the labour supply, which effectively was to mean the new resource provided by the mass mobilization of women.[21] The basic assumption of the negotiations was that women (and all diluted labour) would never equal skilled men in quantity or quality of output so that if the skilled man's level of pay was protected employers would return to their pre-war workers with great relief when war was over. Only Sylvia Pankhurst, organizer of the tiny socialist organization aimed at the East End of London, noticed initially that the agreement of 1915 could cause major problems in holding rates at pre-war levels.[22] The Treasury agreement read: 'The Agreement stated shall not adversely affect the rates customarily paid for the job and the rates paid shall be the usual rate of the district for this class of work'.[23]

The problem was how to define 'customarily' and 'district'. In South London and nearby, there were two customs side by side; in Woolwich and neighbouring Erith and Abbey Wood, all munitions processes were done by men and boys at the Royal Arsenal, while at Vickers, which was privately owned, women worked on fuses and cartridges, particularly in paper and chemical filling, rather than engineering.[24] It was engineering that posed the most difficult problems of definition. Engineers went through frequent changes in the rate at which a job was paid, and the speed expected of each job. Custom could be of a duration less than two weeks.[25]The agreement anticipated the regularity of mass production that war was to create. In effect it left the fixing of wages, especially for dilutees, to negotiation. Hence the enormous importance attached to unionization of war-workers by existing union members.

Nationally this debate was temporarily subdued by the introduction of circular L2. This fixed a guaranteed time-rate to women on men's work of £1 for a 48-hour week, with overtime rates on a proportionate basis.[26] Government thus now took steps to enforce this wage in all munitions industries – a new step in Britain. The debate over dilution has often been characterized as a debate over equal pay. It was widely believed, at the time, that women war-workers had been promised equal pay on men's work, and this belief has been reproduced by some historians.[27] In fact it was not until government orders on pay were consolidated as Statutory Order 885 in 1917, that even dilutees were guaranteed the minimum rate of L2. In many factories, especially ones with new wartime production and therefore neither customs nor a usual rate for the job, L2 created a minimum that speedily became a maximum. Both in theory and practice, women were seen as needing a safety net, to prevent them becoming what contemporaries called 'sweated labour', rather than equal pay. For women trade unionists these negotiations did not deal with the issues that were to be central to their members: actual, rather than minimum, rates of pay; working conditions; the future of their jobs. They also entirely ignored the much greater number of women doing war-work who were replacing men not as dilutees but as substitutes, or in entirely new wartime occupations. This was not seen as a problem until large proportions of these women were organized in trade unions and pressed their claims. In July 1916 they got the same sort of safety net as dilutees. Women on women's work were to get a basic hourly rate of 4½d on time-work, and 4d on piece-work or the premium bonus system. In 1919 it was said that this order, 447, 'aroused more antagonism among employers than circular L2'.[28] This resentment was because there was no shortage of unskilled women workers except briefly over the winter of 1915/16, and they cost as much in extra expenditure on canteens, lavatories and changing-rooms as women replacing skilled men.

The benefits of these proceedings for women were not in the rates, which were very low compared to men's rates, but in the principle of government protection. In looking at discussions of women workers on munitions, the question of whether innovation took place always has to be seen in the context of the discussions about pay. The status of the worker, and therefore her bargaining power, was vitally affected by her relation to a male worker, rather than any independent assessment of her skills. This is underlined by the question of *when* women entered the workforce, since many more did so before they had firm agreements, and therefore government protection, than afterwards.

Women Working for Patriotic Reasons

The workforce altered less than contemporary accounts might seem to indicate. From July 1914 to July 1915, 382,000 entered, while the next year saw 563,000. The change seemed larger than it was because they became a much larger proportion of the workforce; by July 1916 they were already 26.5 per cent, while by July 1917 they were 45.9 per cent. How many of these workers were doing work that was new to women? The Standing Joint Committee of Women's Industrial Organisations (SJCWIO) argued in their 1916 report on the substitution of women that it was irrelevant.[29] They thought there was no real distinction between an increase because women replaced men, or one because the workforce was expanding; or, if women were replacing men, what the category of work on which they were doing so really was. They claimed that the Board of Trade's *Labour Gazette* exaggerated the inexperience of women war-workers, because so much of women's occupational experience was not previously in their sights, being in small, unrecorded workplaces or in domestic work. SJCWIO wrote that the *Labour Gazette* overestimated 'the middle class women who would not normally become wage earners [and] the return of married and widowed women for patriotic reasons'. The SJCWIO argued that the effect of this distortion was to maximize the impression of industrial inexperience and encourage employers to exploit women.

There were large numbers of women who moved within industry. Employers in traditionally female industries complained that they were losing their workers to the lure of munitions. As the Ministry of Munitions monitoring of the labour supply noted in December 1915, 'They do not find the supplies of labour at existing rates of wages adequate to meet their demands and ... in fact there is at present a shortage of women';[30] and in February 1916, 'Although the women who would normally be engaged in industrial work are now all fully occupied, there are large reserves of women, principally married, who have had previous industrial experience, and who could be utilised in *special circumstances*' [emphasis in original].[31]

The impression that government did not know what it was doing is borne out by these quotations, since they simply did not know what would move women back into production. Women were recruited from rural areas, particularly Ireland, and were housed in some munitions areas by building hostels.[32] The major influence on women's recruitment, though, was their relation to the family economy. The Board of Trade reported in 1915 that, because of the high wages earned by men, women did not feel the need to work in munitions areas. A month later they noted women were keeping more at home, 'a fact due to the large number of soldiers billeted in the division'.[33] Servicemen earned low wages and dependants' allowances were low too – 11s 6d for a woman with two children, 6d extra for each child under 10. Areas of high male unemployment were often, though not necessarily, areas of high enlistment; they were often areas of high women's unemployment too.

The debate over dilution focused on women workers as replacements for men at work. But it took place in a fluctuating labour market, and in the context of debate over all women's domestic activity and social roles, as well as their paid labour. By the time government regulated women's employment, most women had made a choice already about how to deal with wartime demands. They had already decided to enter factory work or to move to an area of labour shortage, because they had to do so. Trade unionists were quick to perceive some of the implications of this change, but slow to recognize that some change was in the attitudes, aspirations and mobility of women themselves. Mary Macarthur, for example, addressing a trade union audience, agreed with some of the old attitudes.

> Women could not do the work of men and in some industries that was true. There were occupations that she would be sorry to see women undertake (Hear, Hear) and they were objected to on the ground that they were cheap, and it was a natural objection to be met in only one way, namely where they did men's work they should have men's pay.

The newspaper reporting this speech interpreted her speech as arguing that 'from heavy work women must be barred, while less arduous work must be made easier if they are to do it; but where they do work equally with men they ought to have equal pay for it'.[34] The elision between some unsuitable jobs and all heavy work was common at the time and shows the inflexibility of thinking about women's labour that was still common in 1915. Later in her speech Macarthur pointed out how war had demonstrated society's need for the manual worker. 'They now saw how important the common people were.' Throughout the war, women were to be discussed as Macarthur did here – either in relation to the male workers they replaced, or as heroines for the meantime doing an unnatural job for patriotic reasons.

At the 1915 TUC women's work was unusually high on the agenda. A resolution on unsuitable trades was passed unanimously.

> That, in order to sustain the physique of Britain and to prevent physical degeneration, no relaxation of Trade Union rules shall lead to the employment of women on work of a charter unsuited by
> 1. carrying or turning over weights or operated by heavy foot pressure;
> 2. employment on hot or dusty trades in which lime, oil, grease, fire sand or emery are used;
> 3. or on heavy machinery producing fatigue, or such machines where often male employment produces a large number of accidents.[35]

This was a pious hope. All these conditions occurred in at least one of the trades on which women were engaged. Lloyd George pamphlets on women's work, and the dilution photographs at the Imperial War Museum, show that they were broken by women who were coal heavers, navvies, lathe operators, chemical workers, vehicle maintenance workers, pottery-makers, clockmakers and munition workers. The TUC was not very bothered by the practice of wartime, because of all the agreements which suspended these protections for the duration. When TNT turned out to be toxic, and therefore more dangerous than the explosive lyddite which it replaced, the TUC had little to say. They were in this context fairly reluctant to speak for the national racial stock or other abstractions. The physique of Britain was therefore a highly negotiable concept in wartime, because of the advances for labour possible amidst extreme labour shortage. When they discussed dilution, this centrality of union organization and its dominance over other conditions became clear.

> This Congress recognises the dangers that are likely to arise from the wholesale introduction of women emergency war workers in the engineering trades and is of the opinion that to facilitate the replacement at the close of the war of women by more suitable male labour and the returning of women to industrial pursuits more fitting generally, local committees should be established for each suitable area which should include representatives from the employers' and workers' organisations in the trade together with representatives of the women's labour organisations.

Figure 6.1 Women workers on cranes working with large shells, one of the few groups who got equal pay because they were so visibly doing men's work, in trousers

This resolution clearly separated women from workers and left unstated either the dangers of war-work or the more fitting post-war occupations that were to succeed it. Those who voted against the motion were the general unions, while the craft and industrial unions supported it. On the same day, two resolutions on equal pay and the need for more trade union organization among women were carried with no dissenting voices.[36] But the crucial question for trade unions was who should organize the women? The Amalgamated Society of Engineers (ASE) concluded an agreement with the National Federation of Women Workers (NFWW) that they should organize women war-workers in engineering and that they would assist with recruitment in exchange for the federation's commitment to hand back all diluted jobs done in wartime by their members.[37]

The General Federation of Trade Unions (GFTU), on the other hand, argued for unionization as in the interests of both women and men. First they argued for a war 'ticket' in April 1915 'for women as war-workers on the grounds that unorganised women workers are dangerous, and might be used to reduce the wages of the men'. Appleton, GFTU general secretary, went on to say:

> There is a danger when you have a lot of women in an occupation in which they have not been employed previously, and have no commercial knowledge of the value of their work, that they may be exploited, and not only their conditions but the general conditions made very much worse.[38]

Addressed as a danger and always characterized as affecting men rather than themselves, it is perhaps not surprising that women learned not to be *workers*, new to factory life with all the problems of any novice group of workers, but *women war-workers*, inherently temporary and dealt with as agents in deteriorating the working of their male colleagues in the factory.

There were those who argued against these preconceptions of dilution and of women workers as implicit in dilution. The *Daily Herald* attacked male intransigence. 'Loyalty to any one nation, class or sex is noble only so long as it is a weapon against the oppressor: it becomes a vice as soon as it closes the door of equality against the oppressed'.[39] Alice Smith defended women:

> the average woman worker is an instinctive rather than a conscious trade unionist. Her inexperience leads to a mistrust of officials and she distrusts her own capacity to organise others in her trade union. In my trade union of 22 thousand, 19 thousand are women, all the officers are men.[40]

This defence simply displaced the problem of innateness from work to trade union organization. Women had to create forces for their own protection and simultaneously carry the organization of women in order to protect men's jobs. Inexperience was a transitory phase in an individual's working life, but seen therefore as describing all war-workers however experienced they might be in other forms of industry, and therefore all women.

Dilution was carried out almost without careful monitoring or discussion of principle at all. Lord George Askwith wrote in 1920:

> My view is that in labour matters the Government had no policy, never gave any sign of having a policy, could not be induced to have a policy. The departments never followed any policy in labour matters except of disintegration.[41]

The left feared a policy aimed at attacking union organization and saw the new woman worker as a main weapon in the attack. They were particularly fearful of the extension of government control involved in the entry of government into manufacture through the creation of a Ministry of Munitions. Mary Macarthur, a left-wing member of the ILP, described its introduction as coming 'like a thief in the night'. The introduction of female labour into new forms of work thus became inextricably entwined with debates about state power and the militarism of Britain. 'Dilution of labour was only supposed to increase production. But undoubtedly it has been used to regiment the workers and cheapen labour'.[42]

Employers were encouraged to take advantage of the new supply of female workers by seeing descriptions of every single task newly performed by dilutees, increasingly female in fact, entirely female in propaganda because only a woman doing the task sufficiently dramatized the change. Each dilution officer had a loose-leaf handbook through which the daily novelty of women's industrial innovation could be portrayed. Exhibitions, photographs, and a group of women actually performing tasks toured the country. Two pamphlets, *The Employment of Women on Munition Work* and a companion on non-munitions work, were produced to make the same point. Forty thousand copies were sold or given away. Women's work became visible in a new way.[43] Even posters made women seem central to production *in war-work*: 'Do Your Bit', 'Replace a Man for the Front'. Popular fiction moved from the staple mill-worker or domestic servant to war-work.[44]

Employers were actually quite resistant to this process. They were happy to dilute but not necessarily to introduce women into the workshops. 'Dilution is for the purpose of increasing output and not of reducing labour costs'.[45] Women were increasingly contrasted not with men but with boys – the other group potentially able to make good the shortfall in skilled labour. The comment of a Vickers' works manager was widely reproduced to convince employers that women were better dilutees because they had the merits of not being serious workers:

> girls are much more diligent on work within their capacity than boys ... the boys are naturally expecting to become fully-fledged mechanics and are not content to stay on one job indefinitely; moreover they have great curiosity, and it is impossible to prevent them continually looking

around, whilst the girls, as a rule, do not enter the factory with the idea of staying for more than a few years, and concentrate their attention on attaining dexterity at the particular job they are set to.[46]

Trade unionists were given support for their belief about how highly a worker was gendered in her attitudes to work by these plaudits which emphasized docility and acquiescence. More and more women were classified as dilutees as the definition of work susceptible to regulation as munitions work increased. Skilled workers found it tolerable because of trade union agreement about their withdrawal after war and the commitment to equal pay. In the short term they also benefited directly from increases in output.

> The male operator is responsible for both machines, and the total price paid for the product of the two lathes is the same as was originally paid when two men worked these two machines. The man gives the women every possible assistance and when the total earnings of the two machines are distributed, the division is such as to considerably increase the earnings of the male workers.[47]

Despite this, not all women found it easy to enter a male workplace and many met verbal abuse, and sometimes also physical abuse, on their introduction. Some men argued that women simply could not do the work, although production soared as mass production entered munitions manufacture.

> In many workshops it can safely be said that the women are not a success. As a matter of fact, in some places there has been no attempt to make them a success. They are consequently treated with amused contempt as passengers for the war.[48]

Women union representatives were in the forefront of defining what women were as workers, but they took different tactics for dealing with that sort of contempt. The NFWW dominated the journals, newspapers, government bodies and the TUC, but its policy was more clearly defined by other trade unions than by its members. They revived their paper, the *Woman Worker*, in 1916, and enrolled a large number of wartime organizers. The ASE helped in this drive for members. One slogan was: 'Join the great industrial army. Don't blackleg your man in Flanders'.[49]

There was an implicit maternalism about the assumption that the woman worker was an inexperienced child. Margaret Bondfield, working for the NFWW, told a meeting: 'Every mother must get her daughter a union card'.[50] This was successful in terms of membership levels and a common union interest between men and women. 'Some of our branches have been literally made by the ASE men'.[51] Mary Macarthur, their leader, accepted these constraints as she accepted the need to exclude war-workers after the war. Her philosophy was much like that of other women's organizations at the time: pro-natalist, feminist

Figure 6.2 Women workers in the tailoring shops, doing work traditionally defined as skilled men's work (although it involves sewing and is very like other sorts of women's work) but paid at equal rates by trade union agreement.

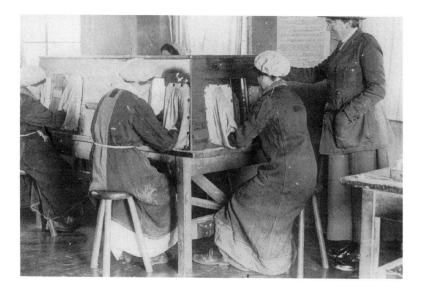

Figure 6.3 Women in the danger buildings with the welfare superintendent, Lilian Barker. Although this was danger work it was actually not men's work; it had been done by women in the district before the war, so it was paid the women's rate.

and pragmatic. 'Women are at heart conservative, but conservative in the best sense of the word. They desire above all else to conserve the race. Big questions of domestic policy will appeal to women insofar as they affect the welfare of children'.[52]

Other organizations for working women shared some of these principles, but rejected the implications about the essential difference between men and women as workers. The Workers' Union (WU) had organized women making armaments before the war, and they too saw war as an opportunity to turn previously unorganized low-paid women into workers. They organized men and women together in some cases in mixed branches, in other cases separately. Julia Varley, their leading women's organizer, argued: 'Both sexes should pay in the same book and both meet in the same room'. The WU saw war as a 'lever for progress'.[53] The editor of the union journal argued in July 1915:

> Then the women's question. The woman is going to stay after the war. Why not? If she has undercut the man in the past it is the man's fault. His conceit of his craft has led him to take up an attitude of contempt and both have suffered in consequence. If the women have been poor trade unionists it is due to the indifference of the men. Generally speaking, the men have not, until the last few years taken the slightest interest in teaching the women Trade Union principles.[54]

As a leading member argued:

> woman is bringing revolution into the industrial world, she is going to be responsible for an amazing increase in the powers of production, one to which that of the 18th century will be clean lost by comparison and she is going to be on our side.[55]

He thus demonstrated yet again, that even for the most sympathetic and enthusiastic supporter of women's industrial labour and wartime innovation in their placing in the workforce, women were not part of the 'us' of the workers, only a group who would be on the same side. Dilution was seen by such socialists as an exposing and educational process revealing the complexities and inequalities of industrial life. It would also tend to lead to unionization and hence also to be welcomed.

The Experience of War

Precisely because war-work was novel and could not be measured against tradition, women workers could exploit the situation to improve trade union strength, or could be exploited by war to weaken trade unionism. The 'experience of war' was then profoundly ambiguous. Women's own experience of war was always mediated by how they entered it, who they worked beside and how far the skills they acquired were transferable. Women entered work, as before, through family and neighbours. Previous work operated in two ways. For married women, it excluded. Housework coarsened the hands and motherhood affected the frame so that sedentary, delicate work was ruled out by the welfare officers who processed new workers and allocated them to workshops. Married women cleaned railways and trams, built a shipyard, mended roads, made rope, and were porters. Many of them directly replaced a family member. Some skills were transferred into war-work. Cooks went into canteens for soldiers or munitions makers; sempstresses and nursery maids did these tasks in 'the wider worlds of the factory'. Organizing or clerical work fitted women for workshop labour as foreman or supervisor, typist or filing clerk. Most women workers in wartime were not new workers at all and even factory workers had often worked before, though very few had made munitions. Of the 110,628 women working in metal trades, excluding engineering and subject to the munitions acts, 53,249 had worked in the same trade before; 18,927 were previously unoccupied or in the household, and about 12,000 each came from other industries or domestic service.[56] In other words, the assumption of novelty was an ideological filter through which war-work was viewed, which affected the record in ways which make the experience difficult to recapture.

The industries which usually employed women complained of shortages of labour attracted away to munitions by patriotism and the high rate of wages.[57] Dilution continued on munitions-related tasks. Many of these women, popularly described as dilutees, were in fact substitutes, and they met both verbal and physical abuse. In Liverpool women were marched into the docks under armed guard but still suffered stone-throwing. This experience only lasted for ten days, but it must have been frightening.[58] Women involved in this process were beginning to redefine what it meant to be a worker, and ignore the banalities of arguments about sexual difference that had caused problems in the past. When women were accused of accepting low pay at the Railway Clerks' conference, a delegate demanded male clerks' help: 'They should work together as workers, not exactly as men and women, to raise the standard of life together'.[59] Tram drivers' unions organized women on trams despite their initial reluctance to believe that women would be safe if they drove as fast as men.[60] The tendency of all this debate was to accept the principle of sexual difference enshrined in the wage system, to assume inexperience and prescribe unionization as the solution. Protectionism was allied to feminist arguments about equal pay and pro-natalism to create a remarkable consensus. Once dilution was well under way the Ministry of Munitions began to address the practices of women workers rather than the theory of their introduction to work. The Health of Munitions Workers Committee charted the activities of women workers in their regular reports. In a pamphlet on the employment of women they recorded:

> [T]he report reveals many instances of the devotion and enthusiasm of women workers. It is notable that this is the characteristic of no one class in a movement which knows no class distinction. These woman

have accepted conditions of work which if continued must ultimately be disastrous to health.[61]

Women in engineering were actually part of a pre-war move towards the introduction of machine tools and the increase in semi-skilled workers to use them. The historian of the ASE sees the 'minor revolution in workshop practice'[62] happening before 1914. W.F. Watson wrote a book called, quite deliberately, *Men and Machines*, about his life as an engineer, in which the war features as a background to strike action but not as a period of women's labour.[63] The growth in the workforce in engineering was from skilled to semi-skilled: while the proportion of unskilled workers remained at 20 per cent, that of semi-skilled increased from 20 per cent to 30 per cent while the proportion of skilled men fell from 60 per cent to 50 per cent.[64] Insofar as women were briefly part of the semi-skilled workforce they were part of this change. However, G.D.H. Cole in his account indicates neatly that the need to make munitions quickly did not encourage certain kinds of innovation at work: 'Even when new factories were built, or new plants installed, specifically for women, the form, design and methods of operation were mainly influenced by traditions made by men for men'.[65]

Cole was, unlike most observers of the period, not tied to any particular interests in this debate, except insofar as his guild socialism led to his favouring some general notion of the workers – which included women but did not privilege them. The question of how far women did enter certain skilled occupations was to cause controversy later in 1918 when a Committee of the War Cabinet assessed women in industry in order to let the government off the hook, as they had broken their promise to give such women equal pay. More than most such questions then, the question of how far women *did* innovate in industrial production needs to be asked very carefully – dependent upon the interests of the witness. The ASE continued to argue that most of what women were doing was women's work anyway and had been before the war, but even they felt that increased welfare provision, greater public scrutiny and the growing confidence of women workers meant that this assumption that not much had changed was untenable. It was argued in the union journal of the ASE in 1915 that 'the innovations [of the shells and fuses agreement] are not so real as they appear, as female labour has been engaged in the manufacture of these products in many parts of the country for some time'.[66]

The 'problem' of women's labour was thus demonstrably seen by the ASE as its trespass upon the work done by ASE members, when it left areas previously designated as women's work. Hence what was actually going on in those areas, where woman had been working before, received very little attention and rarely reached into the deliberations of officials or thence into the historical record. The 'women's work' so much reported in wartime was the work that was likely to lead to strikes, that dilution officers described minutely with photographs to convince employers that women could do it, that was the subject of trade union agreement and discussion. This work was war-work and it was so described and regulated because it was seen as for the duration only, and discussed in the interests of the men they had nominally replaced. Much of it indeed was temporary because it was war production and redundant in time of peace. The mass production of shells, bullets and armour plating ended with the declaration of peace in November. New types of production that women had done in wartime, such as arc welding and large gun making, did continue after the war, as did the development of less flimsy aircraft late in the war. These tasks, with all the technical innovation they had created, were taken by male trade unionists, with the consent of women members of trade unions, especially the Women's Trade Union League, that they were men's work and should therefore be returned to men. This price the unionists felt worth paying for the recognition of women as full members of the trade union movement in peacetime. It was more important to these union leaders to prove that women would not undercut male wages and conditions by staying in these areas of work, than it was to protect the interest of a handful of their members doing these new trades.

Novelty and Technological Excitement

The innovation and the technological change were implicit in the practices of government and employers. The changes were in trade union practice and behaviour, not in the work process itself, which, despite the development of mass production in industries where the task had previously been undertaken by craftsmen with semi-skilled assistants, was little affected by the war. Machinery for war use was not new. Whence comes the impression of novelty, of technological excitement, evident in so many accounts? It derives from many factors. First is probably the novel attention played to technology, particularly that created by dilution. These women were measured as workers, photographed, displayed, praised and held up as heroines – not just as any workers but as dilutees. Their own awareness of their work in oral testimony is all of themselves as replacements for men, doing the men's work as dilutees, although the jobs they were doing, making bullets for example, were actually described as women's work because women had mostly performed the same task, although more slowly, before the war. Even when the task was new it was reduced to male or female work by analogy, as with arc welding, which was completely new and, in wartime, almost entirely done by women. Most women interviewed from the Woolwich Arsenal, and the few from Vickers' works at Erith or Crayford nearby, had enjoyed their work and could reproduce its patterns after sixty years. Most thought they had done a man's job, but only two had wanted to go on working in the same sort of work once peace was declared. Those who were trade unionists had acquired that knowledge in wartime mostly through disputes about welfare supervisors, canteen arrangements or tea-breaks. A few had struck work for equal pay in 1917, but not one spoke of wanting to use or learn new technological skills. The work was their war-work and it was described only negatively as bearing any relation to a future career – in that it ruined some women's chances of domestic work or needlework because of the effects on respectability of war-work in a factory or the direct physical effects of war-work on the hands.

Women had learnt to be workers as part of a vast, de-individuated cohort of women war-workers. They were in uniform, or specialized work clothing, often making the transition between work and outside through an institutional cleansing and transformation of great rigour involving the move from clean to dirty sides of the workplace. They had to leave all hair ornaments, jewellery, purses, cigarettes and lighters behind. One woman even got six months' hard labour for taking matches into her work in the danger buildings. The work was organized for safety to keep it as far away from the normalities of factory life as possible. It was dangerous and its boundaries were very strictly maintained. Women were set apart still further if they worked with TNT which dyed the skin yellow and made them instantly visible as munitions workers. The culture of the workplace, although it was often highly organized in trade unions, and of war factory mass production work itself emphasized the separateness of the workers from everyday concerns and was peculiar to wartime. Although contemporaries worried about militarization of the workplace, they had no need to fear the transfer of these modes of operations into peace, because they had been so specific to the war. Although individual women had learned to think of themselves as workers, most thought of the experience as one that they had enjoyed and valued and yet never wished to repeat. It had been an experience of war rather than of work that they remembered. 'Our place in industry in the future depends upon our determination not to undersell the men or to undermine the family standard of life', argued Mary Macarthur in 1918 at a march for unemployment benefit on equal terms with men called 'The Right to Work, the Right to Life, the Right to Leisure'.[67] This discourse of the social rather than the particularities of differing workplaces explains how far the experience of war shaped the experience of war-work and means that women of very diverse experiences at work did legitimately prioritize their gender rather than their work as the basis for political claims. The change was in the technology of people management and the real beneficiaries of it were the managers, the welfare supervisors and the technicians of health in the Health of Munition Workers Committee. Women munition workers had contributed to that change but they did not have enough time to do more than that to affect technology – a fact for which they were indeed grateful. The women's own contribution was in the formation and support, for a few years more, of female industrial unionism – but this too owed little to technology and much to pre-war factors. Until the significance of political and social factors affecting the employment of dilutees on munitions work is recognized, the experience of that work cannot be measured.

Conclusion

Women's work in wartime is the subject of intense ideological negotiation, not least among the representatives of those women, and it cannot be depoliticized as if the workplace and civil society remain forever separated. To introduce women to areas of work new to them is inevitably to change the women and the workplace but the effects are greater outside the workplace than within it if the introduction is for a period of war, making war materials, because they are no longer necessary once peace is declared. Women's own memories of this period are overlaid with the memories important to them which are those of home, family and friends and then of a brief period in a working life that is also, for them, the war. Even though they can reproduce bodily the activities they did sixty years ago they cannot usually describe them verbally. The pictures we have of the women working on munitions were all gathered for a temporary, pragmatic purpose and the infant science of work study directed towards the imperative needs of war productions. Concerns for women's social role were suspended between 1915 and 1917 because of labour shortage but they were not removed, and they were concerns through which these women too formulated their own reactions to the experience. Although there were a very few who wanted more training and more work and preferred factory work on adjusted machines to their later experience of paid employment, they were a tiny minority and met with virtually no supportive response. The patterns of dilution had been laid down to ensure that there should be no specific work to be taken from war to peace, hence technological change in time of war, limited anyway by the short-term nature of war planning, did not endure into the peace. It is only by assessing technological change in its wider context that we can ensure that the propaganda put out by employers and government does not mislead later generations into ignoring the women's own viewpoint and recollections. Some of the discourse of work is as difficult to understand as other discourses of gender. Labour history has been limited by its own boundaries and by a misleading and disempowering acceptance of separate spheres for too long. One of the most valuable aspects of studying women is the refusal to allow such historic separations to mislead.

Notes

1 Thom, D. (1989) 'Women's Employment in Britain', in Winter, J. and Wall, R. (Eds) *The Upheaval of War*, Cambridge.
2 Thompson, P. (1974) *The Edwardians*, London.
3 Braybon, G. (1981) *Women Workers in the First World War*, London and New Jersey.
4 *Women's Trade Union League Journal*, Oct. 1916, pp. 5–6.
5 Parliamentary Papers 1919, xii, Cmd 135, Report of the War Cabinet Committee on Women in Industry. Parliamentary Papers 1919, xii, Cmd 167, Summaries of evidence to the above.

6 Winston Churchill, Minister of Munitions, in both MUN.5.52.78 and MUN 2.21, cited in vol.VII of the Official History of the Ministry of Munitions, *A History of State Manufacture*, at the Public Record Office. The collection of the Ministry of Munitions files is hereafter cited as MUN, the Imperial War Museum collections as IWM, and the Gertrude Tuckwell collection of documents on women's trade unionism at the Trades Union Congress Library as GT. All sources are in London.

7 Ineson, A. and Thom, D. (1985) 'Women Munition Workers and TNT Poisoning in the First World War', in Weindling, P. (Ed.) *A History of Occupational Health*, London.

8 Watson, W.F. (1935) *Machines and Men*, London, pp. 12–15, 60, 74–5.

9 Cole, G.D.H. (1923) *Workshop Organisation*, Oxford, p. 48.

10 *Labour Gazette*, monthly digest of information from the Board of Trade.

11 For a clear account of the relationship see Hinton, J. (1973) *The First Shop Stewards' Movement*, London.

12 See my unpublished thesis, *The Ideology of Women's Work in Britain, 1914–1924, with Special Reference to the NFWW and other Trade Unions*, CNAA at Thames Polytechnic, 1982.

13 Pankhurst, E.S. (1931) *The Suffragette Movement*, London, p. 506. MUN, 5, 70.26, records of meetings between Lloyd George and Emmeline Pankhurst, 11 and 28 Aug, 1915.

14 Official History of the Ministry of Munitions, henceforward cited as MMOH, vol. IV, pt 1, p. 57.

15 Thom, D. (1986) 'The Bundle of Sticks', in John, A. (Ed.) *Unequal Opportunities*, Oxford.

16 Macarthur, M. 'The Women Trade Unionists' Point of View', in Phillips, M. (Ed.) (1918) *Women and the Labour Party*, London, pp. 18–28, at p. 22.

17 Lloyd, E.H.M. (1924) *Experiments in State Control*, Oxford, p. 22.

18 Wolfe, H. (1923) *Labour Supply and Regulation*, Oxford, p. 20.

19 Drake, B. (1918) *Women in Engineering*, London, p. 17; Cole, G.D.H. (1923) *Trade Unionism and Munitions*, Oxford, pp. 53–4.

20 ASE Monthly Journal and Report, July 1915, cited in Hinton (1973) (see note 11), p. 196.

21 PP 1919, XXIII, Cmd 185, 12th Report on Conciliation and Arbitration, pp. 8–9.

22 Pankhurst, E.S. (1932) *The Home Front*, London, p. 232.

23 *Ibid.*, p. 10.

24 Scott, J.D. (1963) *Vickers – a History*, London.

25 MUN 5.53.91, Report of a visit of Woolwich Shop Stewards to the Ministry of Munitions, 18 July 1917.

26 Circular L2 from Beveridge papers at the British Library for Economics and Political Science, London School of Economics (hereafter cited as BLEPS). Drake (1918) (see note 19), p. 18; Andrews, I. and Hobbs, M. (1921) *The Economic Effects of the War on Women and Children*, New York, pp. 140–6.

27 Marwick, A. (1975) *Women at War*, London, p. 57; Milward, A.S. (1970) *The Economic Effects of Two World Wars on Britain*, London.

28 Drake, B. (1919) Historical memorandum to the War Cabinet Committee on Women in Industry, PP 1919, xxiii, Cmd. 135, pp. 108–12.

29 IWM, Emp. 4, 28/2, Standing Joint Commitee of Women's Industrial Organisations, 'The position of women after the War', p. 4; *Labour Gazette*, July 1916.

30 MUN. 2,27, 11 Dec. 1915, p. 9.

31 MUN. 2,27, 5 Feb. 1916, p. 3.
32 Hammond, M.B. (1919) *British Labor Conditions and Legislation during the War*, New York, pp. 114–15.
33 *Labour Gazette*, Feb. 1915, p. 27; *Labour Gazette*, Mar. 1915, p. 79.
34 *Leicester Mercury*, 22 Nov. 1915 (GT).
35 GT 531, Bristol TUC, *Evening Times and Echo*, 11 Sept. 1915.
36 TUC Report, 1915, pp. 370–5.
37 ASE Monthly Journal and Report, June 1916; ASE Executive Committee minutes, cited in Hinton (1973) (see note 11), p. 72.
38 *Daily Call*, 9 April 1915, (GT).
39 *Daily Herald*, 28 Sept. 1915.
40 GT501, *Cotton Factory Times*, September 1915.
41 Askwith, G. (1920) *Industrial Problems and Disputes*, London, p. 443.
42 *Solidarity*, April 1917.
43 Thom, D. (1989) 'Free from Chains?', in Stedman Jones, G. and Feldman, D. (Eds) *Metropolis-London*, London.
44 IWM Women's employment on munitions collection. Marchant, B. (undated, 1918?) *A Girl Munition Worker*, London.
45 Macassey, I., memo. in BLEPS, Bev., vol.1, Dec.15.
46 MUN 2.27, Dilution Bulletin, Aug. 1916.
47 War Office, *The Employment of Women on Munitions Work*, section 2, p. 18.
48 Murphy, J.T. (1917) *The Workers' Committee*, London, pp. 17–18.
49 Women's Trade Union League (WTUL) Annual Report, 1916, pp. 5–6.
50 *Woman Worker*, Jan. 1916.
51 *Woman Worker*, Jan. 1916, p. 13.
52 Macarthur, M. (1918) (see note 16), pp. 18, 28.
53 *Workers' Union Record*, July 1915. p. 15.
54 *Workers' Union Record*, July 1915. p. 2.
55 *Workers' Union Record*, July 1916, p. 7.
56 *Labour Gazette*, Dec. 1917, p. 438.
57 IWM Emp. 20, Central Advisory Committee on Women's Employment, 1916 report, pp. 6–8.
58 GT, *Liverpool Post*, 17 March, 1916.
59 GT 504, *Birmingham Post*, 1915.
60 GT 504 (no date).
61 MUN 2.27, 12 Feb., citing the Health of Munitions Workers Committee pamphlet, *On the Employment of Women*; the same sentiment is expressed in BLEPS, Bev., vol.V, p. 161.
62 Jeffreys, J.B. (1946) *The Story of the Engineers*, London, p. 122.
63 Watson, W.F. (1935) *Machines and Men*, London.
64 Balfour Committee on Industry and Trade, *Survey of Industries*, vol.II, 1928, p. 152.
65 Cole, G.D.H. (1923) *Trade Unionism and Munitions*, Oxford, p. 217.
66 *ASE Monthly Journal and Report*, April 1915.
67 *Woman Worker*, Sept. 1918, p. 8.

Chapter 7

Gender and Technological Change in the North Staffordshire Pottery Industry

Jacqueline Sarsby

Since the second half of the eighteenth century, the most important concentration of English pottery factories has been in North Staffordshire in an area which is now the city of Stoke-on-Trent, still also known simply as 'the Potteries'. The reason for this is largely to do with the presence of coal. English forests had been steadily cut down from the Bronze Age onwards, as demands for agricultural land increased and, from the sixteenth century, maritime ventures multiplied. The resulting timber famine gave to North Staffordshire, which lay on a coalfield, the advantage of a seemingly inexhaustible supply of fuel for firing kilns. There was also a long-established tradition of pottery-making in the area and, with coal, clay and potters' skills, the eighteenth century saw the emergence of entrepreneurs and the development of canals which were to take Staffordshire wares into a national and international market.

Two centuries of pottery-making have seen change, not so much in the range in size of factories, which in the 1800s, as now, ranged from a handful of workers to over a thousand, but in the way that long-established family firms have been swallowed up, one after another, by international conglomerates with quite other interests than pottery. Although mechanization has taken over in tile-making and sanitary-ware, pottery factories which make tableware still vary very much in the extent to which they are craft-based or mechanized: more mechanization exists in the often highly prestigious factories of the large groups (in spite of the PR which surrounds them with an aura of tradition), but smaller, old-established firms and small new ones, with less fuss, often produce hand-crafted wares, which allow their workforce to exercise traditional skills.

This chapter deals with the areas of the industry, earthenware, china and fine china, where women are mostly concentrated. The other areas are sanitary-ware, tiles and electrical porcelain, but the numbers of men and women involved in these sections are far smaller than in earthenware and china. In December 1990, the Ceramic and Allied Trades Union represented approximately 18,500 workers in earthenware, and 8,500 in china, but only 1,200 in tiles, 700 in electrical

Jacqueline Sarsby

porcelain and 2,500 in sanitary-ware. For most of the twentieth century, more women than men have worked in the industry, but since the 1980s, the reverse is true, as it also was in the nineteenth century. The way that women have increased in numbers in the industry in the twentieth century, and the way that they are now, to some extent, losing their stronghold in it, are complex developments, depending on a number of different factors including technological change, but also including legislated access to education, union attitudes and organization, wartime shortages of male workers and rules about the decoration of ware, boom and slump in the industry, the cheapness of women's labour, and underlying much of this, notions of what is fit work for women, and of their proper place and responsibilities at home and at work. I shall examine some of the factors which have influenced and altered the sexual division of labour in the pottery factories, showing how technological change has meshed in with these factors, and trying to account for the attitudes which underpin women's perennially low wages.

From Clay to Pot

I begin by giving a brief explanation of how the raw materials become pots – cups, plates, teapots and tureens – as they pass through a factory. The clay and other materials are mixed and purified in the sliphouse, emerging finally from the pug-mill as a tube of clay without air bubbles or unwanted particles. Pots are made either by shaping this clay, or by casting liquid clay. Nowadays, a jug, for example, or a teapot, is cast (or 'casted' as people say in the Potteries) by pouring liquid clay into a plaster of paris mould, while a plate is made out of solid clay on a plate-making machine. Plates and saucers are flat-ware, and bowls and cups are hollow-ware, and all are 'made' or shaped in the making department, known as 'the clay end'. Next they are smoothed by sponging and fettling, and then fired at a high temperature in a kiln. They are then in 'biscuit-state', and are cleaned in a vibrating machine, or brushed by hand, and glazed by machine or dipped by hand in a tub of glaze, and fired again in the glost kiln. Nowadays, they are most usually decorated with water-slide transfers by lithographers, and fired again, then selected into first, second, and other quality wares, and packed in the warehouse. Under-glaze prints, as opposed to on-glaze litho-prints, are rubbed on to the wares with soapy brushes, and then the paper is washed off, before hardening and glazing. Recently, American lead-release laws have led to more use of under-glaze printing, in an effort to maintain exports to the United States.

The Early Potteries: The Golden Age of Myth-Making

Information about work in the early potteries is fairly sparse, but suggests that the craft was essentially a male occupation in the early eighteenth century.

Figure 7.1 Wedging the clay: a young woman throws a large piece of clay down on to another over and over again, until all the air has been knocked out of it.

Simeon Shaw, whose *History of the Staffordshire Potteries* was published in 1829, says:

> Up to 1740, in each manufactury, all the persons employed were the slip-maker, thrower, two turners, handler (stouker), fireman, warehouseman, and a few children, and, to be really useful to the master, and secure sufficient employment, a good workman could *throw, turn* and *stouk*.[1]

John Baddeley's *Day-book*, describing a pottery in the 1760s, also suggests that few women were employed, and that their wages were lower than men's. Craftsmen were paid about 9s per week, labourers between 5s and 6s, and two regular women workers between 2s 6d and 3s per week. Wives, working occasionally, earned 1s to 2s, and young people ('lads' and 'wenches') about 1s.[2]

With the expansion of a national market aimed at the aristocracy and the well-off middle class, the decoration of pottery became very important, and by about 1810, the Wedgwood Papers show that women were being taken on to paint, grind colours, gild, burnish and transfer printed patterns to the wares.[3] They also worked in the warehouse, and as 'scourers', an unhealthy job, rubbing the ware with brushes and sandpaper to clean off the flint particles which adhered to it during firing. They retained these as 'women's jobs' throughout the nineteenth century.

This period in the early to mid nineteenth century has become the Golden Age of myth-making about the pottery industry. Work was already divided up into dozens of processes in separate workshops, but it was not mechanized: even turning the thrower's wheel or the turner's lathe was performed by the muscle power of an attendant – who might be male or female.[4] Most of the processes were divided on gender lines, although young boys or girls could be attendants or painters, or work in the warehouse together. The female pottery-worker was archetypically a decorator, or a craftsman's attendant. She was very often a child.[5] Men, on the other hand, performed most of the skilled work in the 'clay end' or making end, working as claybeaters, slipmakers, turners, throwers, pressers, plate-, dish- and saucer-makers, moulders, modellers and dippers. They were also placers and firemen, working in and around the bottle ovens.

The myth, the comforting, collective memory, which is still rehearsed to justify women's lower wages, is that whole families worked together as teams in the nineteenth-century factories, with the husband (who was paid the wage for all of them) as craftsman and the wife and children as his attendants. Tradition, therefore, forbids that she should be paid as much as the craftsman himself, but because the father was paid by the employer for his team, there is some sort of comforting notion of a family wage. Reality was possibly rather different, even at this early stage. A list of workmen shows that in 1811, attendants, who in this case would have been boys, did not share the same surname as the men for whom they worked, and so were presumably not their sons.[6]

Marguerite Dupree has produced evidence which further undermines the cosy image of family work patterns. She says that in 1861 girls tended to leave the industry on marriage, and that the daughter of a miner was more likely than the daughter of a potter to be working on a potbank (pottery factory).[7] This is not to say that some women did not work for their husbands – we know that they did – but that such women were not the only typical female pottery-workers; many, it must be underlined, worked in all-female workshops, painting, gilding, burnishing and scouring, as well as transferring and doing warehouse work.

Scriven's 1842 *Report on the Employment of Children and Young Persons in Staffordshire Potteries*[8] further undermines the comfortable patriarchal image of work patterns by dwelling on the immorality of mixed workshops, 'emporiums of profligacy', and quoting the rector of Longton, who had observed: 'The young girls consorting with males in the works have no sense of the sin of whoredom, or of the bestiality of uncleanness'. In my own research, which deals through oral history with the period that living people can remember (from about 1910), I have found that family work patterns tended to be single-sex groups of mother and daughter or sisters working together.[9] None of this gives any justification for the very poor wages which women earned.

Withdrawal of Child Labour and the Introduction of New Machinery

Pottery factories used large numbers of children until prevented through legislation. The 1810 Wedgwood list of workers shows a workforce totalling 450, of whom 205 were men, 100 women and 145 children.[10] In 1842, Scriven's report to the Royal Commission on the Employment of Children and Young Persons in the District of the Staffordshire Potteries lists 12,407 workers with 978 boys and 522 girls under the age of 13.[11] In 1851, more than half the workforce were aged 18 or younger, and just under a quarter were children.[12]

Twice as many males as females worked in the industry in the nineteenth century. But in the last quarter of the century, the proportion of women increased: from 31 per cent in 1861 to 35 per cent in 1871 and 38 per cent in 1881. Women's labour increased when the output of pottery increased, and the industry was expanding at this time. Two further factors affected women's work: the withdrawal of child labour after the Factory Acts and the introduction of new machinery. Refering to the first, a Factory Inspector's report, quoted in Dupree, mentions 'girls being employed in those occupations which properly belong to boys'. Dupree also quotes the mayor of Hanley, who in 1875 told the Royal Commission on the Working of the Factory and Workshop Acts that the sexes were working more together 'owing to the fact that because of the Factory Act the supply of boys had been narrowed, and workmen had been obliged to get female labour.'[13]

The 1864 Factory Acts Extension Act had a major effect on the industry because, up until that time, the plentiful supply of children had lessened the need to mechanize. Steam power had been used for grinding materials and, in some factories, to turn throwing wheels and lathes, but the absence of machinery had meant that journeymen could work more or less what hours they pleased, and their attendants with them. Hours were now restricted to ten hours a day, no child under 8 was to work in the factories, and those under 13 were to go half-time to school. Women took over some of these jobs left by the wheel-turners, lathe-treaders and jiggerers, and steam power was used more widely, especially in new factories, in the sliphouse and the making-shop.

Mechanized blungers now appeared, and 'jolleys' started to be harnessed by means of ropes to steam engines worked by coal-boilers. The jolley is a machine which makes hollow-ware, such as bowls and cups, out of solid clay, in revolving moulds. Its widespread use in the 1880s brought women into the skilled areas of making in the clay end. If men refused to use the jolley, they discovered that women would be employed to use it instead of them.[14] Women also started working independently as flat-pressers (plate-makers) for the first time. Men objected to their doing this heavy work, but their objection was to women working independently in the clay end, rather than to the heaviness of their work.[15]

In the last quarter of the nineteenth century, therefore, technological change was one of the factors which brought more women into the clay end, but it in turn was the result of a combination of other factors – the expansion of trade, protective legislation and changing attitudes to child labour. It occurred in defiance of contemporary attitudes to women's labour. Men resisted changes in their skilled work, but women took the opportunity to compete for jobs in the making end or 'clay end', the traditional stronghold of men.

The introduction of the pug-mill in the last quarter of the nineteenth century mechanized a task which women had taken over when child labour was withdrawn. Earlier in the century, children had done the very arduous work of wedging, which consisted of repeatedly raising and flinging down large slabs of clay, to get rid of air bubbles. A submission to the Board of Arbitration (13 January 1877) suggests that at this period the lack of child labour led to more women working as attendants on their husbands: 'A good many men had their wives working with them, and it actually paid them to hire a nurse for their families'.[16] Thus, protective legislation had brought husbands and wives more together in the workplace, while children were less in the workshops, and more at home, or out to nurse, or at school. But mechanization could also lead to women working independently in competition with men, earning more than other women workers, but less than male workers.

Technological change sometimes involved a change of skill or deskilling for the craftsman, but could also mean the elimination of very arduous work for his or her attendant. During the first half of the twentieth century, a gradual change occurred from press-moulding to casting. This meant that at one time, men made teapots, for example, out of clay, pressed into shape, and that latterly they were made out of liquid clay or 'slip', poured into a plaster of paris mould. The changeover was gradual, affecting different potteries at different times.

Little Slaves

At the time of my research in the early 1980s, some people could remember pressing, jolleying and casting. I interviewed about seventy women pottery-workers in my research into the work and home lives of women pottery-workers, recording the life histories of twenty-two who had worked between the two world wars. I also interviewed some fathers, husbands and sons of pottery-workers, of whom the oldest was Mr Hilditch.[17] Mr Hilditch, who was born in 1901, told me that he had gone to work as a jigger-turner for a teapot-maker, when he was about 14. The jigger-turner, boy or girl, turned a horizontal wheel all day, so that the maker could make a teapot shape with a regular thickness of clay. The body would be made in two halves: 'You made the bottom half of the teapot. When you had done that, you put it to one side, and then you got another half mould and made the top, see, then connected them both together.' The handle and spout were stuck on after.

Mr Hilditch, recalling the era of jiggering and jolleying, said that the work given to girl attendants was very hard: 'I used to feel sorry for the girls that used to have to jigger-turn, and then the batter-out and mould-runner. The mould-runner had got to run a mile very near.' The batter-out was the girl who knocked a piece of clay flat to the size the maker needed, and the mould-runner would run backwards and forwards, carrying full and empty moulds between the making-shop and the red-hot stove, where the moulds were put to dry. In the 1840s, Scriven had described mould-runners as 'labouring like little slaves', and added, 'It is admitted on all hands that their work is the most arduous and fatiguing of all others.'[18]

In the 1840s, this work was done by little boys. When it became illegal to employ them, the work was done by girls just starting out in the industry. Mrs Farrier, who was born in about 1902, worked as a mould-runner for a cup-maker. She used to have to get clay, make it into a ball, throw it into the moulds of the jolleying-machine, run with the moulds (when the cups had been made in them) into the stove, take out two moulds with dry cups in them, run back and empty them onto a board (or six-foot plank), and put the moulds ready for the cup-maker again: 'By the time you'd finished at night-time, your feet were that sore, you didn't know where to put 'em.' She would walk home in her stockinged feet, too painful for shoes.

Mrs Farrier later became a bowl-jolleyer herself, first being apprenticed to her mother and then taking over the job when her mother gave up to have a baby. Although she described it as 'damned hard' and 'on your feet all day', she contrasted it strongly with the automatic cup-making machine, which was introduced, in her factory, when she was 60 years old: 'Jolleying ... and throwing was the craft. There's no craft in that automatic, you know, there's no craft at all. All they do today is service that machine. They're that machine's slave.'

In jolleying, the maker put her fingers in the ball of clay as it revolved in the mould, and pulled up the clay, before a tool called a 'monkey' came down to

Figure 7.2 Jiggering: the woman attendant turns a wheel for a man making pots.

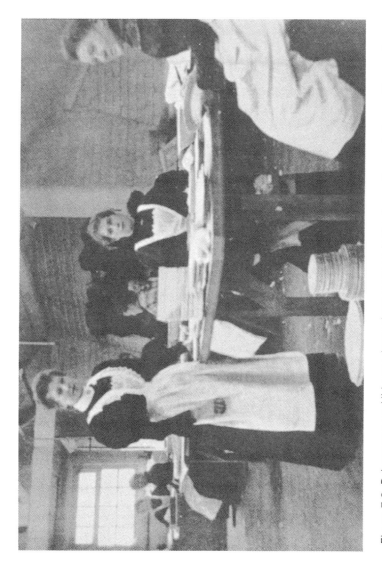

Figure 7.3 Paintresses and lithographers: these women in the decorating end, dressed in smart pinafores like parlour maids, are the elite of the female workforce.

shape the bowl, then she smoothed it with a sponge and water, and scraped off the excess clay with a piece of tin. The arrival of cup roller machines in the late 1950s meant faster work, but the loss of any pride in one's craft. Mrs Farrier refused to work the new machine, and retired.

The jolleyer's skill was replaced by machines which are now mostly minded by men, and this effectively reduced jobs open to women in the clay end. Cup roller machines (making cups) and flat roller machines (making plates) are fast, heavy work, and heavy work is now reserved for men. The design of the machine demands more than average strength, just as in agriculture the size of sacks and bales demands more than average strength. Heavy work also justifies higher wages, but this has only been the case since men have taken over the heavy tasks. When women worked as wedgers, mould-runners, casters and flat-pressers, the heaviness of their work was never seen as a reason for equal pay with men.

Helping Out

Between the wars, as casting came in, women took on this work. Mrs Adams (born in 1923) had been a caster before the Second World War, and she asserted that she had known only women casters in her factory between the wars:

Q: Were there men casters as well as women?

A: Not at that time, no.

Q: No? When did they come in?

A: I think it was soon after the war. After the Second World War, I should think. Because I used to be a caster, and of course during the war I went into the forces, and when I came back, there weren't any women casters, not a lot of women casters at all.

Q: Before the war, did the women do the heavy casting, you know, like the teapots and the big, heavy dishes?

A: Oh yes, yes. There weren't any men, men casters. . . .

Nowadays, casting is a much lighter job than it was between the wars. Casters used big, heavy jugs full of slip to pour into the moulds; nowadays, almost universally, slip is piped to the casters, like petrol from a pump. The Wethered Report of 1924 enables us to compare the wages of men and women casters in 1924. Men received 66s 2d for a 47-hour week, while women casters received 36s 5d. Even though women did extremely hard work, it was always assumed that men should be paid more. Even in the 1950s, the General Secretary of the National Society of Pottery Workers, Harold Hewitt, said that women paid lower union dues and had lower pay 'because they do not have the same responsibilities'.[19] Essentially the same attitudes prevailed in the Potteries then as in 1867 when the Hollow-Ware Pressers told the 1867 Commission: 'Women are better occupied at home'.[20] The priority of women as home-makers and of men as breadwinners remained unshakeable, although throughout the Depression of the

1930s, many women had been indispensable workers to their families, and during the war, women were indispensible on munitions. After the Second World War, when the numbers working in the industry in North Staffordshire were half what they had been before the war, it was 'natural' for men to make gains in the clay end.

Mrs Farrier described to me how she had gone to work in the 1930s, when her babies were only a month old:

A: Me mother used to have 'em right away, see. And when I've left 'em I've gone work crying. . . . You do miss all the niceness of them.
Q: Why did you go to work?
A: Well, half the time he wasn't working, see. Unemployment was vile, those days, see, sometimes we'd both be on the dole together.

Mrs Barness, who was born in 1911 and was a dipper, worked all through the Depression, while her husband was on the dole for seven years, but the way she described it was: 'I used to go out to work to help out'. She was highly skilled:

I progressed through the years to everything from a butter-pat to a fourteen-inch dish – hollow-ware, cups, the lot, everything, there was nothing I couldn't do, and I was made responsible for samples – I did the samples that used to go abroad to get the orders; oh, I got on in me trade. I really liked it, and I would go back tomorrow if I got the chance.

All this was seen by the woman herself as 'helping out', so pervasive was the ideology of the male breadwinner. Nevertheless, in 1935, the labour force of the whole industry consisted of 30,902 males and 37,635 females: women, like apprentices, were cheap labour. Trade union membership figures show that they continued to dominate the industry until the Equal Pay Act and the recession combined to put them in the minority in the 1980s. By December 1991, there were only 14,068 male and 11,861 female members in the union. Even though they dominated the union in numbers in almost every year from 1921, it is noticeable that it was women whose numbers expanded or contracted from year to year according to the vicissitudes of trade.[21] It was not only women's cheapness but the lack of male labour during the two world wars which helped to bring women into skilled work in the making end of the industry. There was very little that they could not do: they made cups and saucers, they did casting, they made seven-inch plates, they dipped, they helped to draw the ovens – and yet women's piece-work prices in 1946 continued to be about two-thirds of men's.[22]

There was no concerted effort to unionize women until the beginning of the twentieth century, and it did not really begin until their labour started to be substituted for men's in the First World War. A woman organizer was officially appointed to the union in 1917, in the year that the amalgamated unions became the National Society of Pottery Workers.[23] Women's earnings continued to be extremely low, but in 1937, the union achieved agreement for minimum rates for women. Nevertheless, in spite of the 1944 Royal Commission on Equal Pay, women continued to be paid considerably less than men in the industry. The 1970 Equal Pay Act has not altered the situation: because of the particular division of labour within any one factory, men and women rarely do exactly the same work on one potbank, and women's average earnings continue to be lower than men's.[24] As has been women's experience in other trades, there are difficulties in comparing the value of different work. Ever since women stopped doing heavy work, this has become the crucial justification for men's higher rates of pay.

One cannot escape the suspicion that whatever are the characteristics of men's work, they will be the ones to which value is attributed, because it is men's work which is considered important. Why should this be so? In the Potteries, the idea of the male breadwinner seems out of step with an industry which has relied so heavily on female labour. One would expect a certain pride and independence in the culture of women who have followed one another, mother and daughter, into skilled work. But the middle-class ideal of the woman at home is very powerful. One might argue that fine china itself, the product which is the pride of the Potteries, carries with it the image of a genteel way of life, of tea parties and dinner parties glowing with gilded tableware, and of fine things over which women hold sway comfortably at home. Reminders of this middle-class ideal are ever present under their fingers. Elizabeth Roberts, however, has suggested that Lancashire women also shared the same ideal, and did not go out to work when there was 'more opportunity for them to indulge their ambition of staying at home'.[25]

One might argue equally well that the decisive factor is the image of work itself. These are areas of heavy industry, of pits as well as pots, and Potteries women have a respect for the hardness and heaviness of men's work in coal-mining and other heavy industries. The idea that heavy work is 'real' work could help to explain why women accept their lower wages now. The weight of tradition certainly does not help: the pottery industry has existed continuously over two centuries and more. Women were always paid less than men, just as they were, for centuries, in agriculture, and the justification for farm-women's lower wages was that, like boys, they did not have the strength to do the work of men – often, of course, precisely because they were on starvation wages.[26]

The Posher Part

Nowadays, the idea that women are 'better off at home' has a sequel, that they are better suited to clean, quiet, 'ladylike' jobs, sitting quietly in the decorating end, rather than 'bashing the clay about' in the clay end. The clay end is noisy; it can be mucky or dusty. People stand to their work and wear overalls. A noisy, mucky place is also essentially a 'man's place', and the idea of the woman as an independent worker in the clay end has been resisted in the industry throughout the twentieth century. A woman is considered to be more suited to 'finishing' – fettling, sponging, smoothing the ware as she has always done, recalling her role as the wife-attendant to the nineteenth-century craftsman. In this role, of course, she does not threaten the job security of male workers, or their solidarity in the face of the threatened loss of their particular skills. Men do not seek to invade this area.

The other preferred image of the female worker – to men throughout the industry including those at union headquarters, and to many women – is as a worker in the 'feminine', decorating end of the pottery. In reality, women have no monopoly of hand-crafted decoration such as freehand painting, and are mostly employed sticking water-slide transfers onto the ware. In the sense that lithographing has largely replaced painting in the pottery industry, women have been deskilled to a very great extent in the decorating end during the course of this century. When it comes to freehand painting, men are employed as artists at least as frequently as women.

Women still do enamelling, which is painting within printed patterns, and they do gilding, and also lining and banding, but one finds only an occasional worker who may exercise these skills, and elsewhere she is replaced by an automated machine. In spite of this, the idea persists that the largely deskilled, monotonous jobs in the decorating shops are 'nice' jobs for women, and there is still a certain superiority attached to these 'feminine' jobs away from the mucky, noisy world of men. The fact that male artists are employed to do freehand painting seems in no way to detract from the integrity of this image of the feminine world of the decorating end.

This superiority through sexual segregation is, of course, no new idea. Middle-class attitudes to the segregation of the sexes were very prominent in the accounts of the nineteenth-century Royal Commissions, which looked at the work of women and children in both agriculture and manufactures, and the idea that it was better for women and girls to be segregated in the pottery factories was voiced by witnesses to Scriven, the Commissioner who took evidence in the potteries in 1841. At that time, there were separate painting-rooms for girls and boys, and Eliza Beech, aged 28, was careful to point this out:

> They do not associate with the boys, but are kept exclusively to themselves. We have no men in the same department. . . . From the experience of many years I can form an opinion as to the general moral and religious character of potters' children in *my department*; compared with others, I think them superior. I never hear anything like vulgar or improper language from any of them; they are respectful, clean and well-conducted.[27]

In the printing-room, by contrast, the association of men and girls attracted criticism from Sarah Proctor: 'Their language is often indecent and profane; this is I think attributable to their associations with young and vulgar men. The printing-room is indeed a bad school for children.'[28] A paintress, born in 1907, had this to say to me about people in the clay end, as she remembered them a hundred years after Scriven: 'The people are different, shouting and gawping at each other – where we have got to be nice and quiet. It's the posher part, you know what I mean? You are quiet and painting.'[29]

Mrs Rugeley, a caster-sponger born in 1939, gave the view from the clay end:

> Decorators go to work all make-up and best clothes and high heels, and totter up and down. Clay end don't: they go tidy, but change – trashers [old shoes] and something as is comfortable, because we have to stand all day, you see, whereas they sit all day.[30]

In spite of the characterization of the clay end as 'rough' and the decorating end as 'posh', many women still work in the clay end, fettling and sponging, handling (which means sticking in handles), and casting. Mechanization has come to casting on many potbanks. Belt casting has further taken away any possibility for workers to feel they are more than a cog in a machine: where this method is used, one group of workers fills the moulds with slip, others tip it out, and others extract the ware from the moulds. In some of the factories in the big groups, plates are made by dust-pressing: there is more mechanization on those firms which must bear the added expense of numerous managers.

The Clean Air Act of 1960 sounded the death-knell of the bottle oven, whose pollution had covered the Potteries with soot throughout the nineteenth century and much of the twentieth. Tunnel kilns began to come in from 1912, fired first by coal and then gas. In the 1960s, some factories were still going over from steam to electricity, facilitating further technological change and mechanization of processes.

From the 1960s onwards, amalgamations and takeovers have led to a situation in which a few large international groups dominate the industry. But with the recession of the 1980s and early 1990s, little firms are mushrooming again, able to respond quickly to changes in taste, able to do small orders and to fulfil the demands of up-market trade. Once again one can find owners capable of turning their hand to almost any process in their works. Mechanization is sometimes minimal, and freehand decoration, particularly sponging, is in fashion again. As the little firms try to find their feet, the giants shed workers, bemoaning the state of the economy both in Britain and abroad.

As the pottery industry tightens its belt, men have won back jobs in the clay end, but as machine-minders. Women, however, do much of the craft work in the clay end. Paradoxically, women are considered suited to the decorating end, but men do much of the most prestigious work in decorating. Management is largely made up of men. The Women's Advisory Committee of the union no longer meets (at the time of writing). Women continue to be paid less than male workers, and to combine paid work with what are seen as their domestic duties. Older workers and part-timers (women) are the first to lose their jobs in a recession. Those that remain work longer hours. It must be concluded that as long as women retain a view of themselves as essentially home-makers who, by preference or necessity, go out to work 'to help out', they will not receive a reward for their work which compares with what men earn. In the past, women have fought against the boundaries of what was considered fit work for women, but have still been paid less than men. In recent decades, groups of women have fought to reduce the difference between their pay and that of men doing similar work: the Wedgwood figure-makers are an example. During a recession, however, women are at their weakest: part-time work is a concession to women's domestic responsibilities, especially childcare. For as long as the necessity for these divided loyalties, to the firm and to the home, is not recognized, women will have precarious jobs and less pay.

Notes

I am grateful to the Nuffield foundation, who supported the original fieldwork on which this research was based.

1   Shaw, S. (1970; first published in 1829) *History of the Staffordshire Potteries*, Newton Abbot, p. 166.
2   Described in Weatherill, L. (1971) *The Pottery Trade and North Staffordshire 1660–1760*, Manchester, p. 104.
3   The Wedgwood Papers, ref. 29126–46, in Keele University Library. I quote from them by kind permission of the Trustees of the Wedgwood Museum.
4   The Wedgwood Papers, ref. 29127–46, 29135–46.
5   *Ibid.*
6   The Wedgwood Papers, ref. 29131–46.
7   Dupree, M. (1981) *Family Structure in the Staffordshire Potteries 1840–1900*, unpublished D.Phil. thesis, Oxford University, p. 145. I am very grateful to Marguerite Dupree for permission to refer to her thesis.
8   Scriven, S. (1842) *Report on the Employment of Children and Young Persons in the District of the Staffordshire Potteries*, Children's Employment Commission.
9   The research is described fully in Sarsby, J. (1988) *Missuses and Mouldrunners: An Oral History of Women Pottery-Workers at Work and at Home*, Milton Keynes and Philadelphia. I mention the way in which older women helped younger ones, especially family members, to get jobs. I also describe the way in which daughters gave their wages to their mothers and helped them with housework – not always gladly – and how mothers looked after their working daughters' children for them, and were paid to do so. The tapes are now lodged at the Gladstone Pottery Museum.
10   The Wedgwood Papers, ref. 29123–46.
11   Scriven (1842) (see note 8).
12   Burchill, F. and Ross, R. (1977) *A History of the Potters' Union*, Hanley, Ceramic and Allied Trades' Union, pp. 29–30.
13   Dupree (1981) (see note 7), p. 336.
14   Burchill and Ross (1977) (see note 12), p. 154.
15   Whipp, R. (1979) 'The Women Pottery Workers of Staffordshire and Trade Unionism, 1890–1905', unpublished M.A. thesis, Warwick University, pp. 24–6.

I regret that I have been unable to find a similar reference in his subsequent book.

16 Dupree (1981) (see note 7), p. 338.

17 Sarsby (1988) (see note 9). This was an oral history study of the work and home lives of women pottery-workers. I was introduced to pottery-workers via the Gladstone Pottery Museum, via visits to various pottery factories, via Radio Stoke and via the Ceramic and Allied Trades Union, especially with the help of the Women's Advisory Committee. I tried to talk to women who had worked in a variety of jobs in different workshops of the potbank (pottery factory), and I also talked to women who had worked in factories of various sizes, making different kinds of ware.

18 Scriven (1842) (see note 8).

19 Burchill and Ross (1977) (see note 12), p. 211.

20 *Ibid.*, p. 148.

21 Census of Production 1935, the China and Earthenware Trade; TUC Annual Reports quoted in Burchill and Ross (1977), p. 177; and CATU membership and employment 1940–75, quoted in Burchill and Ross (1977), p. 261. In 1975, there were 44,404 members in CATU, of whom 53 per cent were female; 75 per cent of the workforce was unionized.

22 The Report of the Royal Commission on Equal Pay 1944–1946.

23 Burchill and Ross (1977) (see note 12), p. 161.

24 In 1991 the average weekly wages of CATU members were as follows: female piece-work, £179.63; female day wage, £140.76; male piece-work, £234.31; male day wage, £183.79 (figures provided by CATU).

25 Roberts, E. (1984) *A Woman's Place*, Oxford, Basil Blackwell, p. 203.

26 Clark, A. (1982) *Working Life of Women in the Seventeenth Century*, London, chapter 2.

27 Scriven (1842) (see note 8).

28 *Ibid.*

29 'Mrs Bede', in Sarsby (1988) (see note 9), chapter 2.

30 Quoted in Sarsby (1988), chapter 2. One of the noticeable differences between most men's work and most women's work in potbanks is that men can move around more, while women remain in one place. This is not true in those jobs where a man is tied to a machine.

Chapter 8

Periodization and the Engendering of Technology: The Pottery of Gustavsberg, Sweden, 1880–1980

Ulla Wikander

The focus of this chapter is the gender division of labour, and especially how it relates to technological change and its periodization.[1] I want to underline the possibilities available for women for equal work with men in some periods, and look at that in relation to technology. The increase and decrease of such possibilities were culturally and socially constructed over time. In order to hold the analysis within the confines of a short chapter, I have excluded class and ethnicity, both of which interacted with gender and technology. The analysis will single out the periods when gender integration, when men and women were working side by side in the same occupation, can be seen as a tendency within a process of reconstructed gender segregation. The two trends, the continuity of segregation during the last hundred years and the discontinuities inside it, are not as contradictory as they might at first appear. The development is a process without sharp time limits, but generally the period from 1880 to 1920 was a period of gender integration, and the period from 1920 to 1950 one of increased gender segregation. After 1950, the two patterns were repeated: first gender integration, later renewed gender segregation. What I am trying to establish are general trends and specific periods for changes in integration/segregation in the gender division of labour. Furthermore I am interested in how such processes ran parallel to societal discourses about women during the last hundred years.[2]

This chapter focuses on one pottery factory, Gustavsberg, in Sweden, during the crucial times after 1880, when a modern labour market in Sweden developed. The period can be called paradoxical, with opportunities opening up and new gender limits being constructed. In Swedish society at large, there were several indications of a change in public opinion, in which women's place was firmly established as different to men's, with both industrial work conditions and democratic and citizenship rights at stake. Beginning in the 1890s, but especially in the period after 1900, there was a turn in public opinion towards a growing interest in racial biology, with a subsequent high evaluation of women's role as the central link in the production of a 'worthy' race.[3] Motherhood came to the forefront in discussions on women's place in an industrial society.

Legal changes were introduced, which meant less favourable conditions for women. Schoolteachers of both sexes had previously, in principle, earned equal wages. In 1906, at a time when the women's movement in Europe had 'equal pay for equal work' as one of its recurrent demands, the Swedish parliament voted for sexually differentiated wages for state-employed teachers.[4] Teaching was considered gendered, and women's contribution of less worth, even if it was of equal value and amount. The minister of education said in the parliamentary debate on the question in 1906: 'Male and female teachers maybe do the *same amount* of work – and certainly *equally valuable* work, but they are of course not doing the *same kind* of work'. Such was the argument for differentiation of wages between men and women doing the same training of schoolchildren.[5] At the same time, there was a serious discussion about the introduction of a legal prohibition against women operating steam engines. After an investigation, that proposition did not become law, but doubts remained in society regarding women's abilities to handle complicated machinery. A prohibition against night work for women in industry was introduced in Sweden in 1909/1911, importing a European legal pattern which had been confirmed by the first International Labour Convention in Berne in 1906 and spread to most industrialized countries.[6] These and other signs reveal a tendency to reconfirm even clear-cut limits between men and women as wage labourers.

Ellen Key was the most eloquent Swedish speaker for the renewed construction of woman as 'the Mother', and warned against abandoning 'women's peculiarities'.[7] She was sensitive to the new eugenic ideas of her time, and firm in her judgment of women's inferiority to men in factory work, declaring:

> The manager of one of the largest factories in the country told me that he has so far never found one single girl who learned to understand the mechanism of the machine she, as an automaton, was tending. On the other hand, it has hardly ever happened that a boy, with the same simple schooling as the girl, did not in a short time comprehend the construction and function of the machine he was operating.[8]

The message in Key's statement was that, while women should not be trusted with technology, they could tend the machinery as unskilled workers. Women could be as good attendants as men. By looking at a specific factory, Gustavsberg, and the engendering of technology there, we will be able to see how the discourse on the societal level was developed in a workplace. A re-evaluation of women was taking place on the factory floor. The process of engendering technology in a factory shows us the changing opinions of the time as clearly as parliamentary discussions or other discourses. The gender division of labour, indeed, was such a discourse, expressed not in words, but in the positioning of women. Key's polemics with feminist demands for equal treatment took place during a period when a discourse on technology and gender was unstable and could assume a variety of forms, even inside a single factory, without being expressed in words. The instability of the relationship between a specific machine and the biological sex of its tender, as well as the gendering of the same technology, was intimately connected to the negotiation and reconstruction of the unequal hierarchical power structure between men and women during this specific historical period.

In my earlier study of the Gustavsberg pottery, I investigated the process of change over the last hundred years, and found above all a 'constancy despite change'. This means that there was a reproduced constancy in the relationship between women and men at work, a recurring subordination of women.[9] Richard Whipp, who studied the British pottery industry, seems to have missed the point of looking at the gender division of labour, if he believes that structural analysis of power relations should mean that female workers are not considered to be acting as 'creative women'. Despite a pronounced interest on his part, he adds little to an understanding of the engendering in the factory, putting all stress on the family connection, notwithstanding enormous changes in technology and work organization.[10] I accentuated continuities. Here I will stress the periods and work processes in which this tendency to constancy was interrupted. I will look towards the discontinuities, the *social* construction of male and female work – a construction that continuously takes place inside a tradition, which might be opposed and changed. Such a construction can lean on new technology. New relations are more easily accepted when material conditions are changing. My intention is to look at the process of gender construction as an experience inside the factory,[11] without touching upon family, civil status or other personal life cycle factors. As with all historical work, this is a construction framed to highlight certain relations and questions. The problem is to follow, and subsequently 'understand', the process of maintaining and reshaping a hierarchically gendered society as it is constructed at an industrial workplace, and to examine processes that still contribute to excluding many women from economic independence and political equality in a democratic system. It will also point to the variability of the engendering of technology.

The Island Factory

The factory of Gustavsberg was established in 1825 on an island outside the Swedish capital of Stockholm. It could only be reached by boat until the 1930s. Its natural harbour, further out in the archipelago than Stockholm, was well suited for receiving the raw materials (coal and clay) imported primarily from England. Until the 1880s, Gustavsberg had a production process almost at a handicraft level, except for burning and clay mixing. In this earliest period women formed approximately 25 per cent of the workforce.

Production was gradually built up around imported 'know-how' and machinery. By the 1880s, potters from England, skilled painters from France, English as well as German foremen and factory managers, together with Swedish capitalists and workers, had made the factory into a flourishing company. The factory then could meet demands being raised by a rapidly industrializing country in transition from classical to organized capitalism,[12] a country where porcelain and pottery were replacing tin and wood even at ordinary people's dinner tables.

This meant a rapid increase of workers, from 466 persons in 1875 to 820 in 1890. From then on, the factory kept an astonishingly stable relationship between the percentage of women and men in production; roughly 40 per cent women, and 60 per cent men.[13] The end-products remained similar over time – a cup is always a cup – whereas the technology changed dramatically, output increased, and work organization was rearranged. This makes pottery an excellent industry in which to study the long-term structural changes in the gender division of labour after 1880 when technological changes first began to be introduced.

At the Gustavsberg factory two periods are discernible which differ from the general tendency of subordinating and segregating women at work. The first of these periods starts in the 1880s, and includes the First World War but is then interrupted. The second period starts after the Second World War, and ends with the late 1960s. It may be noted that this periodization is not congruent with the one Jacqueline Sarsby has observed in the British Potteries. In England there was a continuous period, from the 1870s extending to the end of the Second World War, when female potters competed with men for skilled and well-paid jobs.[14] In Gustavsberg the gender division of labour had been quite rigid during the first fifty years of the factory's existence. According to archive material, women and men worked at different jobs; the men were skilled, and women were often their attendants.[15] There was seldom spatial segregation. On the contrary, women and men often worked in teams interdependent on each other as they shared the same piece-rate, but they did not share it equally. In these teams men usually earned double the wage of the women. Skilled women painters were an exception to the rule: they worked segregated from men throughout the twentieth century, and were only slowly deskilled.

Gender Integration: 1880 to 1920

The 1880s saw the introduction of machines to replace the thrower's wheel. It disturbed the earlier male monopoly of making the standard hollow-ware and flat-ware as skilled handicraft work at a wheel. The work of six adult men could now be executed by one man and a boy attendant, or, as it turned out, by one woman with a boy attendant.

A new technology is never introduced overnight. First a new building was constructed to house the new machines and their workers. The factory expanded. In 1880 it employed 611 workers; in the peak year of 1910, 956 workers. The local labour market was limited. Workers were brought in from the countryside, and were housed by the company. Former farmers, miners and fishermen and their families gathered to receive training in new skills. Labour relations and traditions were altering; very much so in this one factory-village, but also in the whole of Swedish society at a time when industrial enterprises were founded in towns. In those days of turmoil, unskilled women as well as men were trained to work at the new machines, called jiggers or jolleys. It appears as if the old potters refused to leave their wheels. As it was a period of expansion, and as a potter seldom lived beyond his forties or fifties because of silicosis, the transition took place without documented opposition. Women were in a minority as jiggerers and jolleyers, but they were there, trained for a skilled job in the so-called clay end of pottery production. And they earned the same piece-rate as men. Paradoxically, at the same time as women received their chance to become skilled workers at the new machines as equals to men, more women than ever before were needed as attendants in the workshops. As the production rate rose because of the new technology, more and more workers were needed to do the finishing jobs, such as sponging, fettling, sticking-up and handling. These jobs were still performed in the old ways, and were more time-consuming than turning out the ware. As the age below which children were excluded from factory work rose, more and more women were needed to replace them. This finishing-work thus became perceived as 'female'.

New technology was not the only pivot around which new gender divisions of labour crystallized during this period. Engraving had been a male monopoly. The engravers were skilled handicraft workers, engraving on thin copper plates the complicated patterns that later were printed onto thin paper and transferred to cups, saucers and plates. But by the 1880s, four men and four women worked side by side on engraving, and the documents show no differences between the work done by men and women. Women earned somewhat less than men, but still quite well. The gender integration in this small but high-status workshop went on until 1900, when two boys were recruited as apprentices. Apprenticeship had by that time not been practised for several decades in the factory.[16] Its reintroduction must be connected to the exclusion of women. After 1900 no new women were hired, and the last one left the engravers' workshop around 1920. After that time, all engravers were well-paid, skilled and male.[17] The gender integration for twenty to forty years in engraving must be regarded not in the context of technological change, but in the context of the general instability of the gendering of work before the turn of the century. No documents reveal any explicit reasons behind the process of excluding women, but the result is evident, and a strict gendering took place. The influx of women as well as their exclusion has to be understood in relation to the general discourse of women's place in society – or rather as another comment in that discourse: women and men should work in different jobs, and men ought to have the more skilled ones. With the new century such ideas became stronger, but it is interesting to see how contradictory the messages given to women were. Looked upon from the angle of 'work suitable for women', engraving was similar to porcelain painting, not heavy and not demanding much bodily movement, only dexterous fingers. Such supposed qualities were often said to be typical of women's work. Similar reasoning has often been used as legitimization when there has been a need to subordinate women. It was not used to promote women's chances to keep skilled work in Gustavsberg. Engraving was considered skilled work, and maintained its status as such, probably connected to the exclusion of women.

The jolley and the jigger, while mechanical, were controlled by the worker's skill. He or she determined the pace of the work, and influenced the quality of the ware. There had to be a continuous interaction between the machine and the worker, who could put more or less pressure on the handle that formed the ware. He or she had to smooth the surface of the ware with a cloth, or the palm of his or her bare hand, while forming. The process was not automatic in any sense. The machine was an extended tool, speeding up the forming and simplifying it, but it was not a shaper and regulator of the result. As time went by, the worker at a jolley or jigger became the most skilled person in the forming workshops. The old handicraft thrower, the Old Potter, did not exist any more. It meant a rather quick exclusion of women. Female potters became less and less common. Some old men interviewed in the 1960s had started their working life as mould-runners to Big-Ida, a benevolent female maker of saucers. When she had to leave work because of silicosis at the beginning of this century, the period of female makers at jolleys was over, with some insignificant temporary exceptions. By that time the male jolleyer and jiggerer became the 'New Potter', and on him were conferred all the benefits once tied to being the 'Old Potter'. He received preferential treatment, could go home when his daily quota of work was filled, had control over his own work pace, had several attendants, and received better housing than other workers. It is important to keep in mind the engendering of jolleys and jiggers when following the development of more or less automatic machines that were being tested in the 1920s. Automatic machines would gradually take over all of the production of flat-ware and hollow-ware some fifty years later. The shifting gendering of that forming of the ware will be discussed later in this chapter.

Let us, however, first look at the gendering of another new way of producing porcelain and pottery. In the early twentieth century another mode of forming the ware – casting – made its entrance on a grand scale in the workshops. Casting was a method for forming complicated irregular ware, by pouring clay in a liquid state, slip, into a plaster mould. The superfluous liquid was later poured out and, for example, a teapot could be taken out from the mould. Handling the heavy moulds and the slip was hard and dirty work. The new method replaced the older male occupation of pressing clay manually against the mould, a skilled handicraft method, which was now only used for special designs. Both women and men became casters. Differences cannot easily be distinguished as to what ware they each made. Only women cast the very small items, but women as well as men made complicated teapots and profiled urns. The very big ware was often 'casted' by stronger men.

Casting never received high status in the workshops. It took only half a year to become skilled at it, whereas it took a full year to master a jolley or jigger. Contrary to the development elsewhere in the factory, this job remained gender-integrated during the whole period investigated, up until 1985.

In the early decades of the new century, the factory owner also introduced a new printing machine producing a three-coloured continuous sheet of printed patterns, later to be cut and transferred onto pottery and china. One machine took over the work of quite a number of skilled male printers, working at hand-operated printing machines of a simple kind. Only one of them was selected to become the new 'printer' at the continuous machine and was taught all its mechanical sophistications. At that time there was no question that it was a man's job, just as all the former printing had been. The difference from the former work process was that the printer now became more of a supervisor and 'service-man'. The work of the new printer included *both* supervision (being an attendant) of an automatic continuous machine *and* any service it needed to function smoothly. It was all taken care of by one worker. By his side he had a boy or a young man who helped him and could later succeed him. His work had an inbuilt career structure, which was seldom connected to women working as attendants. This work was without any detours a male occupation to start with, and during as much as fifty years a 'male' job with a fairly high status.

Around the turn of the century, the introduction of new machinery and new methods disturbed the older gender division of labour and led to increased gender integration. This new integration turned out to be only temporary for with the new century, the trend was reversed. New technology could lead to both integration and segregation. No consistent pattern existed.

Increasing Gender Segregation: 1920 to 1950

The period from 1920 to 1950 again meant more rigid gender segregation. We will follow the making of the ware to see what happened with the relations between men and women, and automatic forming machinery for pottery. In the 1920s a semi-automatic cup machine was brought from England. It was a so-called upright jolley, on which two cups were formed parallel to each other by two iron 'arms' moving automatically up and down, in a machine rhythm, not steered by the worker's arm like an ordinary jolley. The person working at this machine had to do approximately the work the attendant or the mould-runner used to perform for the jolleyer: put the mould with clay in place for the forming and then take the mould with the ware away when the making was completed. The imported cup machine was on trial for some time, with a woman as attendant, but it was soon taken out of production because it was slower than the old more skill-demanding machinery. The semi-automatic cup machine was experimentally reintroduced now and then during the following decades while improvements were made in its construction. It was always attended by a woman during these test periods. By the early 1950s, with improvements made in the factory's mechanical workshop, a cup machine became such an asset that it was used in regular production. Operating the cup machine was considered women's work as long as the male jiggerer and jolleyer still commanded the most independent skills in the workshops.

In the 1940s, conveyor belts were introduced wherever in the factory they could possibly be of any use. It was mostly women who were put to work at them, doing their earlier jobs in the clay end and in finishing the ware, but now bound to an uncontrollable machine rhythm, making their movements more monotonous. Even the forming of the ware was reorganized, rationalized and connected to a continuous transporting system.

The jiggers and jolleys – still the same old models from the turn of the century – were linked to a new kind of machinery that took care of drying the ware on the plaster moulds. It was a simple kind of conveyor belt, taking the ware from the potter to the attendant via a heated area. The human mould-runner was no longer needed. The drying machine was continuous and placed beside the forming machine, a jolley or a jigger. The maker himself had to adjust to the rhythm of the drying machine. He could no longer speed up at intervals, take a pause and work harder afterwards. Thus even the jiggerers and jolleyers with independent skills had to conform to a machine rhythm from the 1940s. Women stood on the receiving side of the drying machine, which extended to the ceiling and went down on the other side. They unloaded the ware and took care of the finishing and polishing, standing directly by the hot machine all day. Men were still the makers, women were the attendants. The development meant further spatial gender segregation, as well as more monotonous work for both men and women in the factory. The ongoing segregation tended to give the more monotonous work to women.

Some Gender Integration and Renewed Gender Segregation: 1950 to 1985

During the 1950s and 1960s, there were indications that the printing machine, introduced some fifty years earlier, was to become outdated. So far it had always been handled by a man, a printer. Totally new ways of transferring the pattern onto the ware without any paper prints were developed. Gustavsberg did not immediately invest in the new technology, but introduced it gradually. Slowly the so-called Murray printing machines were brought in, one by one. With this machine the pattern was transferred via soft rubber balls from the copper plate to the ware. During the whole of the transitional period of approximately one decade, one woman was allowed to become the printer and another woman took care of the colour-mixing for it, also an earlier male preserve. Of course these women were as efficient as workers as the formerly so-called skilled male personnel. They were allowed into this work because it held no future, and its prestige was on the wane. The printing machine was an ageing technique, soon to be replaced by a more modern one.

Women were placed as attendants at the new Murray printing machines. Some of them were degraded hand painters, others unskilled workers. A couple of male workers were employed as service-men to the fifteen-odd printing machines. The gender relations connected to this technological change correspond to the gender relations connected to the liners for forming, which we will confront further on. Both were definitely introduced during the 1970s and 1980s.

Considering the intermixing of service and attendance at the earlier printing machine, it might be questioned why such a mixed work schedule was not developed for the Murray printing machines which were relatively small. Now this new technology was instead used to reaffirm a gender division of labour, using women as the attendants to the machines and training men to become ambulant service-men, available if there was any trouble. The construction of an image of women as unable to perform mechanical work went on.

The introduction of new improved semi-automatic machines (German so-called Roller machines) resulted in a rapid transformation of the method of forming the ware in the mid 1960s. The male worker was forced to go over to the new semi-automatic machinery. During the experimental period, as we have seen, only women had tended such machines. The following period thus suddenly saw both men and women tending the increasing number of semi-automatic machines for different sizes and kinds of ware. The process was one of gender integration – men were degraded to less skilled work and women continued as attendants, with actually more responsibilities than before. For a period of more than ten years, men and women were gender-integrated at the semi-automatic machines, while these became more sophisticated and included more and more of the external work processes. The work at these semi-automatic machines was not as skilled as the former work at a jolley or jigger, but it can be defined as semi-skilled and varied, and it included many heavy movements of bending, shifting and lifting moulds with clay, wet or dry. Something that was important for the rapid redefinition of the semi-automatic machines, from 'female' to gender integrated technology, was the very *rapid* procedure of changing technology. There was not a long transitional decade – the transition took only a couple of years, which meant that there was little time for the superfluous men to look around for other jobs. Men had to work at semi-automatic machines if they wanted to stay in the porcelain trade at all.

In the early 1970s, more fully automatized machines imported from Germany were introduced for producing simple, round, flat or hollow ware of ordinary size. The machines included the drying of the ware, the handling of the moulds with and without clay, and the central forming of the clay, as well as some of the finishing work and part of the sticking-up of handles (ears) on to cups. The machines were complex, huge (almost twenty metres long and four metres wide) and very noisy.

Only two workers were needed to tend each of them. Women were employed for surveillance and for 'loading' the machine with rolls of clay at the one end, and for the 'unloading' of the ware at the other end, for polishing and piling it in stacks. Both of them performed very heavy work. One woman stood at each end of the two machines. They were attendants, and carried daily a lot of heavy clay and ware. They could not leave their positions unless there was a regular pause. If disturbances occurred in the smooth continuous production, they had to press a button to stop the whole machine before any major production damages occurred. The observation and concentration while working had to be constant and agile. A small disturbance could quickly grow into serious trouble. If a stoppage was necessary the women had to call for a so-called service-man to take over the responsibility. Two service-men were employed for the two big liners forming ware, which were placed near each other in a big hall. They had become redundant at their earlier work on the semi-automatic machines, and had been retrained as service-men. No women were retrained to become service-women. Men's new service work consisted in supervising and controlling the automatized machines, opening them at vital points, sometimes going into them to make rather intricate searches and interventions, sometimes only doing routine correction of details. As long as the machines ran smoothly, they just had to wait, reading papers or drinking coffee. Despite frequent stops every day, they had plenty of time to rest.

At the same time, earlier production methods for making pottery were still used in parallel with the new ones. Not every kind of ware could be mass-produced, even if Gustavsberg had concentrated on long series produced on the liners. Women (mostly) and some men were still working on semi-automatic machines at the beginning of the 1980s. Semi-automatic forming continued, but was losing its earlier gender-integrated character. Only women were staying on at these machines as their importance decreased. The renewed gender segregation was indeed a fact.

Casting was the other dominant method of forming, still used in principle in the same way as before the First World War. In casting there had been gender integration since the early period of its introduction. A caster was doing relatively dirty and heavy work, with less obvious connection to the old forming process. Very little technological development took place in casting. Casting as a job never became highly thought of. The tradition inside the work itself was never disturbed by any rearrangements, and it remained gender-integrated. Casting and engraving were thus the only two jobs being genuinely gender integrated in the 1980s, and casting was the only work process with a long consistent history of such integration. The newest technology, the so-called liner, had on the contrary clearly once again reinstated a rigid segregation between men and women, separating skill and independence from monotony and dependence during the work day. Men's work was better paid, women's work involved more health risks. Men's work as service-men was, in fact, the job with the highest status in the forming department, similar to the status the 'potter' once had.

Conclusions

The reconstruction over a long period of the engendering of the forming of the ware – the work done at the clay end of the production – reveals several things. Women were always a potential workforce for so-called skilled work[18] coming in temporarily at times when they were 'needed', sometimes in work side by side with men, but never on work considered superior to men's. Usually a segregation was introduced later on. In the Gustavsberg factory, as well as in Swedish society at large, there was a tendency to *perceive* a distinction between 'technology for women' and 'technology for men'. At no time, however, was a distinction made consistently in practice. The boundaries were always fluid and random, subject to evaluation more than to strict objective rules or reasons. In general, women were regarded as suitable and consequently readily accepted as workers at machines when they *were perceived to be* the users of the machinery, the attendants. Men were perceived as, and thus welcomed as, active operators, inventors, makers and repairers of machines.[19] There has been, and always is, plenty of room for a subjective historically and geographically bound interpretation of how a particular technology is engendered, depending on whether it is only (perceived as being) tended or (perceived as being) operated.

Comparable gender-determining interpretations can be found in regard to the debates and gender conflicts in connection with the introduction of the Linotype press in printing in the decades around 1900.[20] The debate was actually about how the new technology should be understood and defined with reference to gender. Did the Linotype press require skilled and educated workers or only semi-skilled workers, which meant male or female workers as long as apprenticeship was for boys only? What was the sex of the worker who could be considered skilled? At stake was not who really could work at the new printing machines, but who would be legitimized to do such work.[21]

Five different relations can be observed between technology and the process of gender integration and segregation in Gustavsberg. Firstly, when a technology is new and has not yet received a definitely gendered character, gender integration might be possible. If the new machines are challenging older male monopoly preserves, it is probable that newly trained personnel, possibly women, are being placed on the jobs in the situation of a rivalry concerning productive technologies between the former craftsmen and the employer. Depending upon the situation inside the actual field, as well as the understanding the former experts have of the situation, the former skilled workers might act in two ways: they might agree to the new technology and try to monopolize that too by squeezing out the few women who were let in; or they might hesitate and even try to boycott it. Men may still come in later (as in the case of jiggerers and jolleyers in Gustavsberg). In the latter case, it is not the *same* individual workers, but new men, who come in to share the job with women, as long as it stays gender-integrated. The squeezing out of women later on became a logic inside a gendered perception of technology, which took place only when forming became central and important. In Gustavsberg, around 1900, a local patriarchal society still existed, dominated by the benevolent factory owner, and in that society the old potter had been the aristocrat among the pottery-workers. 'Potters' received special treatment. As the thrower at his wheel disappeared, the new operators at jolleys and jiggers grew into these favoured positions, getting status positions impossible for women to hold.

Secondly, we have the situation when a technique is becoming obsolete. The introduction of new technology often replaces an earlier technique. The older technology then has no future and for this reason is not an attractive occupation to learn, however much skill it might demand to work with it. In such a situation women seem to be welcome to learn what earlier was considered men's skilled work. For a while such jobs can become gender-integrated, with women sometimes being allowed to take over quickly. There were several such occasions in potting. The most obvious case was the work at the printer, which after fifty years could be considered a 'female' possibility, when the machine was on its way to becoming obsolete.

Thirdly, when former work processes are split up and divided between more workers, the technology enters a process of re-evaluation, usually resulting in increased segregation. The classic techniques concerned are of course the conveyor belt, the assembly line and their successors. When conveyor belts were introduced on a grand scale in Gustavsberg in the late 1930s and early 1940s, women were in the majority in jobs directly at the belts, whereas men were employed at jobs as transport-men, fetching the ware, or as supervisors and repairers. This development in Gustavsberg is consistent with the one Miriam Glucksmann points to in her book about women in industries in Britain during the inter-war period. The assembly lines became a new way, a technological way, of segregating women from men and giving the most monotonous and least skill-demanding work to women.[22] At Gustavsberg there was a fourth case of altering the engendering of a job, where technology was not the pivot. This was the case, for example, with engraving. Women were integrated and then again excluded without any other dramatic changes at the workplace. The introduction of round copper rollers to engrave on instead of flat plates occurred after the exclusion of women began. This case, like the ease with which women were introduced in forming and casting in the same period, during the decades around 1900, can only be explained with reference to the spirit of the time, the general stirring up of traditions, even gendered traditions, and the expansion also of this specific factory.

As a fifth, exclusive and positive, case, casting, a less central process, stands out as the only long-term gender-integrated work at Gustavsberg. It was introduced at the turn of this century. Later on it kept the same work process and a tradition of a gender-integrated work process developed and was not changed.

In order to change a gender-integrated character of a work process, new conditions must usually be introduced or developed, which may be taken as a point for renewed segregation. It has been impossible at Gustavsberg for women to stay on in an integrated job if it has become relatively more important with time. A paradoxical factor was the general business expansion of the pottery around 1900, which increased the number of traditional attendant jobs for women and thus increased segregation, at the same time as the expansion gave rise to new conditions and some really new chances for gender integration. In each case we have to look at many external factors involved in the process of the engendering of a new technology. What are the other possibilities of employment for men and/or women? Is the status of the new work *perceived* to be increasing or decreasing, making it attractive for men or not? Is it comparatively important in the work process as a whole? What are the relative employment possibilities available at the specific time and place for men and for women, both in the local labour market and in the factory? What is the general attitude in society to women's waged work and technical abilities?

The engendering of a technology is thus very much a matter of timing; it may have to do with the historical stage of a special technique. But it may equally be connected to the historical period and its conventional judgment of women's work. We have seen the contradicting, paradoxical situation for women at work around 1900; possibilities opened up that were never there before and then, as women's progress was felt as a threat to older gender relations, regulations, laws and discourses brought in renewed strict segregation between men and women. Other factors are also salient, such as the type of technology compared to others, in the factory, in the surrounding area or in existence, and the different occupations that the new technology might help to create. The momentary status of a technique as central might change, depending on the surrounding possibilities, possible future changes and evaluations. Making the work process more or less diversified may not be totally dependent on the technology, but may also depend on how the work is organized. The relativity of the engendering of a specific technology can thus be seen over time and space. Machinery which, during one historical period, in comparison with other machines, seemed *more* automatic was usually *not* regarded as 'male' technology for tending, but it could be considered 'male' for operating and servicing. What was *more* automatic could alter with time, evaluation and comparison with even newer technology. But a low-rated technique could become more highly valued with time, as well as the opposite. Technology perceived as more complicated or more central was considered 'male'. This means, among other things, that, over time, women could be found suitable to use older machinery, once considered only for skilled men, when more modern versions appeared, themselves now considered more sophisticated and suited for men. Also, new machinery could introduce a division of the workforce, thus increasing gender segregation. An economic and geographic, and maybe political, relativity could further be scrutinized by comparisons over regions and countries of different processes of engendering pottery technology. Studies by Marguerite Dupree, Jacqueline Sarsby and Richard Whipp for England, Gertjan de Groot for the Netherlands, and Marie-Hélène Zylberberg-Hocquard for France[23] might make such comparisons possible. Here such possibilities[24] will only be mentioned to point out a road for pursuing an analysis of the technological engendering process. This construction and continuous reconstruction of the engendering of technology is built upon machinery, but has no fixed relation to it. Changes in Gustavsberg never transcended the limits of a recurring subordination of women at the workshop level. Technological change became a pivot for introducing, temporarily disregarding or reaffirming subordination, but always in connection with other specific factors. A less strictly gender-segregated technology did occur but seldom remained and then only at unoffensive, less visible, and insignificant points in the production process; insignificant because of their marginal importance, their low status, or their probable disappearance. Recurrent gender segregation is an integral element in the organization of our society. It is promoted by an ongoing process of reinstating differences, a process which I have followed in one factory. In regard to Gustavsberg, I have found two periods – the decades before 1900, and some decades after the Second World War – when gender integration was easier and took place in several cases. Many studies in women's history indicate that a similar tendency was felt for the first period all over the industrialized world. The second period, however, may be unique to Sweden. To what extent has women's exodus from the home into the labour market meant gender integration, and to what extent only a renewed segregation, in the paid labour force instead of in unpaid housework?

For gender integration at work to become a reality in an overall societal perspective, at least three factors seem crucial. The first is a more general economic and societal change, which lays the foundation for dramatic changes in mentality and societal commotions in which traditions are abandoned or re-evaluated. This was the situation in most Western countries a hundred years ago. Then there have to be agents and organizations which push politically and economically for gender integration, convinced that it is a desirable strategy leading towards a better society that contains political and economic equality between men and women. The women's movement was such a political force a century ago. Women got the vote, but many women yielded to the general and persuasive discourse of difference in the labour market and accepted 'maternal' responsibility for society[25] on the hidden presumption that women's citizenship was of a different kind. It was deemed better to preserve a gendered division of labour, modified for an economic system in transformation.

A hundred years ago, Ellen Key was an early representative of the discourse eventually accepted about and also among women. She was in favour of women's suffrage, but eager not to alter the relationship between men and women in the labour market 'because society needs mothers as well as fathers'.

Notes

1 It is based on Wikander, U. (1988) *Kvinnors och mäns arbeten: Gustavsberg 1880–1980. Genusarbetsdelning och arbetets degradering vid en porslinsfabrik* (Women's and men's work: Gustavsberg 1880–1980. Gender division of labour and degradation of work) Lund, Arkiv. Thanks to Abby Peterson and Joan M. Jensen for valuable comments and linguistic corrections.
2 Wikander, U. (1989) 'Periodisering av kapitalism – med kvinnor' (Periodization of capitalism with women), *Arbetarhistoria* vol. 13, no. 51, pp. 7–11; see also the classic text Kelly-Gadol, J. (1977) 'Did Women Have a Renaissance?', in Bridenthal, R. and Koonz, C. (Eds) *Becoming Visible: Women in European History*, Boston.
3 See Lewis, J. (1980) *The Politics of Motherhood: Child and Maternal Welfare*

in England, 1900–1939, London and Montreal.

4   Wikander, U. (forthcoming) 'Some "kept the flag of feminist demands waving"': Debates on Protecting Women at International Congresses', in Wikander, U., Kessler-Harris, A. and Lewis, J. (Eds) *Comparative Studies in Protective Labor Legislation for Women: Europe, the U.S.A. and Australia.*

5   Florin, C. (1987) *Kampen om katedern. Feminiserings- och professionalisering- sprocessen inom den svenska folkskolans 1860–1906* (Who Should Sit in the Teacher's Chair? The Processes of Feminization and Professionalization among Swedish Elementary School Teachers, 1860–1906), Almqvist & Wiksell, diss. Ume.

6   Wikander, U., Kessler-Harris, A. and Lewis, J. (forthcoming) (see note 4).

7   Women's 'peculiarities' was the English equivalent for the German 'Eigenart', the Swedish 'särart' or 'egendomlighet' (Key's expression). It was used, for example, by the German Alice Salomon in her English speech at the International Congress of Women in London in 1899. See Wikander, U. (1992) 'International Women's Congresses, 1878–1914. The Controversy over Equality and Special Labour Legislation', in Eduards, M. L. *et al.* (Eds) *Rethinking Change. Current Swedish Feminist Research*, Uppsala, HSFR, pp. 11–36.

8   Key, E. (1896) *Missbrukad kvinnokraft och Naturenliga arbetsområden för kvinnan*, Stockholm, p. 23; Goodman, K. (1986) 'Motherhood and Work: The Concept of the Misuse of Women's Energy', in Joeres, R-E. B. and Maynes, M. J. (Eds) *German Women in the Eighteenth and Nineteenth Centuries. A Social and Literary History*, Bloomington, pp. 110–27; Roach Pierson, R. (1990) 'Ellen Key: Maternalism and Pacifism', in Arnup, K., Lévesque, A. and Roach Pierson, R. (Eds) *Delivering Motherhood: Maternal Ideologies and Practices in the 19th and 20th Centuries*, London and New York, pp. 270–83.

9   Whipp, R. (1990) *Patterns of Labour: Work and Social Change in the Pottery Industry*, London, p. 208.

10 Wikander, U. (1988) (see note 1); Wikander (1989) 'Women and men in a pottery industry – constancy despite change in work relations during one hundred years', in *The Sexual Division of Labour, 19th & 20th Centuries. Six essays presented at the Ninth International Economic History Congress, Berne 1986*, Uppsala Papers in Economic History, Working Paper No 7, Dept of Economic History, Uppsala.

11 Baron, A. (1991) 'Gender and Labor History: Learning from the Past, Looking to the Future', in Baron, A. (Ed.) *Work Engendered: Toward a New History of American Labor*, Ithaca and London, pp. 1–46, esp. p. 35.

12 I have borrowed the terms for the periods from Torstendahl, R. (1984) 'Technology in the Development of Society 1850–1980: Four Phases of Industrial Capitalism in Western Europe', *History and Technology*, vol. 1, pp. 157–74.

13 Fluctuations could occur, e.g. in 1880 38 per cent of the workers were women; the proportion increased to 41 per cent in 1890. See Wikander (1988), p. 257.

14 Sarsby, J. (1988) *Missuses and Mouldrunners: An Oral History of Women Pottery- Workers at Work and at Home*, Milton Keynes and Philadelphia, p. 14.

15 'Skill' is a relative but not a totally meaningless term, which of course has strong gendered implications. In this chapter I am using the same definition as earlier, in Wikander (1989) (see note 10) p. 132, when I write about 'independent skills' or 'attendants': 'Firstly – an "attendant" often had to be skilled, that is trained, but she (more seldom he) was always secondary in the work process in question; not doing the main work but helping out doing it. She could not do it all by herself in any situation, whereas the opposite was possible for the person being assisted. Secondly

– a person with "independent skills" knew the whole work-process, but in practice often had to concentrate on the most skill-demanding parts in order to ration his/her skills and thus raise productivity and the profit of the factory-owner. These definitions are not rigid in any sense but I have found them useful.'

16 Baron, A. (1991) 'An "Other" Side of Gender Antagonism at Work' in Baron, A. (Ed.) *Work Engendered: Toward a New History of American Labor*, pp. 47–69, shows the many ways in which apprenticeship could be used in the gendering of work.

17 A young girl was hired in 1980. She worked together with the last male engraver, at a time when the trade was already in decay. See Wikander (1988), pp. 181–2.

18 The first major contribution to discussions of the relativity of skilled work in relation to the sex of the worker is the article by Phillips, A. and Taylor, B. (1980) 'Sex and Skill', first published in *Feminist Review* no. 6, reprinted in Feminist Review (Ed.) (1986) *Waged Work. A Reader*, London.

19 R. Hubbard makes these distinctions in her Foreword to Rothschild J. (Ed.) (1983) *Machina ex Dea: Feminist Perspectives on Technology*, New York.

20 Andersgaard, I. (1982) 'Settersker og typografer – splittelse mellom men og kvinner' (Printers and typographers – a split between men and women) in Blom, I. and Hagemann, G. *Kvinner selv . . . Sju bidrag til norsk kvinnehistorie* (Women on their own . . . Seven contributions to Norwegian women's history), Oslo, Aschehoug; Hunt, F. (1983) 'The London Trade in the Printing and Binding of Books: An Experience in Exclusion, Dilution and De-Skilling for Women Workers', *Women's Studies International Forum* vol. 6, no. 5; Hunt, F. (1986) 'Opportunities Lost and Gained: Mechanization and Women's Work in the London Bookbinding and Printing Trades', in John, A. (Ed.) *Unequal Opportunities: Women's Employment in England 1800–1918*, London; Cockburn, C. (1984) *Brothers: Male Dominance and Technological Change*, London; Cockburn, C. (1986) 'The Material of Male Power', in Feminist Review (Ed.) *Waged Work: A Reader*, London.

21 Cf. Sowerwine, C. (1983) 'Workers and Women in France before 1914: The Debate over the Couriau Affair', *Journal of Modern History* 55 (Sept.), pp. 411–41.

22 Glucksmann, M. (1990) *Women Assemble: Women Workers and the New Industries in Inter-War Britain*, London and New York.

23 Whipp, R. (1979) *The Women Pottery Workers of Staffordshire and Trade Unionism, 1890–1905*, unpublished thesis, Warwick; Dupree, M. (1981) *Family structure in the Staffordshire Potteries 1840–1900*, unpublished D.Phil. thesis, Oxford; Sarsby, J. (1988) (see note 14); Wikander, U. (1988) (see note 1); Zylberberg-Hocquard, M-H., work in progress; De Groot, G., work in progress.

24 Among other things, I imagine that in pottery we should find similar phenomena to those found by Joy Parr concerning knitting machines; men used them in the East Midlands of England, while women used them in south-western Ontario, Canada. See Parr, J. (1990) *The Gender of Breadwinners: Women, Men, and Change in Two Industrial Towns, 1880–1950*, Toronto, Chapter Three, 'When is Knitting Women's Work?'

25 Several studies point to the increasing focus on motherhood in the general debate and also among activist women at this time. See, for example, Sevenhuijsen, S. (1992) 'Mothers as Citizens: Feminism, Evolutionary Theory and the Reform of Dutch Family Law 1870–1910', in Smart, C. (Ed.) *Regulating Womanhood: Historical Essays on Marriage, Motherhood and Sexuality*, London and New York; Lewis, J. (1980).

Chapter 9

Creating Gender: Technology and Femininity in the Swedish Dairy Industry

Lena Sommestad

Figure 9.1 is a photograph taken in a creamery in the Swedish village of Rimbo, close to Stockholm, in 1939. It shows a skilled buttermaker – *a dairymaid* – who has just emptied a large mechanical churn. The butter has slid into the transportation vat below, soon to be wheeled away to the cold-storage room.

The Rimbo dairymaid represents a unique piece of Swedish industrial history. We are used to seeing female industrial workers sitting in long lines in fish-processing, garment and electronics assembly plants, performing monotonous and low-paid work. The Rimbo dairymaid had a very different role. As an industrial dairymaid she was a skilled and authoritative works manager. Not only did dairymaids make high-quality butter and cheese, they were often forewomen and dairy directors, responsible for apprentices and workers, bookkeeping and sales. Their occupational status was confirmed by formal vocational training. As early as 1858 two public vocational schools for dairymaids were founded in Sweden, and during the following century thousands of dairymaids were instructed in schools and training dairies all over Sweden. By 1900 the dairy industry – one of Sweden's most important export industries – depended almost entirely on skilled female labour. Not until the inter-war years did women lose their predominance within skilled industrial dairy work. In that period, the once female art of dairying was transformed into a male industrial profession. As in other Western dairying nations, *dairymen* eventually replaced dairymaids (see Figure 9.2).

Industrial dairying as a female occupation brings to the fore the question of women's relation to science and engineering technology. In the developing Swedish dairy industry dairymaids were machine operators, not machine assistants. Dairymaids knew how to set and operate churns, separators, pasteurizers and cheese vats. They decided the exact time needed for heating the cheese curd as well as for churning the butter and separating and pasteurizing the milk. Dairymaids provided the specialized knowledge needed in dairy production. Machines were tools in their hands, just as milk skimmers and dasher

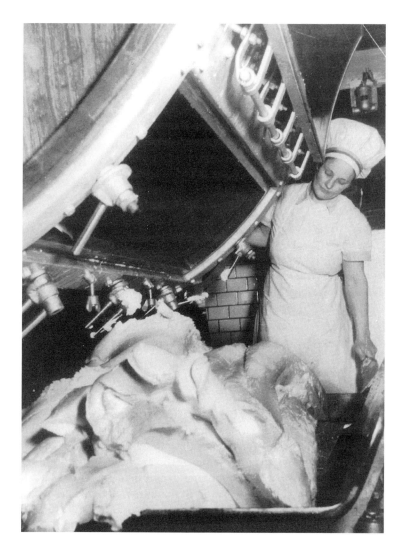

Figure 9.1 A dairymaid in Rimbo empties a large, mechanical churn. Note the characteristic dairymaid's cap. The white cap – often tied with a blue and yellow ribbon – was the professional sign of formally trained dairymaids.

Number of
employees

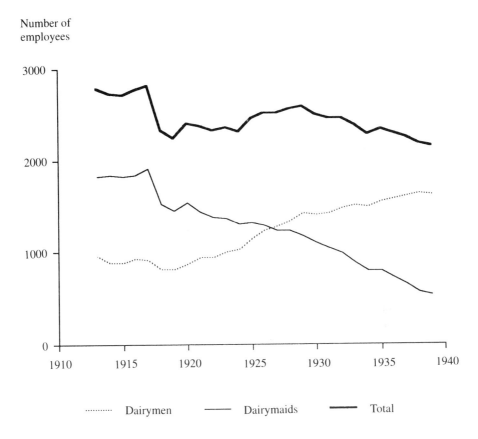

Figure 9.2 Dairymaids and dairymen in the Swedish dairy industry, 1913–1939
Sources: SOS Mejerihantering 1913–1938 (Swedish Official Dairy Statistics 1920–1938); and
Statistiska Centralbyråns arkiv, Jordbruksstatistiska avdelningen, mejeristatistik, Serie HVba,
arbetstabeller 1939, vol. 22 (Archive of Statistiska Centralbyrån, Dairy Statistics, working tables
1939).

churns had been in pre-industrial craft production.

Historically, few female workers have been assigned supervisory and influential positions within industry. The role of controlling machinery and industrial production has been closely connected to masculinity and male power. This has been particularly true in capital-intensive processing industries, where men have directed and controlled all types of production whether steel, paint, dough or paper pulp. How, then, did women in the early-twentieth-century Swedish dairy industry retain their control over mechanized dairy production for such a long time? And why did they eventually lose this unique position as works managers in a modern processing industry?

Gender, Science and Engineering Technology

Changes in the gender division of labour must be understood as historical processes. There are no given economic or biological links between the content of specific work tasks and their gender. People continually code and recode work tasks as masculine or feminine on the basis of their own historically changing conceptions, interests and experiences. In a larger context, the making of gendered divisions of labour is part of the historical construction of gender difference, most obviously reflected in the linguistic categories of the feminine and the masculine. In the historical process conflicting and alternative inter-pretations of gender are constantly confronted with one another, but in the long run these interpretations tend to move towards dichotomies. Femininity and masculinity are differentiated and counterpoised to one another.[1]

In the gender coding of skilled machinery work two traditions may be discerned, one predominant and one underlying. According to the predominant tradition, which we all know, science and engineering technology are associated with masculinity. This tradition has deep historical roots. In the Western world, science and engineering technology were developed by men in male surround-ings, within practical spheres of activity such as metallurgy and warfare or in educational institutions reserved for men. In the course of the centuries science and technology became important sources of male power. Men guarded their near-monopoly in these fields even more carefully as industrialization threatened to undermine established patterns of male dominance. By means of exclusion and ideological pressures, women were prevented from entering scientific and technological fields. Science and engineering technology became primary signifiers of masculinity and male power in the industrial era.[2]

The second, underlying tradition has been much less discussed. This tradition allows for an associative link between femininity, science and engineering technology, not by understanding science and technology as inherently feminine, but by suppressing the masculine, scientific and technological aspects of specific work tasks in the gender coding process. Instead, characteristic traits perceived as feminine have been emphasized. One example is housework. Housework has always been perceived as feminine, even when it has included responsibility for technological devices such as stone mangles (ironing machines), washing machines and sewing machines. The technological aspects of housework have been overlooked, allowing for an unambiguous feminine interpretation. Another example is technically qualified work within health care. This type of work has been so firmly incorporated into a feminine work context – nursing – that the technological aspects have tended to become of secondary importance for its gendering.[3] Skilled industrial dairy work is a third example. I suggest that the reason why Swedish dairymaids in the early twentieth century were allowed to control machinery and production was the existence of an alternative interpretive tradition, challenging the interpretation of dairy work as male machinery work. This interpretive tradition, long predominant, was centred around the notion that milk belongs to the female sphere.

Women and Milk – The Agrarian Interpretation

The idea that milk belongs to the female sphere pervaded many pre-industrial cultures. In Western Europe women were responsible for dairying in most countries before the industrial revolution, and still today, according to anthropologists, dairying is one of the world's most typical female work tasks.[4] In pre-industrial Scandinavia, the feminine coding of dairying was particularly strong. According to ethnologists, Swedish farm women usually performed all daily work chores connected with milk and cows – feeding, clearing the dung out, milking, buttermaking, cheesemaking, etc. Women were also independently responsible for management and the production of knowledge in the field. The exclusiveness of women's control over dairying was especially apparent within cheesemaking. Cheese was often made at seasonal, female work feasts, *ystegillen,* where women worked and enjoyed themselves on their own. 'No man is regarded worthy of attending this women's work, and even if someone nicely asks to be let in, it is of no avail', reported the chronicler Olaus Magnus in the mid sixteeenth century.[5]

The strong feminine coding of milk and dairying persisted well into the twentieth century.[6] This was particularly true in the northern parts of the country, where young women moved to the mountain pastures with the cattle every summer, creating a spatially separated female world of work and leisure. On the farm, the barn was considered an exclusively female space. For example, unmarried women commonly slept in the barn with the cattle. Men seldom approached the female sphere of milk and cows. Milking in particular was associated with strong gender taboos. 'Not only was it improper for a man to milk, it was considered shameful.'[7] Oral histories tell of the surprise and indignation caused by men milking as late as 1900. A southern farm woman claimed, for example, that 'it was so much the case, that when a man had milked, people refused to drink'.[8]

Why did Swedes express such strong feelings about the violation of gender boundaries in milking? Their reactions are easier to understand if we look at dairying in a larger cultural and mythical context. In many pre-industrial societies food preparation was associated with female biology or sexuality. In parts of France, for example, it was believed that marital fertility was related to the art of cooking, and all over Western Europe menstruating women were long considered to have a negative impact on certain foods by promoting processes of putrefaction.[9] In Scandinavia, associations with female sexuality were expressed especially in myths about buttermaking. People argued, for example, that whores had a beneficial influence on the churnability of cream, while witches, on the other hand, could destroy the cream and make it unusable.[10] In some areas nakedness was associated with churning success. An oral history from Finland tells about a woman who churned naked 'and wrapped her vest around the churn'.[11] On a more general level, the associative links between food preparation and female sexuality can be viewed as a part of the comprehensive cultural notion of women's closeness to nature (as opposed to culture). Food preparation is related to products of nature as well as to bodily functions.[12] In this context the feminine character of milk takes on a double meaning. Not only is milk a product of nature, but women themselves are also producers of milk – mother's milk. Furthermore, food preparation can be understood as a technology directly reflecting women's physiology. This interpretation has been proposed by Lewis Mumford, who claims that static and stabilizing processes are associated with femininity:

> the static processes are female and reflect the predominant anabolism of woman's physiology: for they work from within, as in any chemical transformation, and they remain largely in place, undergoing qualitative changes, from raw meat to boiled meat, from fermenting grain to beer, from planted seed to seeding plant.[13]

This analogy, suggested by Mumford, obviously corresponds to popular historical conceptions of gender. The above-mentioned association between cooking and marital fertility, observed in France, is but one example.

Machinery and Science – The Industrial Interpretation

Commercial and industrial dairying developed in Sweden from the late nineteenth century. At this time numerous small, mechanized creameries were established all over the country, and Sweden became one of the world's leading butter exporting nations. In the following decades Swedish dairying gradually developed into a larger-scale industry. This process peaked in the 1930s, when the world agricultural crisis forced a radical restructuring of the entire dairy industry.[14]

With the industrialization of dairy production, skilled dairy work was incorporated into an entirely new context. As a consequence, new interpretive possibilities opened up. Industrial dairy work could be associated with masculin-ity, in line with the strong Western tradition in which technology and scientific rationality – important sources of control and power – belong to the male sphere. The traditional, symbolically charged association between femininity and milk could be challenged by the association of dairy processing with male engineering technology and male science. However, it was a long time before this new interpretive possibility developed more widely in Sweden. Not until the 1920s and 1930s did skilled dairy work finally start to shift from an ambiguously coded occupation – at the crossroads between femininity and masculinity – into an exclusively masculine profession.

The reinterperation process developed along two lines. Firstly, as machinery became increasingly conspicuous in dairy production, it became less natural to associate dairying with milk, and thus with women. Instead, associations were more easily made with engineering technology, and thus with men. The first, important steps in this direction were taken in the late nineteenth century, when separators and mechanical churns were introduced. As buttermaking was mechanized, the relationship between dairymaids and the primary product became less visual and tangible than before. No longer was milk placed in open cans for the cream to rise; nor was it necessary to skim off the cream by hand or to work the churned butter on open table butter-workers. In the separator the cream was separated from the skim milk mechanically, and in the modern churns, butter-working was carried out invisibly in connection with the churning. However, machinery did not completely overshadow milk in the visual appearance of dairy workplaces until the radical restructuring of the industry in the 1930s. At that time, open separators, pasteurizers, chutes and vats were replaced by hermetic separators and by closed pasteurizers, tubes and tanks. Dairying was definitely transformed into a modern processing industry, where milk was seldom seen or touched but instead was handled indirectly, hidden behind tin, enamel and steel.

The rise of scientific milk research contributed to the recoding of dairy work by promoting a radically new attitude towards milk. In the late nineteenth century, chemists investigated the components of milk, trying to explain previously unknown and mysterious physical and chemical processes such as gravity cream separation, ripening of cream, fermentation of milk, and transformation of cream into butter. New, scientifically informed production technologies soon developed within the dairy industry. Methods to check bacterial levels and fat content spread quickly, and the techniques for butter-making and cheesemaking advanced. As a consequence, milk lost its previous status as a respected and mysterious product of nature. In the production of knowledge, oral tradition, myth and experience were replaced by science. This development was closely associated with masculinity. To be sure, dairymaids acquired the new, scientific knowledge and proficiency, but the associative link between milk and women was weakened as the the idea of milk as inherently feminine faded away, at the same time as dairy work could be related to notions of male scientific rationality (in contrast to female intuition). The tools of science offered men a legitimate way of approaching milk, treating it as an interesting chemical solution to be explored and manipulated in systematic ways.

The Process of Gender Recoding

In Sweden as a whole, the masculinization process in dairying clearly paralleled the industrialization process. As the level of centralization and mechanization increased in the dairy industry, so did the proportion of men in the labour force. However, on the local level this correlation between industrialization and masculinization was much less clear-cut.[15] More detailed statistical analyses show that in the midst of the masculinization process, in 1930, more dairymen than dairymaids certainly worked in the largest and most mechanized Swedish dairies, but women still made up a significant minority – approximately one-third – of the skilled workforce in these highly industrialized dairies. I would

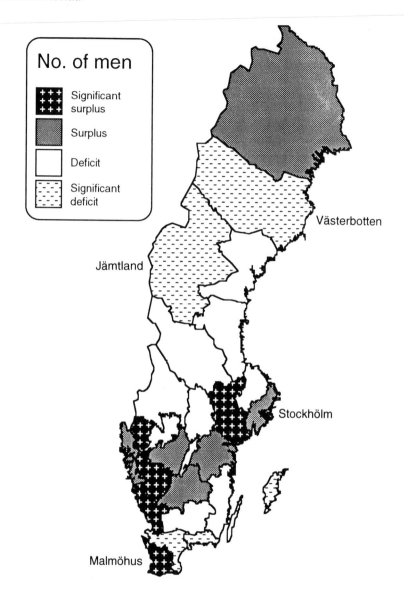

Figure 9.3 Swedish counties with respectively more or less dairymen than should be expected from the level of industrialization* and the type of production of individual dairies, 1930
* Level of industrialization has been measured by type of company, amount of processed milk (scale), and horsepower used (mechanization).

Source: Statistiska centralbyråns arkiv, Jordbruksstatistiska avdelningen. Mejeristatistik, Serie HVa, primäruppgifter 1930 (Archive of Statistics Sweden, Dairy Statistics, primary records 1930).

argue that this locally mixed pattern points to the flexibility of occupational gender coding. People on the local level responded to the centralization and mechanization of dairying in different ways, depending on their own specific personal and social experiences. Some people quickly recoded dairy work as masculine, developing the associative links with machinery and science, while others stuck to the agrarian interpretation, maintaining that dairying belonged to the feminine sphere no matter how scientific, mechanized and large-scale it had become.

Indeed, masculinization spread from dairy to dairy and from region to region in complex and varied ways. Most obviously, the recoding of the gender of dairy work proceeded faster in some regions of Sweden than in others (see Figure 9.3). This regional pattern reflects how individual gender interpretations were shaped by foreign influence as well as by varying economic and cultural surroundings. In the plain districts of south-western Sweden and the Mälar region (surrounding Stockholm, the capital), more dairymen were employed than would be expected considering the level of industrialization and the type of production of individual dairies. In south-eastern and northern Sweden, on the other hand, fewer men than would be expected were employed.

The importance of regional differences is particularly well illustrated by two contrasting dairy regions: the county of Malmöhus in the southernmost part of Sweden, and the counties of Jämtland and Västerbotten in the northern part of the country.[16] The county of Malmöhus, where dairymen soon got a foothold in all types of dairies, was historically receptive to the spread of innovations from abroad, in particular within agriculture. The idea that dairy work could be interpreted as masculine came first from nearby Holstein, a German province where men had already entered commercial dairy production in the proto-industrial phase. *Holsteiner* moved to Sweden as dairy managers and dairy advisers as early as the mid nineteenth century, and they helped to challenge the feminine tradition in Scandinavian dairying by demonstrating the cultural possibility of associating milk with masculinity. Later on, in the 1890s, the first vocational dairy school for men was founded in Malmöhus county, creating a national centre for the continuous spread of new, exemplary dairymen. Furthermore, in addition to foreign influence regional economic and cultural characteristics facilitated the recoding process in Malmöhus county. The agricultural population in Malmöhus was in the minority during the inter-war years. Historically, Malmöhus agriculture had strong ties with nearby Danish and German plain districts, which were characterized by large farms, a late switch from arable to dairy farming, and a low degree of female participation in agricultural work. In this milieu, the feminine coding of milk was weaker than in older dairy districts. In addition, most young women here were not only inexperienced in milking and home dairying, but also culturally alien to the physically demanding character of industrial dairy work. By the 1930s, most women in Malmöhus county had acquired a modern, urban understanding of gender difference, stressing notions of female dexterity and domesticity rather than physical strength.

Figure 9.4 A female dairy assistant monitors the pasteurizer in a large Stockholm dairy in 1930.

Figure 9.5 A dairymaid operates the butter churns in Eskilstuna dairy, a fairly large, urban dairy in central Sweden in 1937.

The counties of Jämtland and Västerbotten provide a striking contrast. Jämtland and Västerbotten, located in the far north, lie outside the historically established routes of innovation diffusion in Sweden. In 1930 dairymaids were still responsible for all types of industrial production, and dairymen were almost unknown. Economically, lumbering and small-scale dairy farming were important. Men were often absent to lumber, fish or hunt, while women managed the farms. Notions of femininity were centred around productive capacities. Farm women were expected to participate actively in all types of farm work; it was desirable for them to be skilled, authoritative, and physically strong. In this milieu, young women were attracted to industrial dairying as late as the 1930s. Dairying offered skilled and independent positions, and it was not more physically taxing than the constant and laborious work on small farms. In addition, the feminine coding of milk was very strong in northern Sweden as a result of centuries of continuous female dairy farming. Men were extremely reluctant to enter this female sphere, and there were few dairymen to exemplify the masculine aspects of scientific and technical dairy work.

Dairymaids as Works Managers and Machine Operators

In the early twentieth century, thousands of industrial dairymaids were given the opportunity to develop specialized and technical skills. How did dairymaids themselves apprehend this unique female opportunity within industry? Interviews with retired dairymaids show that for most of them work was a source of satisfaction and self-confidence. Dairymaids took pride in their ability and in work well done. 'I wasn't afraid of working. And sure, I was strong!' Cheesemaking in particular was regarded as an interesting and challenging task. '[Cheesemaking], it was a rather tough job. But it was fun!' In one of my interviews a retired buttermaker declared that if she could have started her career all over again, she would have chosen cheesemaking. 'I am *tremendously* interested. But buttermaking was interesting, too. It was a shame if your butter wasn't graded as *extra* ...'. Pleasure in work was promoted by feelings of personal independence and work solidarity, especially at small, exclusively female workplaces. As one dairymaid explained, dairying made possible a trespassing of gender boundaries. Dairymaids did 'what girls shouldn't do'. 'In a way, you were your own master in the dairy. You did what you had to do, and then you ran your own business and did whatever you liked.' 'Somehow, you were independent. ... And it was enjoyable, at the same time.' 'And it was kind of fun, too, there were only womenfolk, we had no men with us.'

Tending machinery was part of the daily routine. At larger dairies, where specialist engine-men were often employed, dairymaids were responsible for daily monitoring and maintenance. This included setting and monitoring separators and pasteurizers, carefully disassembling and putting together tubes and machinery, oiling and cleaning. At smaller dairies, dairymaids tended steam engines and other mechanical appliances as well. 'We were responsible for all those things', one dairymaid explained. 'Indeed, even when the pumps broke down, you had to repair them.'

Apparently, dairymaids never gave a great deal of thought to the unusually technical character of their occupation. Since their position within industrial dairying was so well established, they quite simply regarded machinery work as well suited for women. In fact, there are even examples of women who chose dairy work because of its technical character. 'My mother thought it was awful', one dairymaid recalled. 'A 5000-litre churn that thundered awfully, but I was happy! Well, if this had been today, then I would probably have applied for a job in an engineering workshop or something.' However, dairymaids in my interviews most typically talked about machinery work as a natural but nevertheless peripheral part of their occupational identity. Although machinery held an important position in their daily work routine, they tended to play down their own machinery skills. 'It was no great matter to operate the machines', one dairymaid maintained. 'To start the separator, or to start a churn or something. . . . that was no great matter.' 'Sure, one managed those machines all right, the separator and all that', another one recalled. 'Oh yes, because you know, it wasn't much then.'

It is interesting to note that men in the profession had a somewhat different attitude towards machinery. Dairymen often entered dairying through machinery work, for example as specialized engine-men, and in my interviews they typically tended to emphasize the crucial role of machinery in dairy production as well as their own specifically male machinery skills.

> You know in those days, all machines were driven by belts. You had a huge motor, then different belt pulleys to different shafts, to the separator, to the whey pumps, to the churn. . . . Transmission belts, you know, and if one of them flew, you had to mend it. Sure, it was absolutely terrible. . . .

> When things got more modern, dairymaids could seldom manage them. You know, they didn't have this . . . I should say, this understanding of machinery and such things that a man has . . . Well, some dairymaids shouldn't be belittled, but on the whole, if problems arose, they couldn't manage them as well.

We may conclude that the technical aspects of dairy work were crucial for dairymen, who strived to shape a masculine occupational identity within a previously feminine field.

'Get the Women out of the Dairies!'

In 1927, dairymen outnumbered dairymaids in the Swedish dairy industry for the first time, and in the following years, the masculinization process proceeded very rapidly. In 1939, the proportion of dairymaids in the skilled dairy workforce had dropped to only 25 per cent (see figure 9.2 above). Rising male unemployment rates in the 1920s and 1930s contributed to accelerating the pace of masculinization during the inter-war years. In the wake of recurrent male unemployment crises, increasing numbers of men found their way into the dairy profession, while dairymaids, on the other hand, were either pushed aside by male colleagues or voluntarily chose to turn their backs on the dairy industry. State educational policies also promoted the masculinization process. In the inter-war years, dairymen were educated for large, industrial dairies and for independent and leading positions, while dairymaids were educated for small, unmechanized dairies and for subordinate positions. This educational differentiation helped to strengthen the notion of modern, mechanized dairy work as inherently masculine.[17]

In the competitive atmosphere of the inter-war years, the occupational role of Swedish dairymaids was called into question for the first time. In a period of unemployment, why should women stay on in a typically male work task such as skilled, mechanized and supervisory industrial work? The most cutting critique appeared in the professional journal of Swedish dairymen, *Svenska Mejeritidningen*. In a sharp letter to the editor published in 1925, a dairyman demanded that all women leave the dairy industry, considering among other things men's superior 'ability to repair machinery' and the risk of 'standing still' because of women's inability to cope with 'the least little trouble': 'A dairymaid wants an engine-man to attend her, and to be sure, this engine-man must oil the separator and the churn for her, and in any case, even if she is working alone in a small dairy, as soon as the slightest fault or breakdown occurs, one repairman after the other must be hired'.[18]

The disparaging tone of this letter highlights the weakened position of women in the inter-war Swedish dairy industry. Replies from bitter dairymaids soon appeared in *Svenska Mejeritidningen*, but in the following years it became increasingly clear that dairymaids could no longer assert their occupational status. To be sure, dairymaids were still respected for their undeniable contributions during the formative decades of the Swedish dairy industry. However, they were no longer regarded as equals in the profession. Gradually, a consensus of male superiority emerged, fuelled by frequent more or less depreciating comments and statements: 'Of course, the task of tending machinery in a dairy should preferably be assigned to men, since this type of work is not at all suited for women';[19] 'The centralization of dairying, the large-scale production and the mechanized equipment imply that more men are needed in the workforce than has hitherto been the case';[20] 'Men operate machinery better than do women'.[21]

In 1938, the economist Karin Kock noted that young men in the dairy industry had greater opportunities than young women to be trained for machinery work. According to her analysis, male labourers 'start by assisting in machinery work, and then are trained to become dairymen, while women seldom get the necessary training at the machines'.[22] Eventually, thus, young women in the dairy industry had become subject to the same exclusionary policies that other women working in industry had long suffered. In the post-war era, no new generations of women were to follow the Rimbo dairymaid, one of the last representatives of the independent female dairy profession.

The Legacy of Dairymaids – Some Reflections

The new gender division of labour in Swedish dairy work evolved as the result of an economic, political and cultural process, in which multiple developments intertwined. In this chapter I have focused on one particularly important trend: the recoding of the gender of skilled dairy work from a feminine milk-related task to a masculine, scientific, machinery-related task. I have also pointed to the complex interplay between industrial development and occupational gender coding. In order to understand why economic and technological changes result in new gender divisions of labour, we must look at how people interpret work and technology in terms of masculinity and femininity.

In a broader historical perspective, the legacy of Swedish dairymaids allows for several interpretations. On one level, this is a story of conformity and female subordination, a piece in the making of our contemporary, gender-segregated working life. When dairymaids disappeared, so did the alternative model of femininity that they represented. As a consequence, the associative links between masculinity, science and technology were strengthened in Swedish industrial society, while the underlying, alternative tradition – allowing for connections between femininity, science and technology – was pressed back. The opposition between masculinity and femininity was sharpened; the boundary between male and female work was elucidated.

However, the legacy of dairymaids can also be interpreted in more open and optimistic ways. In particular, dairymaids can be viewed as part of a strong, Swedish tradition of active female participation in gainful work. The occupation of the industrial dairymaid was originally shaped in an agrarian context, where women had a crucial role in production. It represents a femininity embracing independence and authority in work, outside as well as inside the domestic sphere. Today, this tradition continues within new occupations. It is worth noticing that in Sweden, the cult of domesticity and the notion of separate spheres never developed as far as in other, more wealthy Western countries which became industrialized earlier. Well into the post-war era, a substantial proportion of young Swedish women were still socialized in rural surroundings, where notions of female domesticity and separateness were largely irrelevant. In Sweden, the family wage system developed late, as a historical parenthesis, and today, women's labour market participation rate is significantly higher than in most other Western countries.[23]

Finally, in contrast to this interpretation of dairymaids as representatives of continuity in working women's experience, we may place the dairymaid as a symbol of change and discontinuity. Industrial dairymaids, skilled and technically able, remind us of the historical flexibility and variability of occupational gender coding. Today, when we look at the photograph of the Rimbo dairymaid, she actually challenges our own limited conceptions of female work, as well as our limited conceptions of femininity. She stands out as a woman doing a man's job, as a deviation from our own expectations of femininity in work. Let us hope that this type of historical challenge may serve to stimulate contemporary discussions on women and technology. In the 1990s, Swedish working women still work predominantly in low-paid jobs and in subordinate positions. At the same time control over science and technology remains centred in male hands. Should women try to capture – or recapture – this male scientific and technological stronghold? Or are there other ways to make working life more equal? History points to alternatives and possibilities. We all participate in the making of new divisions of labour, as well as in the constant re-creation of gender difference.

Notes

A shorter version of this chapter has been published in *Dædalus 1993*, year-book of the Swedish National Museum of Science and Technology (Stockholm, 1992). When no other source is indicated, it is based on Sommestad, L. (1992) *Från mejerska till mejerist. En studie av mejeriyrkets maskuliniseringprocess* (From Dairymaids to Dairymen. A Study of the Masculinization Process in Skilled Dairy Work) (with a summary in English), Lund. More detailed references are given in this book. The most important primary sources used in the study are Swedish official dairy statistics, official reports and government documents, the periodical press, specialist literature, and interviews with experienced, chiefly retired, dairymen and dairymaids. For support and useful suggestions while writing this article I am thankful to Bo Malmberg, Uppsala University: Gertjan de Groot, University of Utrecht; Nancy Grey Osterud, Radcliffe College; Mimi Wessling, University of California at Berkeley; and Ulla Wikander, Uppsala University.

1   Concerning the importance of gender distinctions in the construction of meaning, compare Epstein, C.F. (1988) *Deceptive Distinctions: Sex, Gender, and the Social Order*, New York, pp. 11–16; and Scott, J.W. (1988) *Gender and the Politics of History*, New York, esp. pp. 7, 39–41, 43, 60.

2   For the associative links between masculinity, power, technology and scientific rationality, see, for example, Cockburn, C. (1985) *Machinery of Dominance: Women, Men and Technological Know-How*, London, pp. 20–43; Keller, E.F. (1983) 'Women, Science and Popular Mythology', in Rothschild, J. (Ed.) *Machina ex Dea: Feminist Perspectives on Technology*, New York; Newman, L.M. (1985) 'The Problem of Biological Determinism (1870–1890)', in Newman, L.M. (Ed.) *Men's Ideas/Women's Realities: Popular Science 1870–1915*, New York; and Rosenbeck, B. (1987) *Kvindekøn. Den moderne kvindeligheds historie 1880–1980*, Copenhagen, pp. 67ff. Women's exclusion from educational opportunities in Sweden is discussed, for example, by Berner, B. (1982) 'Kvinnor, kunskap och makt i teknikens värld', *Kvinnovetenskaplig tidskrift* no. 3, pp. 27–9; Kyle, G. (1972) *Svensk flickskola under 1800-talet*, Göteborg, Historiska institutionen, chapter VIII; and Kyle, G. (1979) *Gästarbeterska i manssamhället. Studier om industriarbetande kvinnors*

villkor i Sverige, Stockholm, pp. 117–28; and *SOU 1938:47*, Betänkande angående gift kvinnas yrkesarbete m.m. avgivet av Kvinnoarbetskommittén, Stockholm, pp. 201–9.

3   Compare Cockburn, C. (1985) (see note 2), chapter 4; and Milkman, R. (1987) *Gender at Work. The Dynamics of Job Segregation by Sex During World War II*, Urbana, chapter 4.

4   For the history of women in European dairying, see, for example, Bourke, J. (1990) 'Dairywomen and Affectionate Wives: Women in the Irish Dairy Industry, 1890–1914', *The Agricultural History Review* 38, pp. 149–64; Hansen, B.K. (1982) 'Rural Women in Late Nineteenth-Century Denmark', *The Journal of Peasant Studies* 9, pp. 225–40; Højrup, O. (1967) *Landbokvinden. Rok og kærne, grovbrød og vadmel*, Copenhagen, Nationalmuséet, pp. 64ff; and Højrup, O. (1975) 'Die Arbeitsteilung zwischen Männern und Frauen in der bäuerlichen Kultur Dänemarks', *Ethnologia Scandinavica*, pp. 23–37; Kitteringham, J. (1975) 'Country Work Girls in Nineteenth-Century England', in Samuel, R. (Ed.) *Village Life and Labour*, London; McMurry, S. (1992) 'Women's Work in Agriculture: Divergent Trends in England and America, 1800–1930', *Comparative Studies in Society and History* 34 (April), pp. 248–70; Pinchbeck, I. (1930, repr. 1985) *Women Workers and the Industrial Revolution 1750–1850*, London, pp. 10–16, 33–7, 40–2; Valenze, Deborah (1991) 'The Art of Women and the Business of Men: Women's Work and the Dairy Industry c. 1740–1840', *Past and Present* 130 (February), pp. 142–69; and Wiegelmann, G. (1975) 'Bäuerliche Arbeitsteilung in Mittel- und Nordeuropa – Konstanz oder Wandel?', *Ethnologia Scandinavica*, pp. 5–22. For a comment on the contemporary situation, see Bradley, H. (1989) *Men's Work, Women's Work: A Sociological History of the Sexual Division of Labour in Employment*, Cambridge, p. 8.

5   Magnus, O. (1555, repr. in Swedish 1982) *Historia om de nordiska folken*, Stockholm, Gidlunds, pp. 628–9. A new edition in Latin of this classic book was published in 1972: *Historia de gentibus septentrionalibus: Romae 1555*, Copenhagen.

6   For Swedish women's role in pre-industrial dairy farming see *Ulma 1* in the Ethnological Oral History Collection, Archive of Nordiska Muséet, Stockholm; Ejdestam, J. (1980) *Mannen och kvinnan i svensk folktradition*, Stockholm, pp. 48, 51–3; Lidman, H. (Ed.) (1963) *Fäbodar*, Stockholm; Löfgren, O. (1975) 'Arbeitsteilung und Geschlechterrollen in Schweden', *Ethnologia Scandinavica*, pp. 49–72; Svensson, S. (1942) 'Böndernas tjänstefolk', in Lindblom, A. (Ed.) *Arbetaren i helg och söcken. Del I. Hus och hem*, Stockholm, pp. 121–2; and Österman, A. (1986) 'Kvinor och kor', *Fataburen*.

7   Quotation from Löfgren; O. (1975) (see note 6), p. 54.

8   Quotation from Österman, A. (1986) (see note 6), p. 67.

9   Marital fertility and the art of cooking is discussed in Verdier, Y. (1979) *Façons de dire, façons de faire. La laveuse, la couturière, la cuisinière*, Paris, pp. 19ff, 306–15, 323–5. As for the negative role of menstruation, compare Beauvoir, S. de (1949) *Le deuxième sexe*, Paris, Part I, pp. 202–3; and Gustavsson, A. (1979) *Den nyblivna modern*, Uppsala, pp. 25–6, 44–5.

10   Collection *Ulma 1* in the Ethnological Oral History Collection, Archive of Nordiska Muséet, Stockholm; Højrup, O. (1967) *Landbokvinden. Rok og kærne, grovbrød og vadmel*, Copenhagen, Nationalmuséet, pp. 73–4; and Possing, B. (1982) 'Arbejdsdeling, kvinder og patriarkalisk tradition på landet i det 19. århundrede', in *Årbog*

for arbejderbevægelsens historie, Copenhagen, Selskabet til Forskning i Arbejderbevægelsens Historie, pp. 117–25.

11 Quotation from Frykman, J. (1977) *Horan i bondesamhället*, Lund, pp. 92–5.

12 Women's closeness to nature is an important theme in Simone de Beauvoir's *Le deuxième sexe*, Part I. Compare Merchant, C. (1980) *The Death of Nature: Women, Ecology, and the Scientific Revolution*, San Francisco; and Ortner, S. (1974) 'Is Female to Male as Nature is to Culture?', in Rosaldo, M.Z. and Lamphere, L. (Eds) *Woman, Culture and Society*, Stanford. Food preparation is specifically discussed in Shopes, L. (1987) 'Women Cannery Workers in Baltimore, 1880–1943' (paper delivered at the Seventh Berkshire Conference on the History of Women, Wellesley College, Massachusetts, June 1987), p. 12.

13 Quotation from Mumford, L. (1967) *The Myth of the Machine: Technics and Human Development*, New York, p. 140.

14 For basic information about the rise of the Swedish dairy industry and the development of modern, industrial dairy technology, see for example Eskeröd, A. (1956) 'Jordskiftena och lantbrukets utveckling 1809–1914', in Ingers, E. (Ed.) *Bonden i svensk historia*, Part III, Stockholm; Johansson, T. and Thullberg, P. (1979) *Samverkan gav styrkan. Jordbrukarnas föreningsrörelse 1929–1979*, Stockholm; Juhlin-Dannfelt, H. *Kungl. Landtbruksakademien 1813–1912*, Part I-II, Stockholm; Liljhagen, G. (1901) *Några meddelanden rörande den svenska mejerihandteringen åren 1800–1900 samt förteckning över landet mejerier år 1900*, Stockholm, Kongl. Landtbruksstyrelsen; *Svensk mejeriindustri 1932–1957* (1957), Stockholm, Svenska Mejeriernas Riksförening; and Rosengren, L.F. (Ed.) (1927) *Svenska jordbrukets bok. Om mjölk och mjölkhushållning*, Part I–II, Stockholm.

15 See Sommestad, L. (1992) *Från mejerska till mejerist. En studie av mejeriyrkets maskuliniseringsprocess*, Lund, chapter 4. The detailed statistical analyses include all the 1600 Swedish industrial dairies in operation in 1930. The statistical source used is *Statistiska Centralbyråns arkiv, Jordbruksstatistiska avdelningen, mejeristatistik, Serie HVa, primäruppgifter 1930, vol. 23–24* (Archive of Statistiska Centralbyrån, Dairy Statistics, primary records 1930, vol. 23–24). Information given for each dairy includes location, type of company (farm/manorial, farmers' cooperative or private); amount of processed milk and cream; distribution of processed milk between fluid consumption, butter production and cheese production; horsepower used; and number of employees by sex and occupational category. In the final statistical analysis *the level of industrialization of individual dairies* is measured by type of company, amount of processed milk (scale), and horsepower used (mechanization).

16 The analysis of innovation diffusion and regional differences in Sweden is based on multiple sources, including Erixon, S. (Ed.) (1957) *Atlas över svensk folkkultur I. Materiell och social kultur*, Stockholm, map XXIV; Bringéus, Nils-Arvid (1964) *Tradition och förändring i 1800-talets skånska lanthushållning*, Kristianstad, pp. 92–5; Hägerstrand, T. (1965) 'Quantitative Techniques for Analysis of the Spread of Information and Technology', in Anderson, C.A. and Bowman, M.J. (Eds) *Education and Economic Development*, Chicago; Löfgren, O. (1975) 'Arbeitsteilung und Geschlechterrollen in Schweden', *Ethnologia Scandinavica*, pp. 49–72; Nelson, H. (1963) *Studier över svenskt näringsliv, säsongarbete och befolkningsrörelser under 1800- och 1900-talen*, Lund, pp. 85–8 and *passim*; Nyberg, A. (1989) *Tekniken – kvinnornas befriare? Hushållsteknik, köpevaror och gifta kvinnors hushållsarbetstid och förvärvsdeltagande 1930-talet–1980-talet*, Linköping, Tema

teknik och social förändring, pp. 155–61, 170–2; Szabó, Mátyás (1970) *Herdar och husdjur. En etnologisk studie över Skandinaviens och Mellaneuropas beteskultur och vallningsorganisation*, Stockholm, Nordiska Muséet, pp. 177–212; *Statistiska Meddelanden, Serie A, Band V:8* (1941) Den animaliska produktionen år 1937/1938, Stockholm, pp. 24–5; *Sveriges officiella statistik, Folkräkning 1930*, Stockholm, vol. 3, table 3; *Sveriges officiella statistik, Jordbruksräkningen 1932*, Stockholm, p. 24 and table P; and Utterström, Gustaf (1957) *Jordbrukets arbetare. Levnadsvillkor och arbetsliv på landsbygden från frihetstiden till mitten av 1800-talet*, Stockholm, Part I, pp. 444ff, 547, 559, 830ff.

17 For an extended analysis of Swedish dairy education and its impact on the masculinization process, see Sommestad, L. (1992) 'Able Dairymaids and Proficient Dairymen: Education and De-Feminization in the Swedish Dairy Industry', *Gender and History* 4 (Spring), pp. 34–48.

18 Quotation from 'Manlig eller kvinnlig föreståndare och personal vid mejerierna?' (1925), letter to the editor from 'Gammal mejeriman', *Svenska Mejeritidningen*, no. 46, p. 370.

19 Quotation from Andersson, O. (1925) 'Manlig eller kvinnlig föreståndare och personal vid mejerierna?', *Svenska Mejeritidningen*, no. 50, p. 404.

20 Quotation from Riksarkivet (The Swedish National Archive), Kommittéarkiv, 1 June 1928, Lägre lantbruksundervisningssakkunniga (no. 338), statement from Västmanlands läns hushållningssällskap.

21 Quotation from Riksarkivet (The Swedish National Archive), Esplundaarkivet, Landshövding Axel Mörners arkiv, Lägre lantbruksundervisningssakkunniga (vol. I, no. 288), statement by professor L.F. Rosengren at a committee meeting 21 October 1929.

22 Quotation from *SOU 1938:47*. Betänkande angående gift kvinnas förvärvsarbete m.m., avgivet av Kvinnoarbetskommittén, Stockholm, p. 383.

23 Compare Blom, I. (1990) ' "Hun er den Raadende over Husets Økonomiske Anliggender"? Changes in Women's Work and Family Responsibilities in Norway since the 1860s', in Hudson, P. and Lee, W.R. (Eds) *Women's Work and the Family Economy in Historical Perspective*, Manchester, pp. 157–71; *Kvinnor och män i Sverige och EG* (1991), Stockholm, Statistiska Centralbyrån, p. 7; Lewis, J. and Åström, G. (1992) 'Equality, Difference and State Welfare: Labor Market and Family Policies in Sweden', *Feminist Studies* 18 (Spring), pp. 70–1; and Julkunen, Raija (1990) 'Women in the Welfare State', in Manninen, Merja and Setälä, Päivi (Eds) *The Lady With the Bow: The Story of Finnish Women*, Keuruu, pp. 148–53.

Chapter 10

Cooking up Women's Work: Women Workers in the Dutch Food Industries 1889–1960

Marlou Schrover

If women had dominated the food industries, scholars would no doubt have attributed their prominent role in these industries to the fact that women traditionally dealt with food at home. However, unlike childcare, nursing, and the textile and clothing industries, which were seen as based on work that had traditionally been done by women, the food industries were not dominated by women. Before industrialization, women did take part in commercialized food production. Nevertheless, as soon as food industries emerged, men started to dominate.

Industrialization and urbanization separated large groups of people from the production and processing of their own food. When food production moved out of the household of the producer, it gave rise to food industries. Some products were already manufactured outside the household centuries ago, giving rise to bakeries and breweries. Despite these early forerunners, the food industries are essentially a phenomenon of the nineteenth century. During the end of the nineteenth and the beginning of the twentieth century there was a dramatic expansion in the range of products, a clear change in the methods of production, and an unprecedented increase in scale in the food industries.

In this chapter, I will show that technological change influenced women's work in the food industries, but was seldom the direct reason, or excuse, for the regendering of work. Four Dutch food industries have been selected to illustrate this point. As far as women's work is concerned, there is no doubt that dairying was the most striking of the food industries. Dairying was seen as typically feminine in the non-industrial setting, but dairy factories hardly employed women after 1900. Brewing of beer was commercialized long before the industrial era. It was one of the few Dutch crafts without guild restrictions on women's work, and as a result there were both female and male brewers. Yet, at the end of the nineteenth century, there were relatively fewer women in this industry than in most others. The cocoa and chocolate industry was the most clearly feminized of the food industries. Women constituted a large proportion

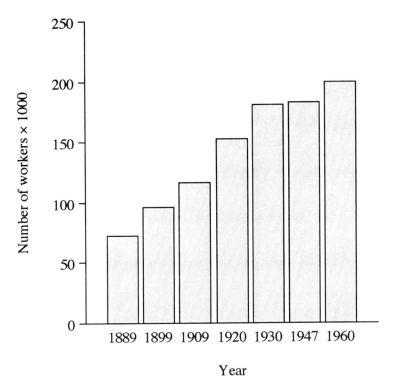

Figure 10.1 Total number of workers in the food and allied industries, 1889–1960
Source: 13th Dutch General Poll, 31 May 1960, part 10-c (Hilversum 1966), table 1.

of the workforce at the end of the nineteenth century, and this proportion rose throughout the first half of the twentieth century. In the margarine industry, there was a sudden influx of women after the First World War, followed by their departure a decade or so later.

With 72,000 workers in 1889, and 200,000 in 1960, food was by far the largest of the Dutch industries.[1] Only a small percentage of workers in the food industries were women, but as the total number of workers was large, food industries employed more women than any other industry except the textile and clothing industries. Figure 10.1 shows the total number of workers in the Dutch food industries, and figure 10.2 the percentage of women in these industries, between 1889 and 1960. The percentage of women employed in the industries rose gradually from 1889 onwards.

Statistics about women's work have to be treated with care. Women's work tends to be underestimated in statistics. Moreover, instructions regarding what is to be counted and what is not can cause apparent fluctuations.[2] Homeworkers are certainly underrepresented in the statistics. This has its consequences for the figures presented here, as homeworking was important for the food industries.

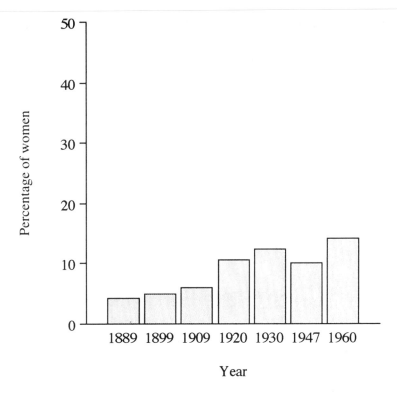

Figure 10.2 Percentage of women workers in the food and allied industries, 1889–1960

Source: 13th Dutch General Poll, 31 May 1960, part 10-c (Hilversum 1966), table 1.

The mechanization of parts of the food production process at first increased the extent of homeworking, and later decreased it. The number of hands needed for cleaning fruit and vegetables, sorting peas and peeling shallots expanded considerably at the end of the nineteenth century and the beginning of the twentieth. This was caused by the introduction of preserved and canned foods, and jams. The peak in home sorting lay around the turn of the century. At the beginning of the twentieth century, the sorting of peas, rice, and cocoa and coffee beans was moved to factories, because it became possible to do this kind of work by machine. Peeling and cleaning remained hand-work. They continued to be done at home throughout the 1930s to 1950s, and sometimes, as for instance with shrimp peeling, even longer. Home-work is often seen as women's work, but it was also done by children who were too young to be officially employed, by unemployed men, and by men and older children after working hours. It is uncertain whether men did much of the home-work in the food industries.[3] They were probably reluctant to admit that they were involved in home-work, as some employers officially forbade it.[4]

The underrepresentation of homeworkers in statistics may cause apparent increases in the number of women employed in the food industries at points when work changed from being home-work to being factory work.

From Women to Men: Dairying

The dairy industry is important for the Netherlands. The exclusion of women from the dairy industry is a striking phenomenon. As figure 10.3 shows, the percentage of women in dairying was in 1889 several times higher than that in the food industry in general. Contrary to the general trend, however, the percentage declined steadily until the Second World War.

At the turn of the century, buttermaking moved from the farm to the factory. Women, as experts in buttermaking, did not make the same move. Farmers' wives may have had clear reasons for not making this transition, but the fact that hardly any women worked in dairy factories is striking. Cheesemaking and buttermaking were typically women's work on farms.

The most common argument for the transition of dairy work from farm to

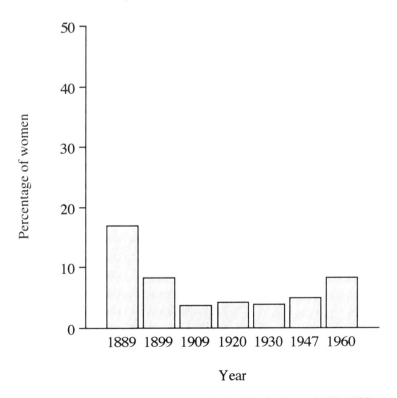

Figure 10.3 Percentage of women workers in the dairy industry, 1889–1960
Source: 13th Dutch General Poll, 31 May 1960, part 10-c (Hilversum 1966), table 1.

factory is that it freed the farmer's wife from the strenuous task of dairying.[5] For reasons of farm management, it was not attractive for the women to move from the farm to the factory. After about 1880, Dutch farming became much more specialized.[6] Peasants, and farmers for whom dairying had only been a sideline, now dropped it. In the ten years before the turn of the century, 800 dairy factories were established. When the factories proved to be successful, farmers for whom dairying had been important also became interested in industrialized butter and cheese production. The butter factories gave farmers a good price for their milk. The women, now freed from dairying, could spend more time on other farm activities such as animal care. Dropping butter production sometimes enabled farmers to do with one maid less. Butter factories made better butter, and provided farmers with a higher income than they had previously obtained from dairy production on the farm. Although this explains why butter production moved to factories, and why farmers' wives did not move with it, it does not explain why dairy factories did not employ women. In an attempt to find an explanation, I shall take a closer look at butter production in farms and factories.

Throughout the nineteenth century, large amounts of butter were made on Dutch farms. The sale of butter was an important source of income for the farmers. In parts of the Netherlands these revenues were the only money income the farmers had. Buttermaking was the realm of women. They were not only in charge of making butter, but often also controlled its sale, either to engrossers or on the local market. Buttermaking was not a skill that was easily learned, neither was there a simple recipe that could be written down. The quality of the milk, the number of hours it had been standing, and the season or the outside temperature, all greatly affected procedures to be followed when churning. Descriptions of churning brim with conditional stipulations.

In the nineteenth century, Dutch butter was widely sold abroad, mainly to England. In the course of the nineteenth century, the Dutch started to lose the English market to the Irish, the French and above all the Danes. In the second half of the nineteenth century the price of Dutch butter started to fall, coinciding with an increase in Danish exports.[7] It was not so much that the Dutch butter had deteriorated, but the Danish was better, and thus sold better.[8] There were two reasons for the superiority of Danish butter. Firstly, there was the adulteration of Dutch butter by merchants and traders. Although much of the declining reputation of Dutch butter was later attributed to the margarine industry, the relapse of Dutch butter precedes the emancipation of butter forgery in the form of a margarine industry by some thirty years. In an attempt to stop the adulteration, the government drew up rules and regulations. This resulted in a slight improvement of the export quality. The second reason for the superiority of Danish butter was that the production of butter on Dutch and Danish farms differed. The Danes were relatively new large-scale producers and exporters of butter. Systematic instruction of farmers, both men and women, on how to improve production had ensured that Danish butter was always of a good quality. Some of the improvements in the production process were simple: hygiene during milking and storing; testing the temperature of the milk with a

Figure 10.4 Woman churning and man playing with a child in a walking frame. This photograph was staged in 1938 to show the way things were in the 'good old days'. The impossibility of combining buttermaking and cheesemaking with childcare, as had been done at home, is often given as an explanation for the failure of women to move to factory dairying. In reality this was, however, not the reason why women did not work in the factories.

thermometer instead of by hand; the use of metal instead of wooden implements. Furthermore, the Danes stored the milk in high vats as opposed to the Dutch wide vessels, and did not let the milk stand as long before taking off the cream. This gave the milk less chance to go bad. The Danes also cooled the milk with ice, following the Swedish so-called Schwartz method that was invented in 1864. Danes furthermore made use of the Laval separator, invented in 1879, a machine which separated milk and cream.[9]

It was not easy to change Dutch farm production methods. Dutch butter, especially the Frisian, had always been praised as the best, and women prided themselves on their skills as buttermakers. Their butter had always been considered good, so they saw no reason to change their techniques. Nevertheless, some of the improved ways of making butter were copied in the Netherlands. Replacement of implements required little investment. The Schwartz method was more difficult for Dutch farmers to use, because they had trouble obtaining the ice. Shorter leases on farms, which were becoming customary in this period, discouraged farmers from making large investments for rebuilding storage rooms.[10] Furthermore, the methods and machines used in Denmark were less suitable for the small-scale Dutch farms. The system of itinerant teachers, who went from farm to farm giving instructions on buttermaking techniques, was copied with some success from the Danes. In 1880, a 19-year-old woman was hired as the first instructor. She received her training in the dairy school of Flensburg. In 1881, the director of this school was brought to the Netherlands as an instructor.[11] The core of the instructor's message was that women should trust not their senses, but the new techniques.

Several Dutch agricultural reformers travelled to Denmark to gather first-hand information. They were most impressed by the Hanna Nielsen enterprise.[12] On her farmstead, Hanna Nielsen trained young people in buttermaking and cheesemaking. From 1866 to 1878 she trained over two hundred women, and about a hundred men. The women stayed half a year, the men eight to thirty days. The women did not only come from Denmark, but also from Sweden, Finland, Germany and Russia.[13]

Around 1890, dairy consultants were appointed in each district of the Netherlands. These consultants were to instruct in butter and cheese production. They organized talks for farmers on improved methods of making butter and cheese. About a quarter of the audience at each lecture consisted of women.[14] In 1889, a Frisian dairy school was set up. The courses lasted three months. Applicants for the school had to be at least 17 years of age, had to have completed elementary school, and to have some knowledge of farm life. One course each year was reserved for women. The school could accommodate eight pupils at a time. The three yearly courses for men were always full, but the one women's course was not. The school board attributed this to farmers objecting to sending their daughters to live in town for the three months that the course lasted. Of the pupils who took the course in the first year, half became dairy factory managers, rather than dairy workers on a farm. For this reason the school adapted its curriculum and started to train managers. In 1892, the women's course was stopped, because no women registered.[15]

In the last decade of the nineteenth century, it became evident that an improvement in Dutch butter would have to come from factory production. Again, reformers looked abroad. The dairy consultant of the Dutch district of Utrecht visited various German factories before undertaking to set up a factory himself. In 1902, he visited three such German factories, all of which made both butter and Dutch-style cheese. Strikingly, these German factories, which were considerably bigger than any he had seen in the Netherlands, all used Dutch personnel, Dutch techniques, and predominantly Dutch machinery.[16]

The first Dutch factories were small, but they were soon followed by larger versions, especially in the north of the Netherlands. The early factories, both in the south and in the north, used machinery that was developed in Scandinavian countries for farm use. These machines were designed for women. The Laval separator was advertised by its Swedish producers with a depiction of an elegant woman leaning lightly on the handle of the machine.

Contrary to later developments, the early dairy factories often employed women. These women were not only taken on for cleaning vats and vessels, mopping floors and washing cloth. Women working in the early factories were often also in charge of buttermaking and cheesemaking. For instance, in 1888 a factory was set up to process the milk of two hundred cows. Soon the business was extended to five hundred cows. The buttermaker in this factory was a woman; a farmer's daughter, and a mother of seven children.[17] Of the five women who attended the first course at the dairy school, two became directors of dairy factories. The products of one of these factories was advertised as made by women. The woman in charge of buttermaking in that factory was a young widow with six children.[18]

The disappearance of women from dairying is not simply a Dutch phenomenon. In this book, Lena Sommestad describes the same occurrence in Sweden, and Joanna Bourke has found the same for Ireland.[19] The parallels between the Irish and Dutch situations are striking.[20] Bourke argues that it was the Factory Acts that made it impossible to employ women in creameries. In 1898, delegates from the cooperative and agricultural societies lobbied to exempt creameries from the general rules regarding female labour. An amendment in 1903 allowed women to be employed on Sunday for three consecutive hours.[21]

It is likely that legislation also excluded women in the Dutch case. In 1889, a law regulating working hours for women and youngsters forbade women to do any work on Sunday. Immediately after the law was passed, dairy owners and managers protested. The protesters claimed that women did work in the dairy industry that could not be done by men. In 1896, the constituent for one of the northern provinces argued that the cooperative factories used to hire a married couple, preferably with children, for dairying, and that this whole family would work in the creamery. Because of the new law, the members of this family could do the work for six days of the week, but a man had to be hired to replace the woman for the seventh day. This was not only inconvenient, but also disadvantageous because the best butter and cheese was made when attended to by one and the same person all the time. Allowing women to work a few hours on Sunday, the representative argued, would not upset their household. The women did not work all day on the other six days of the week, so household tasks could be taken care of as well. Information from other sources confirmed this. On Monday, some women in dairying worked from 5 till 10 in the morning, then went home to do the family washing, and returned to the factory at 4 in the afternoon.[22] The representative pointed out that although forbidden by law, women continued to work in the factories. Some factory managers had already been fined. Furthermore, the board of the factory now only hired the man. His wife was supposed to help him, but this was not in the contract. Judges did not accept the argument that the woman did this work 'voluntarily', and fined the management. Finally, in 1896, the government was forced to change the law, and women were allowed to work in dairy factories for a few hours on Sunday. Dairying was the only industry to be exempted. The change did not only apply to wives of buttermakers or cheesemakers, but to women in general.[23]

From 1889 to 1896, women had not been allowed to work in the dairy factories on Sundays. Factory managers initially felt they could not do without the women's skills. During the seven years that they had to make do without women, however, they found that they could. As a consequence, men came to dominate dairying, which was once so obviously women's work.

From Women to Men: Brewing

Guild restrictions applying to pre-industrial food producers, such as butchers, bakers, and millers, may have influenced the male gendering of these professions in a later period. The exclusion of women from bakeries can be explained by this. Baking was typically masculine long before the industrial era. The Dutch ban on night work for women (since the end of the nineteenth century) may have enforced this, but probably made little difference. As industries became more internationally oriented, guild restrictions in various countries may have influenced each other. This may have had an effect on the gendering of brewing.

The Dutch brewing industry is rather important economically. As figure 10.5 shows, it is a labour-extensive industry. The total number of workers in this industry declined somewhat in the 1920s, and then picked up again. The percentage of women in this industry (see figure 10.6) was strikingly low, and only started to become important after the Second World War.

Brewing has existed since Egyptian times, and from its beginning there are reports of both male and female brewers. In the Netherlands, there were no guild restrictions on brewing, and it was a trade to which women were freely admitted. In the sixteenth century, the staff of a medium-sized brewery consisted of a brewster, who could be the owner or the highest-paid employee, assisted by two well-paid female 'wringsters'. Men, less well-paid, were employed to transport ingredients and beer.[24]

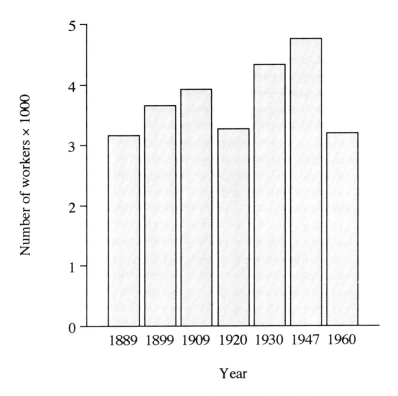

Figure 10.5 Number of workers in the beer industry, 1889–1960
Source: 13th Dutch General Poll, 31 May 1960, part 10-c (Hilversum 1966), table 1.

In the eighteenth and nineteenth century there were large-scale and small-scale breweries. The big breweries, which were usually located in towns, were run by men with considerable social standing. The small breweries in the countryside were as likely to be run by women as by men. The small breweries were often attached to a pub, and only brewed part of the year. The social standing of the owners was generally low. By the beginning of the nineteenth century all the small breweries, not only the ones owned by women, had lost out to the big firms. The big firms could profit from tax measures which favoured the concentration and local monopolization of brewing, making competition for the small firms difficult. The big firms were usually owned by men, but women were not excluded from production.

In the course of the nineteenth century, brewing underwent significant technical changes. The most important of these was the introduction of new yeasting techniques, which favoured renewed increases in scale' and concentration. Around 1870, the bigger Dutch breweries changed to the so-called Bavarian method of brewing. Bavaria, where the Dutch brewers acquired their new technique, had strict guild-like regulations regarding the production of beer,

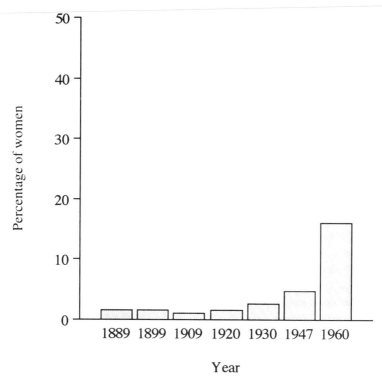

Figure 10.6 Percentage of women workers in the beer industry, 1889–1960
Source: 13th Dutch General Poll, 31 May 1960, part 10-c (Hilversum 1966), table 1.

which tended to exclude women. When the big Dutch brewer Heineken changed to the Bavarian method, a German brewing master was contracted. In 1865 Heineken employed twenty workers, all men and boys. In 1871 there were forty workers, all men and half of them Germans. This German influence remained strong. In 1899, when the workers made demands for wage increases, the spokesmen were the German coopers.[25] Before 1870, Dutch and English machines were used in brewing. After the switch to the Bavarian method, these machines were replaced by German machinery. Because of this German influence, which regarded beer production as a male industry, women never gained a place in the large, new-style factories.

From Men to Women: Cocoa and Chocolate

In the cocoa and chocolate industry there were many complaints about the replacement of skilled male workers by unskilled youths, amongst whom were many girls. At the beginning of the century there were overall complaints about the decreasing age of the workers at cocoa and chocolate factories. The cocoa and chocolate industry was not as important as the industries that have been

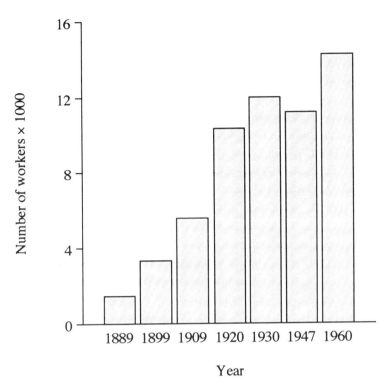

Figure 10.7 Number of workers in the cocoa and chocolate industry, 1889–1960
Source: 13th Dutch General Poll, 31 May 1960, part 10-c (Hilversum 1966), table 1.

discussed so far, but was still one of the larger industries. It was an industry in which women were relatively well represented. As shown in figures 10.7 and 10.8, the number of workers in this industry grew steadily with time, and the percentage of women workers increased.[26]

A distinction has to be made between cocoa factories and chocolate factories. The cocoa factories processed cocoa beans and made cocoa powder. They made little chocolate, restricting their production to that of chocolate bars, which were easy to make. Chocolate factories did not make cocoa, but made both chocolate bars and more fancy chocolate products.

In the cocoa factories, women filled and closed tins of cocoa powder. They also transported heavy sacks of cocoa beans on sack trucks, and carried the heavy metal containers with cacao butter. The roasting of cocoa beans was skilled work, and was done by men. The roaster was usually assisted by boys who filled and emptied the machines. Around 1900, contrary to the practice in other factories, the biggest Dutch cocoa producer, Van Houten, employed girls and women for this work, instead of boys. Van Houten took on the girls for wrapping work, but regularly placed them in a production department after a few

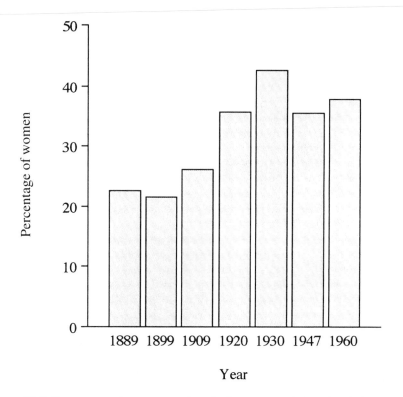

Figure 10.8 Percentage of women workers in the cocoa and chocolate industry, 1889–1960

Source: 13th Dutch General Poll, 31 May 1960, part 10-c (Hilversum 1966), table 1.

weeks. The girls did not like to work in production, and complained repeatedly about this. The work in the production departments was harder and it paid less. Production workers got hourly wages, whereas in the wrapping department they got piece-work wages. With piece-work wages, experienced girls and women were able to earn considerably more. Some of them even managed to earn more than the unskilled male production workers, much to the annoyance of the latter.

Wage differences for young workers were too small to explain Van Houten's preference for female workers in the production department. At the beginning of this century, the hourly wage of women was half of that of men, but wages of boys and girls were rather similar, with the youngest girls earning the same wage as their boy peers or sometimes even more. Nor was the reason for the preference that there was an abundance of available girls. Girls commuted to the Van Houten factory from up to an hour's train journey away. There were complaints that girls were hard to get, and that some of the other cocoa factories drove up the girls' wages. At the same time, boys and men were vainly offering themselves for employment.

Figure 10.9 At the end of the nineteenth century, the chocolate bar became the most popular chocolate product. Unlike the more fancy-shaped chocolate products, the bars could easily be made and wrapped by machines. Women were the main employees on both types of machine. The photograph shows a woman feeding bars of chocolate into a wrapping machine at Van Houten's factory, around 1900.

A reason for Van Houten's preference for female workers may have been that he only had employment for young workers. Within the cocoa factories, there were few possibilities for getting ahead. As women usually left after a few years, Van Houten was spared the uneasy task of laying off workers. The few women who did not leave after a few years were laid off at 30.

The replacement of male workers by youngsters, many of them girls, was even stronger in chocolate factories. The ongoing complaints about women being substituted for men led to a governmental investigation into the matter in the 1930s. The investigators selected thirty factories to which the complaints applied. These were mainly the smaller chocolate factories. The investigators found that there were 346 boys, and 366 girls under 18 (51 per cent) in 1920. In 1925 there were 400 boys and 755 girls (65 per cent). Both numbers had increased, but the number of girls much more than the number of boys.

The chocolate industry had been through many changes since it had evolved in the last quarter of the nineteenth century. As a new industry, it was to some extent modelled on the confectionery industry. Until the turn of the century, confectioners used sugar to make real works of art. It took several years to become a skilled confectioner, and boy apprentices climbed the ladder gradually, each step designated by an impressive French name. In the second part of the century, chocolate was introduced. Chocolate tasted much better than confectionery. As the price of chocolate fell, and incomes rose, people started to buy more chocolate. The confectioners changed from sugar to chocolate, and started to form this into fashionable shapes. The last years of the nineteenth century, however, also saw the introduction of the chocolate bar, soon to become the most popular chocolate product. Chocolate bars could easily be made by machine. From the end of the nineteenth century, the big factories produced machine-made bars of chocolate. Originally, large slabs of chocolate, consisting of several bars, were delivered to the shopkeeper. The shopkeeper would break off a piece for the customer and wrap it. In 1891, the first wrapped bars of chocolate were introduced. The wrapping was initially done by hand, but by 1900 it was already largely done by machines. These machines were attended to by women.

The small chocolate factories specialized in chocolate figures, which were more difficult to make than bars. The chocolate figures were made by men, each seated in front of his own pot of melted chocolate, heated by a gas flame. The difficulty was to keep the chocolate mass at the right temperature. If it became too hot, it went off colour. If it became too cold, it could not be worked with. The chocolatier filled a form with a small spoon, twisting the form continuously to make sure that the layer of chocolate was never too thick or too thin. After the turn of the century, important changes were introduced. A tempering machine kept the chocolate mass at the right temperature. From this machine, the mass was pumped to the filling machine, which filled the moulds. The continuous shaking of a 'toddle table' got rid of the air bubbles. None of these machines required much skill or training to work with. The machine products were not as nice as the hand-made ones, and the chocolatiers shuddered at the sight of a chocolate egg with a seam, but the consumers seemed to care little about that, especially as the price dropped steadily.

In the cocoa and chocolate industry, the effects of the introduction of new machinery are evident. The various chocolate products required different machines. It took until the 1930s before large hollow figures, such as dolls and Easter eggs, could be made by machine. Gradually, new machinery was developed for each product. Each time, this led to the replacement of men by boys and girls. The unions protested against this development, but they were too weak to have any influence. Van Houten did not want any external interference with his business; neither from unions, nor from the government. His competitors at Kwatta, a slightly smaller firm that was mainly oriented towards the inland market, did see advantages in making agreements between factories about, amongst other things, mechanization and the employment of young workers. In 1935, the director of Kwatta threatened to replace some adult workers by youngsters if the government did not come up with a regulation about the percentage of youngsters allowed to work in the industry. Competition forced him to do so, he claimed. Early in 1936, the director started to replace three men per week. As a result, the government started its investigation into the replacement of men by boys and girls in the cocoa and chocolate industry as a whole. This resulted in a law being passed in 1937, which stipulated that a maximal percentage of youngsters could be fixed in several industries. The percentages were to be set after negotiations within the various industries. Twenty-five per cent was suggested for the cocoa and chocolate industry. Kwatta, as one of the initiators of this law, protested, demanding that the wrapping department, where most of the youngsters worked, be excluded from the regulation. In the end, no accord could be reached, and no percentage was fixed. By the spring of 1937, 40 per cent of the more expensive workers at Kwatta had been replaced by young workers. The unions did not obstruct this replacement, because the management said the alternative was to close down the factory as a whole.

In the cocoa and chocolate industry there were many factors favouring women's work. Filling and closing tins of chocolate powder had been women's work from the outset. Changes in production occurred due to the increasing consumer preference for the chocolate bar. Women attended both the machines that made the bars and the machines used for wrapping. As the demand for wrapped chocolate bars increased, so did the demand for female workers. Strikingly, the number of women in the production of cocoa powder also increased, although there had not been many changes in the production process. This may have been a spin-off effect of the rising number of women in other parts of the factory. In the chocolate factories, it was clearly technological change that led to the replacement of old, experienced workers by youngsters, amongst whom were many women.

Creating Women's Work: Margarine

The importance of the margarine industry is easily underestimated, because it was rather labour-extensive. Margarine was invented in 1869, and its production was first taken up by the two main Dutch butter traders of that time: Jurgens and Van den Bergh. Their firms merged in 1927 to form the 'Margarine Unie'. Two years later, this new firm, the world's largest margarine producer, merged with the world's largest soap producer, the British Lever Brothers, to form Unilever, and became one of the world's leading multinationals.[27] As figures 10.10 and 10.11 show, the margarine industry saw a rather sudden rise in the number of workers in the years after the First World War, combined with a sharply rising percentage of female workers. The rapid increase was followed by a steep drop, whereas the percentage of women remained more or less stable.

Margarine began to be produced on an industrial scale between 1870 and 1900. In the beginning, the number of workers was small. In these early years, most work in the margarine industry was done by men. Factories usually only employed one woman – for cleaning. After 1900, changes occurred due to the new way of selling margarine. Until then, margarine had been sold to retailers

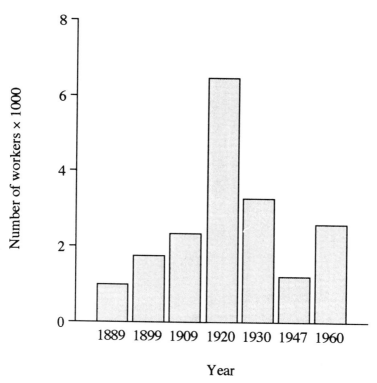

Figure 10.10 Number of workers in the margarine industry, 1889–1960
Source: 13th Dutch General Poll, 31 May 1960, part 10-c (Hilversum 1966), table 1.

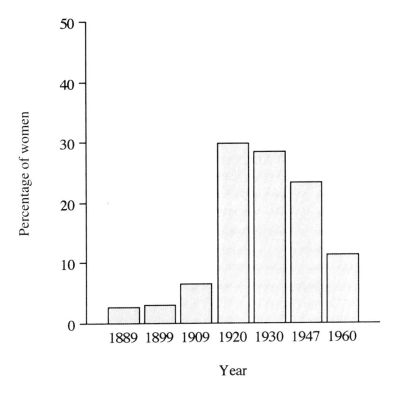

Figure 10.11 Percentage of women workers in the margarine industry, 1889–1960
Source: 13th Dutch General Poll, 31 May 1960, part 10-c (Hilversum 1966), table 1.

in crates or barrels. Shopkeepers would take the amount of margarine the customer wanted out of the barrel, form it into a rectangular shape, and wrap it. Between 1900 and the beginning of the First World War, pre-wrapped margarine took over. This meant that margarine was formed and wrapped in the factory.

Wrapping was labour-intensive. At first, boys aged 12 and 13 were employed for this job. In 1914 the number of boys suddenly declined, and there was an influx of girls and women. The employment of girls and women coincided with the introduction of the first simple wrapping machines. Before these machines, pieces of margarine were formed by hand with the help of a mould. The new machine, which looked like a large egg-slicer, cut a slab of margarine into pieces of more or less the same size.

There were six girls to a machine. The two girls sitting nearest to the machine took the pieces of margarine and rolled them in paper. The next two girls folded the wrapping. The two girls at the head of the table placed the pieces into crates, and replaced full crates by empty ones.

Boys had been doing the packing before the machines were introduced. The introduction of machinery led to their replacement by girls and women. Most of

Figure 10.12 In 1914, there was a sudden influx of women into the margarine industry. This influx was related to introduction of a machine which looked like a large egg-slicer. The machine, shown here, cuts slabs of margarine into pieces of the same size. The invention made packing margarine much simpler. The photograph was taken in the Jurgens factory in Oss in 1914.

the female workers, however, did not replace male workers, but worked in newly created jobs. Jurgens paid the youngest girls a bit more than boys of the same age. As at Van Houten's cocoa factory, the preference for female workers cannot be explained by the fact that they were easily available. Jurgens went through quite a bit of trouble to get the women workers. A foreman was sent out to nearby places recruiting personnel, and the railway company was asked to adjust the timetable of the commuter trains to suit the women workers.

In the 1920s, more sophisticated wrapping machines were introduced, and the number of women and girls employed in the industry was halved from one year to the next. Not only wrapping was affected by mechanization. Throughout the factory, machines replaced workers. Mechanization was not the only reason for the decrease in the labour force. In the 1930s there was a decline in Dutch margarine production. Part of the production was moved to England, following the merger with Lever. Furthermore, the price of butter was low as a result of the agricultural crisis, and part of the population bought butter rather than margarine.

In the 1930s, new machines were introduced which not only formed pieces of margarine, but also wrapped them. Girls took the packages from a conveyer belt and put them into boxes. This work was not difficult, but the pace was hectic. The overall image of packing work, and not only in the margarine industry, is its hectic nature. The movements for packing could be learned in a week or so. However, to acquire the speed which guaranteed a reasonable income could take up to six months. Some girls never got the hang of it, or became extremely nervous. They were placed in different parts of the factory, or left.

As at Van Houten's cocoa factory, the lack of career prospects seems to have been one of the reasons to prefer girls and women for packing. In the margarine industry, a woman could be promoted from being a simple packer to become the main operator of the machine. Women doing this work were called engineers. The requirement was experience and speed in wrapping. The other promotion open to women was to become a mistress or overseer. The mistresses were usually somewhat older, but as the overall age was low it was not uncommon for a woman to become a mistress at 20.

In the margarine industry, it was not a change in the production of margarine that led to the influx of women, but the added process of wrapping. Wrapping was important in many sectors of the food industries. The advent of wrapped products greatly increased the number of women employed in the food industries. The introduction of wrapped products can be dated around the turn of the century, and has since been expanding. Just as in the margarine industry, boys were initially employed for packing in many of the other industries. Later, when the wrapping was mechanized, girls were employed. Although girls did replace boys, most of the girls filled places that had not existed before. Wrapping was new work. In the late 1920s and the 1930s, further mechanization led to a decrease in the number of female workers.

Conclusion

Tradition gendered dairying as feminine. All the reforms and the new techniques of the end of the nineteenth century reinforced this. However, the seven-year ban on women's work on Sunday overcame the effects of a strong tradition and made it possible to relabel the work. In brewing, women were excluded not so much by the new Bavarian technique that was introduced, as by the Bavarian guild-like restrictions that were imported together with the technique and the German workers. In dairying and brewing, technological change had an indirect influence on women's work. There were many technological changes in dairying. None of these directly led to the regendering of work. Changes in dairying, however, did result in the transition of production from farm to factory. When women were subsequently forbidden to work in factories on Sunday, dairying was regendered. Dairying, however, seems to have been the only industry thus affected by legislation. Brewing, which was initially not restricted to men, became an exclusive male occupation when foreign guild-type restrictions were imported together with new brewing techniques.

In the chocolate industry it is clear that the introduction of machinery made the skills of the old workers obsolete. This meant that they could be replaced by youngsters, including many women. A consumer preference for chocolate bars, which were machine-made by women, led to an increase in the number of women employed. The introduction of women into the cocoa factories, which until then had a mainly male workforce, may have had its consequences on parts of the factory that were not affected by technological change. Once women had been introduced in one part of the factory, it became easier to introduce them in other parts as well. The effects of technological change were much more direct in the chocolate industry than in dairying and brewing. Developments in the cocoa and chocolate industry almost fit the classical image of the results of mechanization. Making chocolate figures by hand required experience and training. When the chocolate products could be made by machines, women replaced men. However, this simple process was not the only cause of the increase in the percentage, or number, of female workers. The growing popularity of the chocolate bar strengthened the feminization of the industry. Government and unions tried to halt this development, but failed.

An important change in the food industry was the introduction of the wrapped product. In wrapping it is inaccurate to speak of the regendering of work, because wrapping was new work. The effects of the introduction of wrapping were most apparent in the margarine industry. As the demand for wrapped margarine rose, the number of female workers in margarine boomed. This trend, however, was not sustained, because wrapping was soon mechanized, and the number of women dropped. The example of the margarine industry shows that women's work can be both created and destroyed by mechanization, without affecting male workers. Mechanization in this case led to many changes, but not to regendering of the existing work.

In all these cases there appears to have been a direct reason for regendering the work. Although the reasons are very different, it is evident that work was not gradually regendered, but that technological change often provided a rather abrupt excuse for regendering. Thus technological change provided an excuse to introduce shifts in an otherwise rigid distrubution of work between men and women.

Notes

1 Thirteenth Dutch General Poll, 31 May 1960, part 10-c (Hilversum, 1966), table 1.

2 Eijl, C. van, (1994) *Het werkzame verschil. Vrouwen in de slag om arbeid 1898–1940*, Hilversum, chapter 2. See also: Pott-Buter, H.A. (1993) *Facts and fairy tales, about female labor, family and fertility. A seven-country comparison, 1850–1990*, Amsterdam.

3 *Onderzoekingen naar de toestanden in de Nederlandse huisindustrie*, p. 67; Schrover, M. (1991) *Het vette, het zoete en het wederzijdse profijt, arbeidsverhoudingen in de margarine-industrie en in de cacao- en chocolade-industrie in Nederland 1870–1960* (The Fat, the Sweet and the Common Good: Labour Relations in the Margarine Industry and in the Cocoa and Chocolate Industry in the Netherlands 1870–1960), Hilversum, p. 115.

4 Sluyterman, K.E. (1983) *Ondernemen in sigaren. Analyse van bedrijfsbeleid in vijf Nederlandse sigarenfabrieken in de perioden 1856–1865 en 1925–1934*, Tilburg, p. 138.

5 Croesen, V.R.IJ. (1931) *De geschiedenis van de ontwikkeling van de Nederlandsche zuivelbereiding in het laatst van de negentiende en het begin van de twintigste eeuw*, Den Haag, p. 85.

6 *Ibid.*, p. 42.

7 Rinkes Borger, J. (1878) *Boter- en kaasfabrieken. Eenige praktische denkbeelden over hedendaagse landbouwtoestanden*, Leeuwarden.

8 Croesen (1931) (see note 5), p. 46.

9 *Ibid.*, p. 84.

10 Wiersma, J.P. (1959) *Erf en wereld. Over de agrarische toestand in Friesland na 1870. De doorbraak der cooperatieve gedachte. De opkomst van de Friese landbouwcooperatie en haar ontwikkeling tot in onze tijd*, Drachten, p. 33.

11 *Ibid.*, p. 40.

12 Rinkes Borger (1878), p. 35.

13 Wiersma (1959) (see note 10), p. 30.

14 Regional archive Utrecht, archive dairy consultant 123, nr. 9, diary of dairy consultant T.J. Swierstra 1897–1904.

15 Spahr van der Hoek, J.J. (1952) *Geschiedenis van de Friese landbouw*, Drachten, part II, pp. 248–9; Croesen (1931) (see note 5), p. 108.

16 Regional archive Utrecht, archive dairy consultant 123, nr. 9 diary of dairy consultant T.J. Swierstra 1897–1904.

17 Wiersma (1959) (see note 10), p. 93.

18 Spahr (see note 15), part II, pp. 248–9; part I, p. 563; Wiersma (1959), pp. 125–6, 161, 177; Lodder, T. (1989) 'Boterbereiding en boerinnenverzet in Friesland, 1880–1910', in Backerre, F. *et al.*, *Vrouwen van het land. Anderhalve eeuw plattelandsvrouwen in Nederland*, Zutphen, pp. 45–65.

19 Bourke, J. (1990) 'Dairywomen and Affectionate Wives: Women in the Irish Dairy Industry, 1890–1914', *Agricultural History Review* 38, pp. 149–64.

20 *Ibid.*, p. 155.

21 *Ibid.*, p. 157.

22 Wiersma (1959) (see note 10), pp. 125–6, 161, 177.

23 Minutes of the State General Meetings, 18 July 1895, p. 389, 19 July 1895 p. 399; 7 February 1896, pp. 295, p. 303. Supplement to the minutes of the Second Chamber 1896–1897 no. 100, pp.1–5.

24 Hallema, A. and Emmens, J.A. (1968) *Het bier en zijn brouwers. De geschiedenis van onze oudste volksdrank*, Amsterdam, pp. 51, 59.

25 Korthals, H.A. (1948) *Korte geschiedenis der Heineken's bierbrouwerij Maatschappij N.V. 1873–1948*, Voorschoten, pp. 51, 243; Schipper, H. (1992), 'Bier', in Lintsen, H.W. (Ed.) *Geschiedenis van de techniek in Nederland. De wording van een moderne samenleving 1800–1890. Deel 1. Techniek en modernisering. Landbouw en Voeding*, Zutphen, pp. 171–214.

26 The description of the cocoa and chocolate industry is based on part of my dissertation (Schrover, 1991, as at note 3), especially pp. 172–233.

27 This description of the margarine industry is based on part of my dissertation (Schrover, 1991), especially pp. 34–170. See also Schrover, M. (1992) 'Buttering Up Labour Relations in the Margarine Industry, Social Setting versus Industrial Setting', *TvSG*, Summer, pp. 425–38; Schrover, M. (1990) 'Labour Relations in the Dutch Margarine Industry', *History Workshop Journal*, Autumn, 53–62. See also, for a company history of Unilever, Wilson, C. (1954) *The History of Unilever*, London.

Notes on Contributors

Harriet Bradley is Reader in Sociology at Sunderland University. Her doctorate, which provided the data on which her essay in this book is based, was a study of the history of industrial relations in the British hosiery industry. She is the author of *Men's Work, Women's Work: A Sociological History of the Sexual Division of Labour in Employment* (1989). She is currently engaged on a research project on gender differences within trade unions.

Gertjan de Groot was research assistant at the department of Economic and Social History at the University Utrecht in the Netherlands. He has written articles on women and trade unions, social policy and industrialization. He is currently finishing his book titled *Men's work, women's work. Gender segregation and labour organization in Dutch industry between 1850 and 1940*, to be published in Dutch in 1995.

Marianne Rostgård is Associate Professor at the Institute of Development and Planning at Aalborg University, Denmark. In 1991 she published her Ph.D., *Teknologiudvikling og kønsarbejdsdeling indenfor tekstilindustrien i Danmark ca. 1830–1915* (Technological Change and the Sexual Division of Labour in the Danish Textile Industry between 1830 and 1915).

Jacqueline Sarsby (Hon. Research Fellow, University of Exeter) is a social anthropologist and a photographer. Her doctoral thesis investigating the history of marriage based on romantic love and young people's attitudes to love and marriage was published as *Romantic Love and Society* (1983). Government research into the transmission of deprivation led to *A Cycle of Deprivation?* (1980) written with Frank Coffield and Phil Robinson. In 1981, she did oral history fieldwork in North Staffordshire, and published *Missuses and Mould-runners: An Oral History of Women Pottery-Workers at Work and at Home* (1988).

Marlou Schrover is a lecturer at the Economic and Social History department of Utrecht University. She has published articles on the Dutch food industries. She wrote a Ph.D. on labour relations in the margarine and cocoa and chocolate industries published as *Het vette, het zoete en het wederzijdse profijt, arbeidsver-houdingen in de margarine-industrie en in de cacao- en chocolade-industrie in*

Nederland 1870–1960 (The Fat, the Sweet and the Common Good: Labour Relations in the Margarine Industry and in the Cocoa and Chocolate Industry in the Netherlands 1870–1960) (1991).

Lena Sommestad is Assistant Researcher at the Department of Economic History, Uppsala University, Sweden. Her publications include: *Mjölk och människor* (Milk and Men: Life and Labour in an Uppsala Dairy, 1871–1985) (1987); and *Från mejerska till mejerist* (From Dairymaids to Dairymen. A Study of the Masculinization Process in Skilled Dairy Work, with a summary in English) (1992).

Deborah Thom is a historian who is a Fellow, College Lecturer in History and Social and Political Sciences, and Admissions Tutor at Robinson College, Cambridge. She has published articles on women's employment and trade unionism, feminism and psychology and education. Publications include: 'The Bundle of Sticks', in John, A. (Ed.) *Unequal Opportunities* (1988); 'Free from Chains? The Image of Women's Labour in London, 1910–1920', in Feldman, D. and Stedman Jones, G. (Eds) *Metropolis – London* (1989); 'Tommy's Sister', in Samuel, R. (Ed.) *Patriotism: The Making and Unmaking of British National Identity*, volume II, *Minorities and Outsiders* (1989).

Ulla Wikander is Senior Lecturer in Economic History at the University of Uppsala. She is editor and co-editor of books in Swedish on women's history as well as more general social history. She did research on industrial work relations and the gender division of labour especially in factory work resulting in *Kvinnors och mäns arbeten: Gustavsberg 1880–1980. Genusarbetsdelning och arbetets degradering vid en porslinsfabrik* (Women's and Men's Work: Gustavsberg 1880–1980. Gender Division of Labour and Degradation of Work in a Pottery) (1988). With co-editors Alice Kessler-Harris and Jane Lewis, she is currently working on a book on comparative studies in protective labour legislation for women in Europe, the US and Australia.

Meta Zimmeck lives in London, and has worked both as a tape transcriber for the Royal Courts of Justice and as a researcher, most recently in the field of housing. She has published articles on the employment of women in clerical occupations, particulartly the British Civil Service. Publications include: 'Marry in Haste, Repent at Leisure: Women, Bureaucracy and the Post Office, 1870–1920', in Savage, M. and Witz, A. (Eds) *Gender and Bureaucracy* (1992); '"Get Out and Get Under": The Impact of Demobilisation on the Civil Service, 1918–32', in Anderson, G. (Ed.) *The White-Blouse Revolution: Female Office Workers since 1870* (1988); 'The New Woman in the Machinery of Government: A Spanner in the Works?', in MacLeod, R. (Ed.) *Government and Expertise: Specialists, Administrators and Professionals, 1860–1919* (1988).

Index